D0962329

French Fried

Also by Harriet Welty Rochefort

French Toast

French Fried

THE CULINARY CAPERS OF
AN AMERICAN IN PARIS

Harriet Welty Rochefort

THOMAS DUNNE BOOKS

ST. MARTIN'S PRESS ✼ NEW YORK

www.stmartins.com

Title page illustration used courtesy of Artville™

BOOK DESIGN BY VICTORIA KUSKOWSKI

Library of Congress Cataloging-in-Publication Data

Rochefort, Harriet Welty.
French fried : the culinary capers of an American in Paris / Harriet Welty Rochefort—1st ed.
p. cm.
Includes bibliographical references.
ISBN 0-312-26149-7
1. Cookery, French. 2. Food habits—France.
3. France—Social life and customs. I. Title.
TX719 .R617 2001
394.1'0944—dc21

00-047047

First Edition: March 2001

10 9 8 7 6 5 4 3 2 1

To Philippe

☕ Recipes ☕

☕ Contents ☕

CONTENTS

— 4 —
Foraging for Food

Meandering through markets · *La Mouffe* · A stroll through a
French hypermarket · Designer delicacies · The chocolate counter ·
The growing yogurt
85

— 5 —
À la campagne

La maison de campagne · The Fête de St. Lô · An American
connection · Good times and good food · A family tradition ·
A typical Sunday lunch in the country · Making mirabelle alcohol ·
Some dental work at lunch · How do they eat like this and not
get fat? Or . . . no doggy bags.
105

— 6 —
À la ville

Give us this day our daily meals · Twice a day ·
And in courses, please
121

— 7 —
Body Parts or: Is offal awful?

The French eat everything in the animal · A butcher store
and a rabbit head · A horsemeat surprise · Making blood sausage ·
Brains in the microwave · *Le porc*
134

CONTENTS

CONTENTS

☕ Acknowledgments ☕

Many people helped me with this book. As it took shape, Judy Fayard, Jan Tabet, Angenette Meany, Clara Jane Lake, Andrea Tulloch Girma, Soyo Graham-Stewart, Susan Rosenberg, Karim Bitar, and Sarah Colton Villeminot made greatly appreciated contributions in various ways. Family friend Micheline Simenel sent memorabilia from the Normandy Inn and shared her recollections of Shenandoah days. My sincere gratitude to all of them, as well as to Adrian Leeds and Betty Rosbottom, who were instrumental in inspiring the title for the book.

When the manuscript was just about finished I handed copies of it to Sue Ellen Black, Dorie Denbigh Laurent, Marcia Lord, Janet Lizop Thorpe, and Nancy and Pierre Sayer. Not only were they unsparing with their time but they pored over it carefully; their astute observations and suggestions immensely improved the manuscript. Special thanks to each and every one of them for their invaluable input.

My American family, Miriam Welty Trangsrud and Chuck Trangsrud, John Welty, Ward, Jane, and Ryan Welty, all chimed in with lively encouragement. Miriam, a professional editor, spared me many an error of syntax and spelling. My parents, especially my mother, who made many trips to France and admired the French way of dining, would have loved this book. It is written with them always in my mind.

My French family, Marie-Jeanne Rochefort, Martine and Alain Therade, and Tante Françoise, are, as you will see, an important part of this book. Tante Françoise and mother-in-law Marie-Jeanne taught me everything I know about the basics of French cooking and how to get a French meal on the table in no time at all. My sister-in-law Martine, one of the best cooks and most hospitable hostesses I know, was kind enough to contribute some of her truly delicious recipes.

The bright spirits and moral support of the three Rochefort boys, Nicolas, Benjamin, and David, sustained me through the writing of this book. David, the last "at home," would frequently cast his eagle eye on the manuscript and keep me on track when I was threatening to leave it.

French food and wine professionals Philippe Alléosse, Christian Constant, Robert Linxe, Gerard Margeon, Michel Moison, Scott Serrato, Alexandre Viron and his father, Philippe, the staff at Le Cordon Bleu, especially ebullient chef Christian Guillut, the staff at Lenôtre cooking school and Lenôtre pastry chef Alain Blanchard allowed me to enter their specialized worlds for a brief time. I called these people out of the blue, simply explaining that I was writing a book and would enjoy meeting them. Their willingness to set aside time to see me was gratifying and greatly appreciated. This book would not be the same without their contributions.

I could not possibly personally acknowledge all the French people who have invited me to their homes to share good conversation and good food and good wine, the three indispensable elements of a French meal. In lieu of that, I salute the French in general for the importance they attach to high standards and to *le plaisir*.

Mille mercis to my editor, Melissa Jacobs, who possesses a winning combination of the "right touch" and the "light touch," and to my agent, Regula Noetzli, for her steadiness and professionalism.

This book could not have been written without Philippe, not just for the interviews with him but for, as always, his unfailing backing and good humor (well, almost) every step of the way.

Introduction

I've written about cultural divergences between the Americans and the French before, both in newspaper and magazine articles and in my book *French Toast*, but never extensively on the one thing that illustrates those cultural gaps so radically—the different relationships the two cultures have with food.

This book began when I started reflecting on my three decades of living in France, making and eating French food.

It seemed important to write this personal memoir of my observations if only to attest to the cultural differences that still separate French food and French eating habits from American ones at this particular point in time. As the French become more and more American or globalized in what they eat and how they eat, there may be fewer and fewer of these differences in the future. I thought it worthwhile if only for historical record to recount what it was like in my day, a period stretching from 1971 when I first found myself cooking in France, to the present (as Philippe would say: "That's *only* about twenty thousand meals").

Change is inevitable, bringing with it a mixture of good and bad. The French have opened their arms to foreign food in a big way. I remember the days when a takeout pizza was unheard of, a muffin a funny foreign word, and a brownie exotic. No more! Asian and Italian cooking have posed no problem influencing French cuisine: the French always seem to manage to take the best of everything and make it singularly and distinctively their own. Service in restaurants is improving and a smile is no longer something you have to wrest from a waiter. On the home front, the French still sit down to family meals on a daily basis, something that is almost unheard of in the States.

As the French embrace the new and the foreign, though, they may be abandoning the wonderful traditions that have made French food the best in the world. They may be abandoning them because no one seems to have the time anymore. In fact, some Americanized French people I know think their compatriots devote entirely too much attention to talking and thinking about food. As an American living in France, I admire the French concern with what one puts in one's mouth and the effort expended going to the market to pick out exactly the right product. When, many years ago, my American family crossed the Atlantic to visit my future in-laws, my mother-in-law-to-be crossed Paris to get *the* right salad greens for our gathering. She wanted my family to have a good meal, a tasty meal. She knew, as the French know, that to honor your guests, you need (in this case, literally) to go out of your way.

Frozen *bœuf bourguignon*, vacuum-packed salads, and industrialized cheese wrapped in plastic have all come to France. I am the first to say that they are certainly a help in today's busy world. But they'll never replace the real thing, the stew that has cooked for hours, the salad fresh from the garden, the cheese that speaks to you with its own particular aspect and fragrant, sometimes flagrant, odor. Some French children unfortunately don't know what a homemade *blan-*

quette de veau or *pot-au-feu* tastes like. *Quel dommage!* The French are going to have to work hard to maintain their culinary traditions. Since the French have a way of taking the worst from the U.S.A., I fervently hope the day will never come when they adopt the American habit of eating from the fridge.

In this book, I hope to capture the immense joy I experience as an American living in France and eating and making food the French way.

Will this pleasure vanish as globalization and standardization invade the Gallic kitchen? Will the French continue to take their time? Will the fishmonger continue to allow a line to form while he patiently tells you how to prepare the fish you just bought? Will the *fromager* still be there to lovingly choose the Camembert that you want to eat tonight and not in two days? Will the vegetable lady still pick out that perfect avocado for the salad you're making tomorrow? Or will the French become believers in the bottom line? Will we all drink Coke and eat Velveeta? Will the delight disappear?

Who can say? But I've lived in France long enough to think that the French won't let it happen.

Here's hoping I'm not wrong. And if I am, this book will at least tell you what the French and their food were like back when.

—HARRIET WELTY ROCHEFORT
Paris, March 2000

1

The Beginnings

Shenandoah, Iowa

On the bedroom wall of my Paris apartment is a black-and-white photo of Main Street, Shenandoah, Iowa, 1878. The storefronts are wood and look like facades built for a Western. The dirt street is wide and runs west into emptiness. On the piano in my living room I have another photo, also black-and-white. It is of the beautiful Victorian house I grew up in, a large turreted home with thick carved walnut doors and stained-glass windows built at the turn of the century by David Lake, the founder of the seed and nursery industry in Shenandoah. The only people to live in the house before my father purchased it were Lakes, which is why it was always referred to as the Lake House even when we were living in it.

My father bought the Lake House when I was three years old and it was so much bigger than our small house on Crescent Street that I managed to promptly get lost in it. Filled with nooks and crannies, a basement with many unexplored rooms you could barely crawl into and a creepy attic with playful mice that pattered over your head at night but that miraculously disappeared when you went up there to play, it was a house made for children.

After my father died when I was fifteen, my mother moved to Minneapolis and sold the house. Although I have seen it from time to time from the outside on my infrequent visits to Shenandoah, I have not entered it since my sister's wedding, which was held there in 1968. I have often traveled through its rooms in my mind, though, and prefer to remember it the way it was: a house with many books and a grand piano that was constantly in use, a house filled with young people of all ages and good smells coming from the kitchen, a house that was impeccable yet comfortably welcoming, a house in which everyone could find his or her own space. The kitchen—especially compared to the one I have today in Paris—was huge, with a pantry and a dining nook where we ate when not in the formal dining room.

My bedroom was at the head of the back stairs directly up from the kitchen where the smell of bacon frying was often the only thing that could wrest me from my bed in the morning. The fragrance of fresh baked cookies, especially chocolate chip and ginger, my favorites, was another surefire way of getting me to emerge from my upstairs hideaway.

Without doing it on purpose, my mother contributed to my early interest in France. She chose a turquoise-and-white wallpaper pattern called Monique, and decorated my bedroom window with turquoise café curtains bordered by a harlequin pattern. She certainly could not have guessed what far-reaching effects those seemingly prosaic decorating choices would have on my life. Perhaps because I loved my room so much, I associated France with all things pleasant.

It's all far away now, a continent away, in fact, but I keep those images in my mind and those photos in my home in France to remind me of where I came from and who I am.

So what does that have to do with a book on French food?

Everything.

First of all, in regard to food in general, I didn't grow up in the age of fast food. In our family, my mother set the table with real silver and linen tablecloths, sometimes for lunch and always for dinner. My brothers and sister and I were expected to attend all meals, and to carry on some semblance of civilized conversation. My dignified father sat at the head of the table, elegant in a white shirt and tie, my mother at the other end, refined and soft-spoken. When I went out into the big wide world, I discovered that my parents were about as far from the stereotype of the Iowa farmer as you could find, yet both of them came from farm families and were the first to come "to town."

My father's great-grandfather, Andrew Jackson Welty, settled in Shenandoah in 1870 and "saw the town grow from its birth in the wild prairie grass," according to his biographical sketch. Andrew Jackson's claim to fame, other than his name, was the "leading and fearless part" he took in the fight to keep saloons and spirits out of Shenandoah. My illustrious ancestor surely would have been horrified to think that one of his issue (me) would so much as sip a glass of wine let alone participate in the distilling of it (more on that in the chapter on *à la campagne*).

My maternal grandmother, who was born and raised on a farm and married a farmer, was a teetotaler as well. The family story is that she only asked two things of my mother. The first was that she attend college. This is because when my grandmother was ten years old, her mother died so she had to stay at home to take care of her father and brothers and never even had the opportunity to finish high school. A highly intelligent woman, she regretted her lack of schooling and my mother's education therefore was of the utmost importance to her. The second request, equally serious, was that my mother never sit on a barstool at the local country club! For my reserved ladylike grandmother, who had never been to the country club and surely imagined it as a den of iniquity, that was the worst possible thing that could happen to her daughter. My mother satisfied both of her mother's wishes, finishing Iowa State Teacher's College (now the University of Northern Iowa) and never sitting on a barstool or drinking anything more than a half a glass of sherry from time to time. Knowing how our sprightly grandmother felt about liquor, we four grandchildren would on an annual basis spice the Christmas fruitcake with rum or whiskey, naively hoping to get her tipsy. To no avail!

It may seem strange to talk about drink when the matter at hand is food, but there's a link. Teetotalers or not, it's hard to imagine either of my parents' mothers having a cocktail hour with all the work they had to do on the farm preparing gigantic repasts of meat, mashed potatoes, gravy, and salads for their men and all the hired hands. Drink was strictly out, and food was serious. Even though my parents left their respective farms and moved to town after they were grown, they maintained a respect for and a tradition of regular meals—major meals—that farm families have. (When my children were young, we took my mother, the picture of decorum, to a Burger King in Minneapolis. She never would have set foot in there on her own but was a good sport about accompanying me and the kids. We watched with amazement as she carefully set the Dastardly Thing down on her tray, divided it neatly into bottom and top sections, and proceeded to eat it with a knife and fork! After that experience, we abandoned any attempts to perpetrate fast food on her. It just wasn't her style. One of the reasons she loved visiting us in France, she told me, was the way the food is served, one course after another, in small portions. This appealed to her genteel sense of the way things should be.)

Perhaps this respect for mealtime is one reason I feel so at home in France.

A "French connection"

Besides my own family, another influence was our town's own French restaurant. This was not a restaurant that called itself French but a real restaurant run by real French people. In addition to two local drugstores (Jay's and Rexall's), two cinemas (the State and the Page), various dress stores and offices, including my father's busy real estate and life insurance agency, Shenandoah had a restaurant scene as well: Simpson's café and the Spot for a quick bite and for a "real meal," the Delmonico Hotel and the Tallcorn Motel. But the crown jewel for a few years in the '50s was the Normandy Inn, a French restaurant run by the parents of our family friend, Micheline, a war bride who married an air force officer from the Midwest.

What she thought about being transported from Le Havre, a city on the west coast of France, which had been so badly bombed during World War II that it had to be totally rebuilt, to a small town in the cornfields of Iowa I never knew until I questioned her about it one day some forty years later; suffice it to say that coming from an urbane French family where she was a beloved only child with a nanny and English governess, it was a shock to find herself in the southwest corner of Iowa where she even took work in a factory for a time. But Micheline never looked back. Shortly after she arrived, she sent for her mother and father who had been left financially destitute after the Occupation and the ravages of the war. The news of their arrival was duly published in our local paper, *The Shenandoah Evening Sentinel*, with the headline: "French Couple Will Make Their Home in Shenandoah."

I have the old newspaper clipping, which Micheline sent me, and it brought back memories of how *everything* was reported in a small town newspaper. This event was, certainly, not an everyday one and our paper made sure we got all the details about the French family who was moving to our town. In a 1949 write-up, the *Sentinel* reported that Mr. Simenel, Micheline's father, "is not a stranger to the U.S.A.," that he first came in 1906 and stayed three years in different states of the Cotton Belt and that for twenty-three years he had been the official sworn expert for cotton at the Tribunal of Commerce of Le Havre but retired during the American Depression. In an article in August 1954, the paper announced that the Simenels had become citizens, having been called to appear before the federal court of justice in Council Bluffs to take their oath of allegiance. "After the ceremony," the newspaper related, "they were guests of the Council Bluffs chapter of Daughters of American Revolution and of Chamber of Commerce women at a luncheon at the Chieftain Hotel."

The Normandy Inn

Meanwhile, the Normandy Inn had been born and we Shenandoahans had been introduced to a touch of class. To my child's eyes, the restaurant combined foreign and cozy with its red-and-white checkered tablecloths and a candle on each table. A display of beautiful antique plates rescued from the Simenel's house in Normandy, a home occupied by the Germans for four and a half years, lent yet another foreign note. Micheline's father, who had never cooked before other than as a hobby, presided over the restaurant with his pretty petite wife, Madeleine. Surprisingly, though Micheline recalls my family having lunch at the Normandy Inn every Sunday, I have very few vivid memories—the influence of the restaurant was surely subliminal.

I do have one reminiscence that is firmly implanted in my mind, though, and that is the Simenel's "Swiss steak Normandy," which became my Proust's madeleine. Granted, Swiss steak is not French, but the person cooking it was, and what a difference it made! Years later, in a Paris restaurant with a Shenandoah friend, we started talking about the Normandy Inn. "Do you remember the Swiss steak?" my friend asked, and we each rolled our eyes blissfully as we conjured up its delicious taste. Memories are tricky things, however—my brother doesn't remember the restaurant but recalls the family unpacking their goods and exclaiming "ooh la la" every time they came upon a broken object. As for me, as the years passed, I started thinking I had dreamed up the Swiss steak until I contacted Micheline, who now lives outside of Washington, D.C. Not only did she confirm my few memories but she sent me a Normandy Inn menu on which Swiss steak was prominently listed at the modest price of eighty-five cents!

An "almost French" stepgrandmother

My first experience with French food and French people was, then, in Iowa. I had never laid eyes on anyone as different as the beautiful black-haired, green-eyed Micheline, her tiny white-haired mother, Madeleine, and her tall good-looking father, Bernard, who, in spite of his perfect English, was obviously not a native midwesterner. They blended into the community and at the same time were special members of it: three exotic French birds in a sea of corn!

Experience number two was, as I recounted in my book *French Toast*, the marriage of my grandfather, after my grandmother passed away, to Blanche Schweitzer, who had been a French professor at Grinnell College, one of the most respected schools in our state. With her white hair, blue eyes, and kind nature, my stepgrandmother, whom we called Aunt Blanche, was another major French influence on me. From the books she brought me to read, I learned that there were boys named Jean and not John, girls named Jeanne and not Jean, places called Brittany where people slept in beds with doors that shut them in at night.

In this day and age of the Internet and CNN, none of this would perhaps seem so alien, so alluring, so romantic. However, in the early '50s in a small town in Iowa where most of my hours were spent in the comfortable confines of the Shenandoah Public Library immersing myself in other worlds, this was *crucially* unfamiliar territory. Merely the sound of the French language transported me elsewhere. My Aunt Blanche taught me the first French words I ever learned: *fourchette*, fork, and *cochon*, pig. The latter was not because of pigs on the farm, but a particular pink stuffed pig she brought me as a gift. I was enchanted. I can't recall it, but I surely heard Micheline and Madeleine speak French together (Madeleine had a delicious French accent in English—I often think of her when I get self-conscious about my American accent in French and can only hope that my accent in French is as charming as hers was in English). At any rate, all these influences must have sunk in to a deeper part of me because by the time I got to the University of Michigan, there was only one thing I wanted to do: go to France.

A defining moment and a detour through Italy

The summer between my junior and senior year, I got my wish and went to France with Denise, my college roommate. In terms of a defining experience, that trip made all the difference, transporting me from the safety of home to the insecurity and fun of travel adventure. As hard as it is to imagine now, I was more than reluctant to leave home (and I especially didn't want to fly!) but then we were on our way, and I discovered France and found myself under its spell.

Our travel was not limited to France. We hitchhiked in Scotland and were amused to find that neither of us could understand what the lorry drivers were saying, nor could they understand us, I presume. Denise would push me into the cab first so that I would be the one who had to keep up the conversation. In exchange, though, she took care of all our finances, leaving me the comparatively more pleasant assignment of being our PR person. This ended in several fiascos including a memorable one in which we naively got off the train in Italy with a good-looking elderly Italian gentleman who suggested we see his village. He even knew a good hotel, he said. We could stay the night and get back on the train the next day. "Fantastic!" we exclaimed, in our incredible innocence, neither of us suspecting for one second that the motive of this man, who was old enough to be our grandfather, was to parade his American "catches" around the village—and more, if possible.

When our Italian friend tried to break down the door to our

hotel room, we suddenly (oh how brilliant we were, how quick on the draw) figured it all out. With great glee, we constructed a hastily made barricade in front of the entrance to our room and after a giggly night in which we tried to imagine the technical details of an elderly man taking on not one but two young college girls, we skittered out of there the next morning. Thank you, EurRail Pass. We also solemnly decided that my future PR efforts would be limited to English and French as I obviously had no clue about what was going on in Italian.

Trying out my French on the French

Far from the clutches of the old lecher, France seemed safer and I could try out my rudimentary language skills. To my surprise and to their credit, the French proved tolerant. *"Oo ay lah twahlet?"* (Where is the bathroom?) was about the extent of it at that point, but it was useful. Seeing that I could actually make myself understood, after two years of high school French and only one in college, I was overjoyed. When you are twenty years old and emerge from the Midwest and a sheltered life in college and find yourself in a simple hotel in the Latin Quarter overlooking the roofs of Paris; when you go down in the morning to buy your fresh croissant and are hit in the face by the smell of strong coffee; when you peer at the people and they look different, talk different, and act different—you might have one of several reactions: You might feel ill at ease and want to go back home where everything is familiar; you might not care much either way; or you might, like me, be so totally enthralled that you want to *be* those people, speak their language, eat their food, and drink their wine. I didn't want to return home and shop for French food in specialty stores or speak French from time to time when the occasion would (rarely) arise. I had made up my mind: I wanted to be in France—forever!

Dutifully, I returned to get my B.A. from the University of Michigan but my heart by now was miles away. After having seen France, my last year of college was anticlimatic, a parenthesis in time before I could return. In an attempt to dissuade myself from the admittedly crazy idea of going to France to live, I did however make one intense last-ditch effort to entice a handsome young law student to marry me and take me back to Chicago with him, where we would live together happily ever after in bourgeois paradise. Destiny wouldn't let me off the hook: after all my wily arrangements to get him interested in me, he announced that he was getting engaged to someone else. I spent a despondent five minutes contemplating Life After College Without Marriage—in those days this was no small matter—but I was quite sure everything would work out in the end, and besides, France was out there. It was time to get on the move.

Arcueil-Cachan and the *pension de famille*

While my friends busied themselves getting married and then getting jobs or not (that was the order in those days), I arranged to stay in a *pension de famille* in the working-class suburb of Cachan south of Paris and bought a one-way ticket to the French capital.

The husband of the lady who ran the *pension* would pick me up at the airport, I was told. Not to be caught unaware and not to let him know that my French was minimal to say the least, all through the long ride from America, I had repeated what I would tell him when he asked me the inevitable question—Did you have a good flight?

"*C'était très bien*," I would reply.

He was a white-haired gentleman driving a sardine-can Citroën 2CV, and he did indeed ask the question, as I had thought he would. When I replied, I even added an innovation. I had noticed that French people often punctuate phrases with an exclamation-question, "*Ah, bon?*" Every time he would rattle on in French which I absolutely did not understand, I would wait for him to pause, and then knowingly place my "*Ah, bon?*" It worked like a charm. Jean, we'll call him, chatted merrily away as we drove through a series of nondescript suburbs to Cachan. I was given a tour of the *pension*, during which time I was informed that there were no other English speakers, and that my sheets would be changed every two weeks (my French was good enough to understand *that*). By eight o'clock that evening, now far away from *l'Amérique*, I sat dazed in front of a table laden with good things to eat. Lots of good bread and, it seemed to me, lots of wine. Jean gestured for me to watch him.

"This is how you do it," he pronounced in what I thought was beautiful French, cutting a piece of creamy, slightly runny Camembert to spread on a piece of his baguette. He brought it to his mouth slowly with one hand and with the other picked up his glass of *vin rouge* to wash down this savory bite. I sat across the table from him, watching in utter fascination. What he was doing looked so *French* I couldn't believe it. Was I in someone's dream? Then I imitated him, slicing into the Camembert, spreading it on my bread, chewing on it very slowly, and washing it down with the wine. I later learned that this way of eating cheese would not exactly stand up *chez la marquise* but since we weren't in any way, shape, or form *chez la marquise*, it didn't make any difference. I was learning about French food first-hand and loved every minute of it.

La rue des Volontaires and the concierge with the onion soup

Another crucial eating experience took place a few years later in the late '60s with my concierge in a bourgeois (i.e., respectable) building in the fifteenth arrondissement where for a time I rented a maid's room on the seventh floor. She called me Mademoiselle Wetly instead of Welty and was very interested in which of my boyfriends would eventually become my husband. She rejected the suspicious-looking, oddly dressed, unshaven, leftist types and cast her vote for the polite well-dressed Englishman in tweed who turned out to be French and did indeed become my husband.

Perhaps her most outstanding characteristic was that she drank like a *poisson*. Her demeanor was that of a pug but perhaps the bulging eyes and red nose and smashed-in features were the effect of too much wine. However that may be, my concierge and I took an instant liking to each other and so it was that one day I had the privilege of being beckoned into her tiny courtyard kitchen, separate from her living quarters, to partake of her homemade onion soup, which was, naturally, accompanied by massive amounts of red wine. As with Jean and the Camembert, I couldn't have been more pleased to have been included in what for me was a truly French moment. The soup was hot and flavorful on that cold rainy evening, the wine, although by this time even I could tell it was *ordinaire*, just the ticket. I couldn't really understand much of what she was saying because my French still wasn't all that good, but I was starting to figure out that any kind of human contact in France that was accompanied by a sharing of food, no matter how modest the surroundings, was to be considered special.

La rue Mouffetard—an irate neighbor

The food-sharing experience I remember most, though, happened in between the *pension de famille* and the concierge experiences. It was on the rue Mouffetard where I rented an almost-civilized studio apartment for a year, a world record for me in my single days.

I had only lived on the rue Mouffetard about a week when my downstairs neighbor banged on my door, his face crimson and contorted with anger. Looking like a bantam hen or a *coq gaulois*, he shouted at me in French, phrases I did not understand other than the word *sabots*. He pointed accusingly at the wooden clogs I was wearing. They were Dr. Scholls and a wonderful remedy for sore feet, I thought. He didn't think they were so wonderful. Through an elaborate series of gestures, he demonstrated that my marching on top of his head was driving him insane. Since I've always believed in placating people when I can, I assured him in my broken French that this wouldn't happen again—I'd take the *sabots* and throw them out the window if need be! I even pantomimed it. Grumbling, he returned to his second-floor apartment. I thought that was the end of the story.

Mais non! A few minutes later he popped back, asking me if I would like to join him and his wife for some soup. Given the smells of fine cooking coming from their apartment, I had surmised early on that she shopped for food at the rue Mouffetard market unlike undomesticated me. Over a conciliatory bowl of delicious vegetables in broth, my neighbor made a confession to me, probably the only American he had ever seen in such proximity. Drawing himself up and staring me straight in the eyeballs, he announced in a tone which was definitely a proclamation and not to be argued with: "*On n'aime pas les Américains, mais on les admire."* We don't like Americans, but we admire them.

He set his soup spoon down defiantly and waited for my reaction. Aha! Did I turn my soup bowl over and run out? Was I horrified by this display of anti-Americanism? No! I finished the broth and contemplated the meaning of the declaration of which he seemed so proud. He obviously wasn't telling me he didn't like *me* and there was certainly nothing I could do about his or anyone else's anti-Americanism. Since it seemed to be his problem and not mine, I decided to cool off this particular Franco-American bilateral relationship before it got hot by flashing a big smile, thanking them, and bidding them good-bye. I relegated my wooden clogs to my closet and for the remainder of our time as neighbors, we had no more tiffs. A few months later, they moved to a modern apartment in the suburbs of Paris. I missed the smell of their soup and hoped for their sake that their new neighbors weren't Americans and didn't wear *sabots*.

. . . and cops in the closet

By this time I was beginning to get a glimpse of real French life, living right there on the rue Mouffetard, which, you might say, is almost a tourist cliché of a place. It wasn't so much then. Now renovated with a speaker phone and all the modern accoutrements, my building on the rue Mouffetard was then a real dump. Authentic and seventeenth century, but still, to all intents and purposes, a dump. Being American, of course, it was my dream of what France was. You entered the building through a passageway. On the right was an old wooden door that looked like it was going to fall apart (and, I reckoned, must have been there since the seventeenth century as well). Trash cans were lined up on one side of the entryway, the mailbox on the other. There were only four apartments in the building, one on the second floor, and three on the third floor. And here's the kicker: the toilets were *sur le palier*, on the landing, and my shower was in the kitchen. Looking back on it, it seems almost inconceivable that I would tolerate these conditions, but when you are twenty years old, what would seem outrageous or at the least downright inconvenient was *romantic*.

The practical result of having the toilet on the landing was that I would wait until the last possible moment to execute my needs. In winter, I would put on the biggest bathrobe and the warmest slippers I could find before slipping out my door and into the freezing hall, hoping against hope that none of the other occupants had had the same idea. I would open the door and steel myself for the blast of icy air coming from the window, which was always left open. Worse than the cold and the open window, though, were the pigeons who flocked there to roost and coo in a ghastly manner right above our heads. Years later, even today, I admit, I go to the bathroom about five times before really going to bed. I am convinced this odd habit is a direct consequence of my rue Mouffetard experience and to this day I can't look at a pigeon without thinking of that WC.

This was 1967, mind you, and as I said, it's unbelievable even for then that this kind of toilet still existed. Someone out there was making money out of innocent (dumb) foreigners who found all this alluring and put up with highway robbery for the privilege of living on this picturesque street in such conditions. My two neighbors turned out to be foreigners like me and one was even a fellow midwesterner. Quite obviously the place was a magnet for the likes of us. It *was*, I have to admit, Paris as I'd dreamed it, toilet on the landing and all. Where in the U.S. can you look out the window of a centuries-old crumbling-down building onto a street crowded with throngs of people straight out of a Breughel painting merrily weaving their way with straw baskets and string bags in hand to buy fresh fish, oranges and apples and pears from neat pyramid piles, slabs of meat of every imaginable cut, dates so succulent looking you could taste them even before putting them in your mouth, every imaginable kind of olive, and bouquets of flowers of every tone and hue? So who cared if the toilet was on the landing and the shower stall in the kitchen? At least I *had* a shower—and a kitchen.

Joe, my Italian-American neighbor on the third floor, decided that he'd had enough of being the innocent American abroad. "I got my apartment measured," he confided to me before pausing to announce triumphantly, "and now I have the proof that I'm being had and I'm sure you are as well!" He explained to me the complicated French system of the *surface corrigée* in which you can get your apartment officially measured to see if it corresponds to the actual number of square meters you have. If it turns out that you have been given misinformation about the exact number of square meters in your apartment, you not only start paying the correct amount of rent but recuperate your surplus back rent as well. Joe's plan was simple: I was to get my apartment officially measured and once we had the results, we would state our case to the owners (whoever they were) through the rental agency.

I did so—and found he was right. I only had twenty square meters as it was and was paying for about ten more meters than I actually had! It was time for battle.

Joe and I made a beeline to the Préfecture de Police where an *inspecteur* listened to us carefully. To our surprise, instead of dismissing us as the insane Americans we were, he seemed impressed by our knowledge of French real estate laws and promptly started thinking out loud about how we could help him apprehend the people who were cheating us.

But before anything else, he said, he needed to visit our apartments to "case the joint" for action. Mine was tailor-made for what he had in mind. The entryway gave onto a small kitchen to the left. In it was my sink and shower (yes, my shower!). In the main room a lone window looked directly over the rue Mouffetard. One entire wall was taken up by a closet with sliding doors that were covered in beige burlap.

"Aha!" he said, fairly rubbing his hands together and sliding the doors back and forth. "This is where I will hide. And Inspector B.," he said, pointing to his colleague, "will go there." He pointed to the shower.

He quickly laid out his plan. The next time the real estate agent contacted me, I was to say I was sick and couldn't come to the agency to pay the rent. Could Mademoiselle collect it at my place? Once she assented, I was to call the inspector to inform him of the day and time. He and his colleague would come to occupy their respective hiding places before she arrived. Apparently our inspector was an old hand at such showdowns for he felt it necessary to warn Joe and me that in cases like this people had a tendency to faint or have heart attacks. But, he reassured us, not to worry.

I wasn't worried. I had always had a flair for the dramatic and now I found myself a bit player in my own drama.

Everything went as designed. When the agent called, I asked her to come by and we set a date. A few minutes before her arrival, Joe strolled casually over to my place. He was there to pay his rent as well—in cash, naturally. That was the way we had always done it:

neither of us had ever questioned the arrangement or tried to pay by check or get a receipt—until that moment.

When Mademoiselle arrived, I greeted her cordially and asked her to sit down on the crummy fake-leather couch that had come with the place. A fairly young, black-haired, diminutive French-woman, she chatted with me for a few minutes. Then we got down to business. I had received precise instructions as to what I must make her say. If I didn't utter certain key words that would make her respond with other key words, those cops would remain in my closet and shower forever and the whole elaborate process would have been for naught.

"Do you have the money?" she asked.

"Oh, yes," I said, smiling, "but I need a receipt this time and from now on because it's my mom who's paying."

She shook her head with sincere regret. "*Vous savez*, I would like to give you a receipt but I can't. It's because of taxes."

The magic words! Out sprang the two inspectors, one from the shower stall, the other directly in front of her, appearing from the closet as if he had walked through the wall. She did not faint or have a heart attack but seemed to get even smaller as they handcuffed her and led her downstairs to where her accomplice was waiting for her in the car. They nabbed him too.

As befits life in France, Joe and I brought out one bottle of Champagne to celebrate immediately and kept another in the fridge to share with our cop friends later on.

By the time I met my husband to be, I could truthfully brag that I may not have made any food in my miniscule kitchen on the rue Mouffetard, but that I had hidden a French cop in its shower. How many people can say that?

La rue Duvivier and a fatal moment

It was on the rue Duvivier that I learned that the size of the kitchen in France (with or without shower and with or without a cop in the shower) has absolutely nothing to do with the quality of the cuisine issuing from it. Over the years I have lived in France, I have marveled at the exquisite meals that have sprung forth from rooms with barely enough counter space to cut a *saucisson* on.

It was a good thing I wasn't picky about kitchens or much of anything else (as we have seen with the toilet on the landing) or I never would have moved in with Mr. Englishman Tweed on the rue Duvivier in the seventh arrondissement. The kitchen in the place he rented there was almost big enough for one person to turn around in and with two people in its confines . . . it gave new meaning to "two's company, three's a crowd." *Two* was a crowd.

His apartment was a second-floor four-room affair in a total space of about 160 square feet. The walls were made out of plywood or some kind of material that let in all the noise from the other apartments, dogs barking, babies wailing, a complete caboodle of sounds. Squished into those 160 square feet was an entry hall, a minuscule bathroom, a kitchen that I never intended to use, and the main room with a window looking out over the rue Duvivier.

It was small and sonorous, but I didn't really care because 1) I was young, 2) there were only two of us, and 3) every night we headed out to dinner with friends or just the two of us for a romantic *tête à tête*. Ah, life in Paris. How gay, how insouciant!

One night as we awaited the bill at one of our favorite hangouts, which was not French but Chinese, Mr. Englishman Tweed, who I now called by his real name, Philippe, gave me a strange look. He sat back, lit up a cigarette, and took a puff.

"How much do you think I earn?" he asked.

I had never given any thought to the question and was in fact wondering for the thousandth time why the French smoke so much. I reflected a moment and then came out with an approximate figure. He guffawed and nervously took another puff.

"No, that's not it, not it at all," he said, shaking his head.

He marked a slight pause before delivering the blow.

"It's time to start eating at home."

If he'd announced he didn't love me or was dumping me for someone else, I wouldn't have been more surprised—or horrified. Eating at home? Making food? In France? Me? Oh, my God. You can run but you can't hide. Real life, even in France, had finally caught up with me.

 INTERVIEW WITH PHILIPPE

HWR: Did you ever think that I would rise to the challenge of getting in the kitchen and making French food on a daily basis for *twenty-nine years*?

PhR: That is only 21,173 meals.

Soupe à l'oignon à la concierge

When I sat down with my concierge on a rainy cold night some thirty years ago to eat her onion soup, I was delighted to find myself sharing her food and wine. Not being a "foodie" (forgive the horrid term) now or then, I didn't dissect the soup or ask how she made it. I simply ate it and it tasted good. To me, it's the quintessential homey dish to restore you on a cold night. No wonder it was so popular with the big, beefy workers in Les Halles when that neighborhood was the stomach of Paris. There are many, many ways to make this French classic, which is a meal in itself. Some make it with white wine, others with water, others with both. Some people add cognac, others sherry. Still others put in a dash of nutmeg, and I saw one version which called for a clove of crushed garlic. Some recipes call for straining the broth; others say to add an egg beaten with port to the bouillon right before putting on the croutons. Certain ingredients are not subject to debate: you definitely need onions, croutons, and grated cheese! After trying several variations on the theme, I have decided that the following simple one is probably what my concierge served me.

But first . . . an important food note

In this book, from time to time, when the spirit moves me and when there's a reason, I'll share a recipe for a dish I particularly like. I'm not a food professional, though, and these recipes in their converted form have not been tested in a lab. You may need to adjust the measurements as recipes have a tendency to turn out differently when they are transposed from liters to cups, from kilos to pounds. I have of course made all the recipes I'm presenting here—but using the metric system. This is because, as I'll explain in this book, since I live, shop and cook in France, out of sheer necessity I quit thinking in ounces and pounds a long time ago.

Different ingredients give different tastes as well. Ask any of the American women living in France who have tried to bake chocolate chip cookies "just like home." The ones made in France are definitely not the same and it isn't because they're homesick! Same for the vinaigrette I make in the States: I use the same proportions of vinegar and oil and mustard, but the resulting vinaigrette does not resemble the one I make in France because the oil is different, the vinegar is different, and the mustard is different!

So now you've been warned. If any of these recipes doesn't quite make it in your kitchen, adjust! And especially, enjoy!

Soupe à l'oignon

1 pound of onions
3 big tablespoons of butter
1 tablespoon of flour
6 cups of boiling liquid (this can be 3 cups of water and 3 cups of white wine, or 6 cups of water to which you have added a bouillon cube, or better still, the liquid from a pot-au-feu you've made the day before, but that's getting rather ambitious, isn't it?)
A tablespoon of cognac
A baguette or pain de campagne
½ cup grated Gruyère
Salt and pepper to taste

Cut the onions in small pieces.
Stir them in the melted butter until
they are transparent.
Sprinkle the flour over them.
Keep stirring while you add the 6 cups of liquid.
Add salt and pepper to taste.
Lower the flame, add the cognac.
Cover and cook for 20 minutes on a
low flame.

Quickly brown some round slices of baguette or *pain de campagne* in the oven (or toast them in the toaster), pour the broth into the bowls, place the croutons on top, and sprinkle the grated Gruyère over them. Grill in the oven until the cheese melts. Eat piping hot and be careful not to burn your tongue. Serves 4.

2

A Cultural Clash in the Kitchen

The plastic sandwich · Learning to cook with la cocotte minute · Potluck and leftovers à la française · Sauces and seasons and strange things to eat · Bring out the tofu · A very special American in Paris

Can anything prepare an American woman for life in France and in particular the life of the wife of a Frenchman who is used to eating the French way? My short answer to that one is: no.

The French way, I can assure you, is *not* the American way. If you want to know what the difference is, get a group of French and Americans together and stick them on a desert island—or at least have them on vacation together, which is my experience. The main preoccupation of the French group will be what they will eat and when. The American group won't think about food other than as an afterthought.

The French think about lunch and dinner from the moment they've finished breakfast and sometimes even before they've started it. As Kristina Didouan, the American wife of a Frenchman put it: "I love my mother-in-law dearly but when she starts in on "What are we going to eat for lunch?" at 7:00 A.M. while I'm hovering over my coffee and prunes, it is a bit much." I myself have often been surprised that the first order of the day, before, during, and sometimes just after breakfast but never later, is "What are we going to eat for lunch?" This is *very* French. We Americans are the opposite: we always profess that we aren't hungry and relegate thinking about meals and mealtime to the bottom of our list of priorities. What this translates into in terms of Franco-American vacations is that the French make the food and the Americans eat it! I say this as one of the worst offenders.

Take a lovely holiday we had in the south of France with another French–American couple and three other Americans. When Philippe and the other Frenchman were there, right after breakfast they would start talking about what to eat for lunch. We would then make an excursion to the market or to the small village for groceries. Thanks to our French husbands, we sat down to a sumptuously tasty four-course lunch at around one every afternoon and dinner between eight and nine in the evening (I can see the French people reading this shaking their heads and saying: So what?!).

The minute our two cooks and representatives of France returned to Paris to work and we Americans were left alone, you'd better believe that even the *idea* of shopping and making meals flew right out the window. Chaos reigned! Ironically, I was the one who made myself lunch and ate it alone because everyone else claimed they weren't hungry. One wandered off for a nap, the other for a swim, yet another went off to read a book. I on the other hand had heard the familiar French signal that now goes off in my head when the noon hour approaches. Lunch = *sit down* for an enjoyable moment, even if you're alone. So there I sat with a simple lunch and a glass of wine, enjoying my solitary meal immensely. My French husband would have been proud.

Which gets me back to my theory: it isn't that we Americans don't like food or eating. Not by a long shot. In fact, we champion grazers eat all day long. Maybe this is because, unlike the French, we don't have several centuries of structured mealtimes behind us so there's nothing in our reptilian brain that tells us it's *time* to eat!

The French have no problem with this. Or at least they don't so far. Perhaps globalization will eradicate centuries of sitting down to the table and turn them into snackers and grazers as well. For the moment, though, they still view mealtime as a congenial moment not only to eat but to discuss the day and relax.

French women in the kitchen

American women to whom I recount my life as the wife of a Frenchman and what that means in terms of kitchen duty are generally nonplussed, depending on their age.

"How is it possible that it's always the women who are spending all the time thinking and worrying about food?" they expostulate. This question comes from women who are under the age of fifty or who are still seriously into women's lib, or who don't have children and so don't know the *pleasure* of feeding your offspring.

Here's my personal take on the situation. Yes, French women spend a lot of time in the kitchen, certainly more time than American women do. No, I've never heard any vocal griping about this. But then I've never heard a lot of bean counting between French women and French men in general. They seem to like each other, as I said in *French Toast*, and kind of get on with things. Food being a pleasure, I don't think anyone in France could imagine fighting about it!

There are, to be sure, certain cultural differences this particular

American wife had to get used to. One Saturday, we were sitting at the table for lunch and I started getting some gentle gibes about the meal which was composed of ham and rice—sick people's food because I was a victim of intestinal flu and didn't feel like either shopping for or making food.

"You certainly aren't subtle," said Philippe. "In case we hadn't guessed you didn't feel good, we know it now."

"How can I make food when the thought of it makes me want to vomit?" I asked.

"Well, if you were Latin and Catholic, you would make us something good and watch us eat it."

"Yeah, right," I replied. "Well, I'm Anglo-Saxon and Protestant and there's no *way* I'd make you guys something delicious while I sit here eating my boring slice of ham and this tasteless bowl of rice!"

"We noticed."

I checked out this cultural difference with my French friend Françoise, who said: "I'm French and I'm Catholic and I'm like you. I can't stand to make food when I'm out of order." Ah, thank heavens for reality checks.

But the whole episode illustrated four things to me and they were all positive. The first thing is that my dear husband is a tease and that I shouldn't take everything he says seriously. I now check out his version of things with at least three French friends to see if what he is saying applies to all French people or if it only applies to him. The second thing is that he can kid me about bad meals because they are so rare (hey!). The third thing is that I don't mind his occasional quips because he often takes over in the kitchen. The fourth thing is that—and this is an answer to the horrified feminists—we both do what we do in the kitchen because we like it. There aren't any victims in this house. And we're not keeping score.

Antecedents: the plastic sandwich

As I've explained, though I didn't come from a tradition of fast food, French food, other than the Normandy Inn of my childhood, was still something I knew next to nothing about. When I started living real life in France, I was a blank slate upon which all had to be written. Food to me was something your mom made for you or you shared with friends in restaurants.

My cooking skills were so slim, family lore has it—and I confess it's true—that when my sister brought her fiancé home to introduce him to the family, I made him a cheese sandwich (quite nice of me, I thought) . . . with the plastic wrapping still on the cheese! He married her anyway, but my reputation had been made.

The plastic sandwich episode behind me, my contacts with the world of food were limited to waiting tables in and shortly after college. Fortunately for my fellow students and restaurant patrons, I never had a hand in the making of anyone's meals. But I kept getting closer to the kitchen: in San Francisco I worked for a time as a hatcheck girl at the Fleur de Lys restaurant. There, I had the same delicious meals the customers ate, but with the staff in the basement. This job, which a French friend found for me, gave me the opportunity to see firsthand the absolutely professional standards this restaurant maintained in its cooking and its decor. Everything was harmonious, everything went together. I, for example, was dressed in a beautiful skirt that was made out of exactly the same French country material as the drapes.

"Oh, she's so cute," murmured a customer to my boss, thinking I was French and didn't understand. "She goes with the curtains!"

And so it was that I leaped up in the world from Plastic Sandwich Lady to a Cute Curtain in a French restaurant.

At least by the time I got to France and married a Frenchman, I'd had some exposure to French cuisine even if I was only hanging around it. But from there to settling down in another country and putting two three-course French meals on the table every day was another giant step.

Regular meals—on both sides of the Atlantic

The French really are into regular meals! My father-in-law was the busy proprietor of Rochefort Papier Peint, a thriving Paris paint and wallpaper supply business. He came home every day for lunch, which, believe me, wasn't a sandwich (see my book *French Toast* for the episode in which my mother-in-law and I attempt to foist one off on him!) but a complete hot repast which my mother-in-law had waiting on the table. Anything less would have been unthinkable. Of course, I have to say in all honesty that on the other side of the ocean it wasn't that different. My father also returned every day from his busy real estate and insurance agency on Main Street to our home at 200 South Center Street to a full meal in the dining room with four children who came home for lunch, which my mother served without fail. After it, Dad would retire to the living room to sit in his favorite chair and take a ten-minute nap before returning to work. My mom always took a daily after-lunch nap as well, probably to get over the exhaustion of dealing with four wee ones and all those meals! In the evening the six of us sat around the dining room table with Mom at one end and Dad at the other. There was no question in our house of dashing out the door during mealtime. Years later, several of my friends told me how much they liked to come to our house because of the civilized ambiance at the dinner table. Although in college my eating habits became chaotic, at least from having grown up in such a family, I knew what the word *mealtime* meant. (I belabor the point, perhaps, but it is because the French somehow think that all Americans grab food out of the fridge and never sit down to the table. I protest!)

A meal is a meal is a meal

So it wasn't a terrible shock for me to learn that the French take eating so seriously. What I didn't realize, though, was that, to paraphrase Gertrude Stein, *a meal is a meal is a meal*, with a beginning, a middle, and an end. An American meal does not compare to the French meal in which the various dishes are served in courses. We Americans consider a sandwich a meal, for example. My French husband doesn't: when he comes home from the office and says he's starving because he didn't eat any lunch and I question him closely, it turns out that he had a sandwich, which he doesn't consider lunch!

Times have changed now and the French, especially the Parisians, have loosened up and eat sandwiches and light salads for lunch, but as I pointed out above, back in the early '70s when I first began cooking in France people like my traditional in-laws wouldn't have considered such a thing. Actually they still don't. I have *never* in all the years I've lived here, including the most recent ones, seen a sandwich appear at the Rochefort family table, even at lunchtime. And speaking of lunch, according to a recent study by the Centre de Recherche pour l'Étude et l'Observation des Conditions de Vie,

Research Center for the Study and Observation of Living Conditions, four out of five Frenchmen eat at home at midday every day of the week, a pattern that hasn't changed over the past ten years!

What did all this mean for me? In those first years in France, it was good-bye American eating habits! Good-bye snacks all day long and Coke (which I never liked anyway) and a quick sandwich at lunch, not because Philippe came home but because my children did, and having French genes, they wouldn't let me get away with throwing a mere sandwich at them. I did at one point consider staging my own French Revolution by simply overthrowing the rules and getting everyone to eat out of the fridge. As time went by, though, I adjusted—to the great amusement and wonder of my single friends who lived in France. They were free to eat what they wanted when they wanted or not at all. In the end, though, I didn't regret changing my eating habits, mainly because I ended up losing weight with the French way of eating (but that's another story). Deep down in my American heart, though, lurked the thought that the constant preoccupation with food and menu planning required some kind of a saintlike devotion mixed with military planning that doesn't come naturally unless you have ten centuries of French food culture in your bones.

Don't get me wrong: It's not that I didn't like living in France or eating good food. It's that when confronted with my having to *make* the food on a daily basis, it became another kettle of fish!

In those early days, I couldn't quite fathom that most of the next two decades of my life would be spent on that earthshaking but necessary question: What are we going to eat (today, tonight, tomorrow, next week)? But that quickly became evident. Fortunately, at the time my live-in announced that we would be eating at home, we lived right around the corner from the rue Cler, a delightful market street in the seventh arrondissement which I loved to stroll down to admire the precisely aligned colorful piles of vegetables and fruits.

Admiring, though, was one thing. Putting these wonderful products to culinary use was another. There was, admittedly, a gap to close.

Learning to cook with *la cocotte minute*

I could see that no matter how hard I tried I wasn't going to get out of cooking. Philippe had definitely stated that we were going to be eating at home and seemed to mean business. He had unveiled his financial status, thereby giving me the idea that he was serious enough about me to make such a revelation and making it quite obvious that it wouldn't be possible to continue eating at restaurants every night for the rest of our lives (more's the pity, I thought at the time). You know how it is with love, though. One does make sacrifices and efforts one wouldn't ordinarily make. So off it was to the tiny kitchen (remember the one where I said two was a crowd and which I never had any intention of using?) to figure out what on earth one could possibly concoct in it. I soon learned, and it was confirmed several small kitchens later, that you can work wonders in a *cuisine* the size of a galley in a boat.

Even if you only have two gas burners, you can cook in a *cocotte minute*, a pressure cooker. My mom used to use a pressure cooker but I don't know of many Americans who do these days. Invented in the '50s in France, it is one of the most popular cooking vessels not only in France but throughout the world. SEB, one of the leading brands, has sold some 50 million *cocottes minutes* in more than fifty countries, I read in one of my favorite cooking magazines. A French friend of mine told me that when the *cocotte minute* first came out, it almost brought a revolution with it. The idea of cooking long-simmering traditional dishes like the *bœuf bourgignon* or a *pot-au-feu* in a pressure cooker was shocking! And yet what could be more convenient for working women who want to make good food but can't spend hours doing it? Still today, the *cocotte* is not universally accepted. Some people don't know how to or like to use it. Others swear by it. I love using one because you can make almost everything in it from meat and fish to vegetables. It enables meats to keep their flavors and juices and vegetables to hold on to their minerals— and since it attains a high temperature in a matter of minutes, it cooks the food in about half the time it would normally take. It's a good way to have decent healthy meals without having to spend an inordinate amount of time on them. Therefore, I became great friends with my *cocotte minute* and the recipes that accompanied it in a book by Françoise Bernard called *300 Recettes SEB*, or *300 SEB Recipes*.

Françoise Bernard is one of those no-nonsense cooks whose simple, quick recipes have bailed out thousands of people just like me. My *300 Recettes* is now completely dog-eared and stained. When Philippe bought me a brand-new *cocotte minute* a couple of years ago, I was delighted to see that a new book by Françoise Bernard came with it. And even more interested to see, on a tour through a bookstore, that she had recently collaborated on a book of 208 easy, convivial recipes with six-star chef Alain Ducasse. What a meeting of the minds, one the veritable voice of French gastronomy, and the other the voice of practicality personified. In the Bernard–Ducasse book, each takes a product and gives a recipe. I checked out the recipe for endive, one of my favorite vegetables. Françoise Bernard gives her recipe for endives with a beaufort (Savoy cheese) gratin, *endives au gratin au beaufort*; on the opposite page, Alain Ducasse presents his recipe for cooked and raw endives with truffle, *endives cuites et crues aux truffes*. Same product, different approach. As you can imagine, Bernard's recipes are more appropriate for everyday cooking. Ducasse's make you dream.

With *La Bonne Cuisine, 208 Recettes Faciles et Conviviales*, the author of my *300 Recettes SEB* has risen even higher in my opinion. After all, thanks to her, I've made everything from lamb stew to *riz au lait*, a delicious sweet rice-and-milk dessert, in my tried-and-true pressure cooker. I couldn't live without it.

There are only two problems with the *cocotte minute*: one is that the time given for some of the recipes is really ambitious. I, for one, do not believe in the four-minute cauliflower!

The second problem is that in the days before the new safety valves, you did have to be careful or this handy pot might blow itself—and you—to kingdom come. A concierge once told me that he was calmly sitting in his place on his day off when he heard a tremendous commotion. He raced out the door to find the debris of one of the occupant's Sunday lunch strewn all over the common grounds when the *cocotte* had exploded. To be sure, this didn't happen often, but still it was best not to be absentminded when opening it, and make sure that all the steam had been evacuated.

Perhaps I was thinking of this story the day the lid of my trusty old *cocotte minute* refused to budge. I rushed downstairs to consult my concierge, whose husband, an unparalleled handyman, happened to be there. He turned it this way and that until, to my great relief, he somehow got the top off. I decided at that point it was time for a brand-new one that was less temperamental. With my new *cocotte minute*, I no longer fear that in a forgetful moment I'll jet out of here on a cloud of steam. For sentimental reasons, though, the old one is still with me. We've been friends for too long to part company.

Potluck and leftovers à la française

At the same time I was learning to cook in the *cocotte minute*, I was discovering all kinds of other things—and so were my friends. We were in some kind of giant culinary boot camp in which we learned that . . . guess what? Unlike the States, where anything goes, in France there are *rules*. There are rules for the way you make food, but also the way you serve food, and even the way you talk about food. Most of these rules are learned from experience—and goofs.

We American transplants had to get used to things we'd never even thought about before, whether it was cooking or serving, inviting or thanking people for being invited. For example, inviting people to dinner for spaghetti . . . This may not shock you but I learned that you don't invite French people, unless they are best buddies, of course, for spaghetti and garlic bread, my good old favorite meal! I am of course talking about Paris and people my age (old!) but my twenty-year-old son David opines that whatever the social milieu, if you're over the age of twenty-five, you don't tell people to stop by for a bite. The idea is that if you're going to invite people, bring out the best. And, by the way, when the French say "come for potluck," be prepared. Their potluck is our fanciest dinner!

As the humorous writer Pierre Daninos's fictitious character, Major Thompson, an Englishman in France, explains in *Les Carnets du Major Thompson*, when the French say that the meal will be *à la fortune du pot* it's not quite the same as in England. "That potluck, of a skeletonlike thinness in England, in France takes on the most generous forms. It even throws light on the whole problem: for you understand, when you see the French inviting you for potluck with their best dishes, why this improvisation must be . . . prepared ahead of time. Never would one of our housewives succeed in this without working on it for several months."

When it came to making food at home, I soon found out that Philippe and I had varying views on leftovers. This isn't necessarily a cultural clash because I think everyone has different views on them. There's the throw-them-away school and the keep-everything school and the keep-some, throw-out-others school. I'm of the school: keep-them-until-you-can-figure-out-what-to-do-with-them-and-if-they-are-still-around-a-week-later-toss-them. Philippe and I did not see eye to eye on this from day one as his grandmother, an excellent cook, was the queen of leftovers. If she had made a *pot-au-feu*, the remaining beef would end up in a delicious cold beef salad with pickles, shallots, fresh parsley mixed with a good vinaigrette and be the next day's main fare. The beef might also end up in a *hachis parmentier*, a delicious combination of the chopped beef and mashed potatoes baked together. Philippe can never get over my penchant for forgetting what is in the fridge and going ahead and shopping for whatever I feel like eating.

"You don't eat what you feel like eating," he explained to me early on in our marriage. "You eat what's in the fridge!"

"Oh, really," I replied, "how utterly and consummately boring."

It took me more than twenty years to get the message, and to want to dive into the contents of the fridge to see what is in there that would make a meal. I'm not quite at his grandmother's level but I'm making progress. A simple example: if you have eggs and milk and *crème fraiche* and bacon or ham, you've got the makings of a quiche, *et voilà!* One night after we'd had a pot-au-feu and had plenty of leftover meat, I remembered his grandmother's wonderful salad and I made:

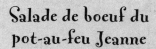

Salade de boeuf du pot-au-feu Jeanne

Leftover meat from pot-au-feu
Shallots

Pickles (preferably corni-chons)
Fresh parsley

Take the leftover meat from the *pot-au-feu* (recipe in Chapter 13) and cut into 1-inch cubes.
Take a few shallots and slice them.
Take some pickles (dill so they are like French cornichons—it's even better if you can find French cornichons) and cut them into pieces.
Take fresh parsley and chop it. Mix the meat, shallots, pickles, and chopped parsley in a bowl with a good homemade vinaigrette.

Delicious!

Below you'll find the recipe for homemade French vinaigrette, which is essential to the success of this and most French salads.

Vinaigrette

The best thing about this, other than its taste, is that you're sure no one has thrown any sugar into it, which is what they do in almost all commercial dressings. A simple French vinaigrette salad dressing. Ready?

1 teaspoon mustard (Dijon is best)
1 tablespoon vinegar (good-quality red wine)
a dash of salt and pepper
3 tablespoons of oil (olive or cooking depending on what you're making and your personal taste buds)
Stir (if you stir with a fork, the sauce will have a better consistency).

For more, keep the ratio of 1 vinegar to 3 oil and you're on!

Although Philippe definitely approves of the beef salad served with its delicious vinaigrette, I found that he has definite opinions on what is fit to be served again and what is not. For some reason he won't touch a day-old potato and is the first to shun vegetables that have been cooked and served once. He also wouldn't consider drinking warmed-over coffee (neither would I). But since I know French people who drink warmed-over coffee and eat day-old potatoes, I've concluded that attitudes toward leftovers are more linked to personal taste than national preferences.

French Fries

You may not believe it but in this land of foie gras and Champagne and exquisite delicacies that other nations can only envy, French fries are the Frenchman's favorite food. I may eat and make all kinds of French food but on this score, I'm definitely a failure. I simply don't have the French-fry reflex, and not only that, I associate French fries with *fat*. Yet what could be simpler than cutting up potatoes, plunging them into oil, and taking them out when they are golden brown to serve with a fresh green salad and a steak (as in the ubiquitous *steak frites*, France's most popular dish). Some French families do this several times a week. When our children were young, Philippe would say:

"Let's have *frites*." And the boys would chime in: *"Oui, oui, des frites, Maman!"*

Sadly, it was to no avail. I just couldn't seem to get into that kitchen and make French fries. It was one French thing it seemed we were just never going to have, not in our home, at any rate.

Hoping that I would become more enthusiastic if it seemed easier, Philippe offered me a *friteuse*, a French-fry maker. I plugged it in, gazed at its wire basket and stainless-steel container, admired the sophisticated controls that would bring the oil to the perfect temperature. It then sat on a counter where it was never used.

Rather than heave the machine, Philippe appointed himself Head French-Fry Maker. I think that deep in his heart he's still hoping that I'll adopt this French custom someday. And who knows? His homemade fries aren't soggy or greasy: they are a crisp, golden delight. In the beginning, I didn't eat them. Now I eat them all. It might, I have started thinking, indeed be worth a try.

Someday.

Language and food

The way the French talk about food and drink is different as well. As Daninos writes: "The French have such an epicurian way of evoking good things that it allows them to have a feast of words between meals. It's an incomparable pleasure for a foreigner to be able to observe this as a guest. On their lips, the mere names Pommard or Château-Margaux sound so rich, so soft—as if already brought to room temperature—that all of a sudden they yield the fluid treasures of Burgundy and the secrets of the Bordeaux vineyards."

Ah, the importance of language. One American married to a Frenchman told me that she wrote a thank-you letter to her mother-in-law after a good meal, telling her that she had *bien mangé*. The next time her mother-in-law saw her, she called her over and explained to her that *manger* is used for animals. *People* dine or *déjeunent*, lunch; they don't *mangent*. I was relieved by this story because I had done something even worse, which was to exclaim in a burst of enthusiasm to my mother-in-law that I had *bien bouffé*— the equivalent of stuffing your mouth!

Unpeeled asparagus and a French hamburger assembly line

But casting around for the right vocabulary is nothing compared to those first disastrous dinner parties. When she was a young bride, my dear friend Dorie, whose husband, Jacques, was out of town on business, spent the day preparing a meal for their guests, an unsuspecting provincial notary and his wife. Since Jacques wasn't there to advise her, she did the best she could as she struggled to prepare some lovely white asparagus. There was only one problem. "Did he tell me you had to peel those babies?" She laughs as she recalls: "I served them *unpeeled* to my guests who sat there politely spitting out the filaments of asparagus. I don't think they ever got over it. I've never seen them since!"

All these years later, I still find that the French dinner party is quite a production. Even when you've learned how to cook French food and know the order of courses and have the procedure down pat, the truth is a French dinner party takes a lot of time and planning.

I am not even talking about extremely formal occasions. I am talking about a "normal" meal with friends, which is very different from our American version. In the States, it's "Come on over," and then you serve sandwiches or hamburgers or chili. You all sit around and it's great. Food isn't really the point.

In France, it is very different. Take as an example a dinner party I recently had with some really good friends. With my son David that meant seven at the table. I decided on a simple menu. As an entrée, a light salad of avocado, shrimps, and peeled grapefruit (not so simple because it takes a lot of time to get the skin off each segment of grapefruit), followed by a *lotte à l'américaine* (monkfish in a wine-and-tomato sauce) and rice (not very creative, I admit), salad, cheese and dessert. The first glitch in my perfect planning was that when I went to the market, I saw that for the price of the monkfish that day I could buy a new car (just kidding). I had to change my menu right there at the market. I decided on a veal sauté Marengo for the good reason that when you have a stew like this, you can make it ahead of time and don't have to keep popping back to the kitchen. I bought the veal, I bought the salad, I bought the cheese, and I went to the best pastry shop I could find and bought two wonderful cakes. Then I went to the bakery to buy the bread. Philippe took care of the wine. When you think about it, since I bought the cheese and the dessert, there wasn't that much work. Right? Wrong! I figure that between the shopping at the market and elsewhere, the polishing of silver and setting of the table, the cleaning up the apartment before and cleaning up the whole mess afterwards, it was a three-day affair! And you wonder why the French don't launch casual invitations?

The point of this for foreigners who are invited to French homes is that they should be aware that the hostess has in the majority of cases invested a lot of time and thought and energy in the dinner. A dinner party is a social event, not a happening, not something that has been thrown together at the last minute or came from some kind of divine inspiration. One night in our country place we were invited to the home of friends. All of us, including the host and hostess, were dressed casually in our country clothes and it might have been a simple country meal, which would have been fine. It turned out, though, that our hostess had gone to a lot of trouble for us. Her first course in particular was stunning: beautifully presented baked oysters on the half shell in a delicate sauce. A wee dark green spinach leaf adorned each oyster shell. Then we had a succulent *coq au vin*, chicken in wine sauce, and potatoes, the cheese plate, and a homemade *baba au rhum*, a sponge cake soaked in rum. I know that the oysters alone must have taken her hours! But we had been invited three weeks ahead of the date so she had had plenty of time to think about and devise her menu strategy. One reaction to this could be: Why go to so much trouble? Having lived in France so long, I've come to understand "where she's coming from" in the sense that if you invite people, you want to make it a very special occasion for everyone, one they will remember with pleasure.

One culinary disaster, which wouldn't happen today, occurred when I decided, in 1976 (prehamburger days in France), to have a casual American party at which the guests would assemble their own hamburgers. First of all, I had to explain to the baker what a bun was. He made them especially for me and they were much better than any bun I have ever had before or since. Then I had to explain to my French guests (I reiterate: this was pre-McDonald's and the invasion of American food) that since the buns were there and the meat was cooked, all they had to do was put the two together and add catsup, mustard, pickles or whatever they wanted. They had never done this before and must have thought it was totally crazy. But being extremely polite, they executed, and stood around awkwardly nibbling on their hamburgers which they seemed to like in spite of having to hold them in their hands, constantly watching to make sure catsup didn't ooze out of them. Even more than the oddness of the hamburger, the idea of inviting people over only to make them construct their own dinner must have seemed strange to them because in France when you invite, the idea is to spare your guests ↡ any work! So much for being *that* casual.

Sauces and seasons and strange things to eat

How cooked one likes meat and what one puts on it is another cultural difference. One American told me that her French husband once took a large group of American businessmen to a highly recommended Parisian restaurant. He had to ascertain that the meat would be well done and translate to the waiters that the Americans had asked for catsup in spite of the fact that the *tournedos*, a thick round cut of steak from the tenderloin, were served with an incredible sauce the chef had probably spent hours concocting. "The waiter returned with the catsup and pushed the offending item toward the oblivious culprits in a great moment that said it all," my friend said with a laugh, noting that the incident happened twenty years ago and happens with less frequency today as many American palates have become more sophisticated.

It works both ways, of course. I once invited some very unadventurous French people to whom I gave corn bread, chili, and brownies. The chili and brownies were strange enough but when I passed around the corn bread, one of my guests could barely conceal his astonishment. He clearly could not make the connection between "corn" and "bread." Of course one must remember that until recently the French thought corn on the cob was strictly limited to farm animals.

The French in the States are up against their own problems of cultural culinary shock. Janine Hopkins, a Frenchwoman who has lived in the States since 1951 and considers herself well adapted to

American life, says that it took her "a good long while to get used to or like sweet potatoes, corn, broccoli, even the bread stuffing of the turkey and all those gravies." As a Parisienne, *"bifsteak pommes frites* is my favorite," she confesses. She says she still doesn't care for breads that stick to the roof of her mouth, cheddar cheese, and not surprisingly, "French" dressing. But she likes peanut butter, dough-nuts, and hamburgers.

Sauces are a great source of Franco-American or Franco-foreign gaffes. Unless (and even if) your meat is clearly grilled meat, the French like sauce and they don't like their meat dry. "One night a Frenchman asked me if there was sauce to go with the lamb and when he saw there wasn't taught me how to do it right on the spot," admitted a friend. Speaking of lamb, don't ever serve a Frenchman mint sauce with lamb. They *hate* it.

But how about when the meat isn't cooked at all? Steak tartare is one of my favorites, but I can understand how people not used to it might find it revolting. Some tips on steak tartare, which is, very simple, seasoned raw beef: If you make it at home be sure that the meat has been chopped *right in front of your eyes* at the butcher shop. Once you've brought your meat home—and here's a tip from my mother-in-law—consume it immediately, i.e., in the next hour or so. Form a small mound of meat with a hole in it into which you put an egg yolk. Then add (to your taste): chopped onion, salt, pepper, capers, chopped parsley, Dijon mustard, Worcestershire sauce. Some people also add a dash of tabasco. Mix well and serve with home-made French fries and a tasty red wine. If you eat steak tartare in a restaurant, make sure 1) the cow in question wasn't English—oops, that was a low blow—there have been a few cases of mad cow disease in France but not nearly as many as across the Channel and 2) you are eating it in a very reputable restaurant.

....

The absolute best opportunity for cultural misunderstandings is Thanksgiving. I have yet to find a French person who sincerely can say he or she likes pumpkin pie. The French like pumpkin soup, but pie doesn't seem to make it. My kids, who, as I said, are thoroughly French, consider Thanksgiving a really weird meal. Cranberry sauce? Sweet potatoes? Wild rice? Pecan pie? All of these are my most favorite things but my kids, in spite of laudable intentions, find them too foreign for their French taste buds. What's an American mother to do, I ask myself each Thanksgiving?

Every American married to a Frenchman has her own story about Thanksgiving. Andrea Tulloch Girma, who lives in the States with her French husband, says that she's not normally a great fan of candied yams, baked oysters, chestnut soup, or mincemeat and pumpkin pies but at Thanksgiving eats and loves them. But not her French mother-in-law, who, Andrea told me, "had always wanted to experience Thanksgiving, and finally arranged to be in California with us for the holiday several years ago. Because we had all been invited to the home of a family friend for the event, I could not eliminate the foods that I knew would offend her. She got past the cranberry Jell-O mold by not eating it, she even used the paper napkins with a picture of a turkey on it, she was game enough to pick out and pour salad dressings from a selection of bottles after we told her to pick Italian because it was the closest to a vinaigrette."

Her mother-in-law, continued Andrea, even ate a forkful of the sweet potatoes without making a face and the turkey (although she later declared it had been overcooked) but she had reached her limit when she was served pumpkin pie. "*En principe*, you never eat vegetables as dessert," she asserted loudly in French, and everyone of course wanted to know what she had said. "However, no one needed a translation to understand the desperate look on my mother-in-law's face as she frantically pushed the pumpkin pie plate as far from her as possible," Andrea recalled.

Christmas and Passover bring cultural surprises as well. As my friend Barbara Katz explained: "A French Jewish Passover is different from an American one in which you get gefilte fish and all kinds of specialties served with horseradish. Here they serve you oysters and *foie gras*!" An English woman told me that after twenty years of celebrating Christmas in France with a typically English meal, her French friends admitted, under the influence of a tad too much to drink, that in all truth they couldn't stand the English pudding they'd been politely eating for the past two decades! The English woman told me that by the same token she can't stand the traditional French *bûche de Nöel*, Christmas log. *Touché!*

And when summer rolls around, there's the myth of "vichyssoise." As an American, you think it's typically French—but I and many of my friends have met French people who've never heard of this "typically" French cold soup. Kind of like French toast, which for the French is *pain perdu*, lost bread, and which hardly anybody in France ever eats anymore!

Bring out the tofu and other food phobias

We once had a German baby-sitter who was such fun that we asked her if she would like to come along with us on a vacation to Provence. She was delighted to come, but once there, looked at me and said, "I forgot to tell you something."

"What is it?" I asked, instantly conjuring up images of her being pregnant or in trouble with the law.

"I don't eat garlic or onions," she announced.

Actually, this confession was almost worse than if she had informed me of pregnancy or jail. Not eating garlic or onions in the south of France is like not eating seafood on the seacoast or not eating fondue in the Savoy or not eating *choucroute* in Alsace. Can you imagine a ratatouille without onions and garlic? I decided to put her food phobia to the test and served her a ratatouille redolent with the flavor of onions and garlic. She ate it all, with gusto. After that success, all summer long I blithely threw onions and garlic into everything. I simply made sure she could never see them or crunch them!

Cultural differences crop up not just about what is being eaten but how and when it's being eaten. After some young Americans had stayed in her home, one hostess confided to me that she was mystified because "they were so incredibly ill at ease about food and even sitting down to the table—they dissected everything and were incapable of *enjoying*," she said, obviously more troubled by their lack of enthusiasm than their refusal of any particular food. I've heard barrels of tales such as these, including one about a young American visitor who, on her first day with a French family, presented a complete list of the things she didn't eat to her hostess—who still hasn't gotten over it—and another about a young American who declined a French family meal starring a succulent *pot-au-feu* because his diet consisted solely of tofu and frozen yogurt!

Having lived in France for so long, my American friends and I cannot for the life of us understand why so many young visitors, especially our own compatriots, have to analyze everything before they eat it (in the event they consent to eat it). They seem to think only of fat content and allergies. Has food become such an enemy in the U.S. that no one can enjoy it anymore? And did it ever kill anyone to taste something new and different?

Fortunately, many visitors are only too delighted to try new things. There are many foreigners who visit France and who do not have food phobias, who do not insist on peanut butter, and for whom it is a real pleasure to cook. We've had many a guest who ended up wanting to live in France forever after having tasted wonderful new cheeses and wines and realizing that if you live here, you can have a pleasurable food experience *every single day.* To ring out the twentieth century, my entire family came from the States. They ate and drank absolutely everything that was put before them. They especially loved French cheese and French wine. What a treat to have appreciative guests. My brother-in-law's nephew (get that?), a young American high school student, was exquisitely well mannered. Not only did he look forward to the meal hour, but he tasted absolutely everything. He wisely only took small quantities in case he didn't particularly like what he was tasting but his open-mindedness was a marvel to see. Although only sixteen, he tasted the wine as well but was mature enough to keep his consumption down to a glass. A French friend of mine told me she had a young American who, on the contrary, liked wine at mealtime so much that he nearly drank them out of house and home!

A very special American in Paris

Writer Edith Wharton had no problems with French food. This American in France loved not only what the French ate but the way they dined. A member of the *haute société*, Wharton was an ardent Francophile who lived in France for more than ten years. During World War I, she was instrumental in helping refugees and running hospitals in Paris, activities for which the French government awarded her the Cross of the Legion of Honor in 1915. She lived in France a total of ten years and died in 1937 at her home at Château Sainte-Claire.

An admirer of the French table, the author of *Ethan Frome* and *The House of Mirth* would surely have approved of an Edith Wharton theme dinner I had the honor of attending at a U.S. embassy residence on a rainy September evening as the twentieth century drew to a close. Huge palm trees decorated the rooms, gilded candelabra set off the table, indeed the entire decor evoked images of the table and the dining rooms of Edith Wharton's time.

As for the food . . . young chef Philippe Escoffier, who claims he doesn't know whether he is related to the great French gastronomist ("He's surely being modest," one of the guests whispered), prepared the following feast:

Langouste à la parisienne
Clawless spiny lobster with a vegetable garnish

Quenelle de brochet aux ecrevisses
Pike dumpling with crayfish

Faisan en Chartreuse
Pheasant in a Chartreuse sauce

Pudding Malakoff
Malakoff pudding

Each sumptuously decorated dish was presented on a silver platter along with a commentary on the contents of the course; it was mind-boggling to think how much time must have been spent in the preparation of each one. When I asked Escoffier how long it took, he told me that it was hard to calculate because all the various operations involved in the preparation of the different dishes are done at different times. Escoffier, who is thirty, has worked in several prestigious restaurants as well as being a freelance cook for such notables as the late president François Mitterrand and former culture minister Jack Lang. He then decided on a career as a cook for *maisons bourgeoises* (wealthy private homes or official residences). Not many chefs choose to go this route. (And not many homes can afford private chefs.) Escoffier told me there are only about eighty-six chefs like this left in the whole of France.

Escoffier noted that no one these days would eat the kind of heavy food that people ate in Edith Wharton's times but that a dinner like this is exactly the kind of challenge he loves. He graciously gave me the recipe for the Pudding Malakoff. When you see the ingredients, you see what he means by heavy: the base is a compote of apples and pears, then there are raisins which have been marinated in kirsch, a cherry brandy, and shredded almonds, all of this topped with a *crème anglaise* (egg yolk custard cream). I personally went wild over this dessert, but it's true that it's not exactly light.

Heavy food or not, as the fourteen guests chatted around the table, it was almost as if Edith Wharton's spirit was floating above and around us, or that we were participants in a dinner that could have come straight from the pages of *The Age of Innocence*. Although the kinds of food we eat now and the way of preparing them has changed, French formal dinner table rites have remained the same. In *French Ways and Their Meaning*, a pamphlet Wharton penned to explain French customs to GIs coming to France to serve in WWI, she explains that:

Dining is a solemn rite to the French, because it offers the double opportunity of good eating and good talk, the two forms of aesthetic enjoyment most generally appreciated. Everything connected with dinner-giving has an almost sacramental importance in France. The quality of the cooking comes first; but, once this is assured, the hostess' chief concern is that the quality of the talk shall match it. To attain this, the guests are as carefully chosen as boxers for a championship, their number is strictly limited, and care is taken not to invite two champions likely to talk each other down.

As the French expression goes, *"Plus ça change, plus c'est la même chose."* Regarding the "sacramental importance" of dinner giving, indeed nothing has changed a whit since Wharton's day.

SOME DO'S AND DON'TS

For Americans:
- When you visit France, **don't** look at food and say "it's fattening" or moan about the pounds you're going to put on.
- Whether you're in France three days or three weeks, **do** taste a bit of everything and enjoy yourselves.
- A helpful tip: **Don't** eat *anything* in between meals. That way, you'll enjoy your food much more—the way the French do.
- If you aren't hungry for a full meal and only desire a salad or a sandwich, **don't** go to a restaurant. Restaurants are for full-fledged meals. That's how they make their money. For a salad or an omelette, go to a brasserie.

For the French:

- **Don't** look at American food and think that it's all bad. That hasn't been true for some time. You can easily find excellent restaurants and good food in the U.S.A. today.
- On the other hand, **don't** take the worst from our society, our all-day snacking, our compulsive addiction to sugar and soft drinks and fat-free foods, our never sitting down to real meals, our fondness for gigantic portions, or you'll end up with 25 percent of *your* population obese.
- **Do** take a leaf from our book on smoking in restaurants. You'll live longer.
- **Don't** *ever* buy plastic-wrapped cheese!!!!

SOME AMERICAN FOOD THE FRENCH FIND STRANGE, MYSTIFYING, OR DOWNRIGHT DISGUSTING

Pumpkin pie—The French generally eat pumpkin in soup.

Broccoli—You see it more now but some French people still don't like it. I haven't been able to figure out why, though.

Jell-O—They actually think it's quite funny and like the fluorescent colors but can't imagine that anyone would *eat* it.

Coffee—Too weak, and they can't understand why we prefer drinking weak coffee all day long as opposed to two or three small strong cups.

Pies—They can't understand why there's a top crust.

Salad dressings—They can't understand why there are so many of them.

Overcooked meat—They can't understand why you would do that to good meat.

Milk as a drink with a meal—They can't understand why you wouldn't prefer wine, especially as it lowers your cholesterol!

Processed cheese (Velveeta, etc.)—They can't understand why anyone would eat cheese wrapped in plastic—unfortunately they are starting to do it themselves. . . .

Peanut butter—There are a few French people who like it, most don't.

American mustard—They are not familiar with it and don't appreciate the sugar that's in it.

SOME FRENCH FOOD THE AMERICANS FIND STRANGE, MYSTIFYING, OR DOWNRIGHT DISGUSTING

Escargots, snails—Some Americans will eat snails if they don't think too much about what it is they're eating.

Oursins, bulots, and bigorneau, **sea urchins, sea snails, and winkles**—They tend to find them slimy.

Gésiers, **Gizzard**—An acquired taste that not many (except me!) acquire.

Huitres, **oysters on the half shell**—They say "Are they *alive?*"

Lapin, **rabbit (!)**—They say "What a pity to eat a poor bunny rabbit!"

Salade de museau, **calf-head salad**—They say *"No Way."*

Langue de bœuf, **beef tongue**—Yuck!

Boudin noir, **blood sausage**—Gross!

Crête de coq, **cockscomb**—Are you kidding?

Tripes, **tripe**—No, thank you.

Foie gras—Some Americans like this and some love it. However, some don't know the difference (and ensuing difference of cost!) between *foie gras* and *pâtés* so pay heed: *foie gras*, or goose liver, is an expensive delicacy that the French generally reserve for special occasions (i.e., you don't sit down to a normal family meal and start with foie gras! However, sales of *foie gras* explode around Christmas and New Years). *Pâtés* are molded meat or fish pastes and can be made with various kinds of fish and various kinds of meat (duck, rabbit, liver). Depending on how they are made and where you buy them and what is in them, they range from affordable to expensive, but in general, they are always less expensive than *foie gras*.

Cuisses de grénouilles, frog legs—Most Americans find this disgusting.

Organ meats, brains, balls, intestines, heart, kidneys, chitterling—*All* Americans, except me and a few other crazies, find them disgusting.

Café, coffee—Too strong or too bitter and too small.

Tartes, pies—They can't understand why there's no top crust.

Vinaigrette, salad dressing—They can't figure out how there can be only one kind of salad dressing.

Les fromages qui sentent très fort, strong smelly cheese—How can people eat cheese that smells like stinky socks?

Sanglier, wild boar—They find it strange but might eat it, considering they have quite a bit of game.

Ris de veau, sweetbreads—I hear Americans are starting to appreciate this delicacy.

Pieds de cochon, pig's feet—This falls into the disgusting category again.

Tête de veau, veal head—Served with a *sauce gribiche* composed of blended hard-boiled egg yolks, capers, and herbs mixed with chopped hard-boiled egg whites, the *tête de veau* is a real test of character. I'd like all Americans who have tasted this to stand up and be counted.

Steak tartare, raw beefsteak—This is unusual but is becoming accepted in some quarters. I don't however know *gobs* of Americans who like it.

 INTERVIEW WITH PHILIPPE

HWR: I read in a French magazine that some of the French may have adopted or may be about to adopt our U.S. custom of Sunday brunch.

PhR: Let them eat cake.

HWR: Wouldn't you like to eat brunch here on Sunday instead of our normal four-course Sunday lunch?

PhR: Over my dead body. It's a dumb concept, too big for breakfast and too small for a civilized lunch so by three in the afternoon, you're starving and you eat a pizza.

HWR: I still don't understand why you refuse for us to bring out paper plates and cups when we have more than ten guests.

PhR: Because you threaten to put wine or Champagne in them! And while we're at it, why not paper food? *Quelle drôle d'idée!*

HWR: I guess that's why you don't like picnics?

PhR: The history of mankind is the overcoming of cold, uncertainty, fear, and wild beasts. Those are all the ingredients of a picnic.

HWR: One last thing: how many centiliters in a deciliter?

PhR: Do you know how many square inches there are in a square mile? The metric system was adopted by the leaders of the French Revolution so that even the dumbest peasant could figure it out. Everything is a multiple of ten.

3

The Dire First Meal at Home

Reading recipes · Thinking in French · Famous authors and French food · Some help from Robuchon (on TV) · Going to cooking school and banishing food phobias

The dire first meal at home was not made in a *cocotte minute* but in an oven! As it turned out, there actually was a stove in that lilliputian kitchen on the rue Duvivier; it was so small that I hadn't seen it!

"What shall we make?" I asked Philippe excitedly. After all, this was going to be my first attempt at a meal *chez nous*. For some odd reason we decided upon a *pied de cochon*, pig's foot. Philippe, however, had omitted one important detail. Although he had eaten many a *pied de cochon* in his life, he had never actually cooked one! I didn't learn this until the *pied* was in front of us and it was too late. So there we stood, two clueless people facing down that porcine hoof and wondering what to do with it.

"Simple," he said. "We'll wrap it in aluminum foil and grill it."

"Sounds good to me," I agreed in my total ignorance. Common sense should have warned me something was inherently wrong with this solution but no warning flags appeared.

In went the *pied* and we waited . . . and waited, until the tantalizingly fine smells of pork cooking began to waft through the apartment. We opened the oven, took our creation out, and were surprised to see that underneath the aluminium it looked quite nice, verging as it was on golden brown, with a pretty pink inside. However, when we continued trying to undo the aluminium foil, it stubbornly stuck to the bread crumbs that encased the foot. I remember nothing else about that first meal at home other than that we laughed a lot, pulled out some emergency *saucisson*, drank great quantities of wine, and vowed we really must ask someone how to do a pig's foot properly.

Frankly, I never attempted a *pied de cochon* again, not because of that first failure but because there were so many other things to make and it kind of slipped my mind. To my surprise, I recently ran across a recipe for *pied de porc au génepi*, pig's foot with artemisia, by chef Marc Veyrat, known as much for his trademark floppy *sapé*, the traditional hat peasants in the Savoy wear, as for the wonders he works with the herbs of his native Alps. I couldn't believe it: a pig's foot elevated to such a status! I then studied the recipe carefully and looked at the accompanying picture. First of all, the foot didn't look like one anymore. It had been attractively reconstituted into a round shape. Secondly, it was accompanied by some artistically carved carrots and served with what looked like a light cream sauce. Philippe's and my *pied de porc*, had it survived the abominable treatment we gave it, would never have come out of that oven looking like anything other than what it was—a *foot*. I am quite sure that at my level of cooking in 1971, I never would have been able to master such a recipe, and now, almost three decades later, I admit I've lost my motivation!

Reading recipes

The Veyrat recipe for the pig's foot is one of many recipes I've read but haven't made. I've always liked to read cookbooks as a hobby because this way I can get the pleasure of imagining the finished product without doing any actual work.

In France, I've found that many people don't even have cookbooks, as recipes are transmitted from one generation to the next. When my mother-in-law and sister-in-law go in the kitchen to prepare a meal, there are no books around, not *one*. This is because they are doing things they've done for years and know how to do. Do you remember my sister-in-law from *French Toast*? She's the one who *never wears an apron*. She didn't when I wrote *French Toast* and she still doesn't. She is very pretty and very lively and thinks nothing of wearing silk blouses and high heels when she cooks. I think of her every time I hit the kitchen to make dinner. The first thing I do is tie on that apron. How does she manage? The mystery remains. Also, how does she not lose her cool when she has a group of ten to prepare a meal for? Not only does she not lose it, she rises to the challenge, creating new dishes, setting the table with candles and flowers. She enjoys it. Okay, I admit. I'm in awe. When I contemplate the idea of having ten people to dinner, my immediate reaction is to commit Hari-Kari. Anyway, when we have ten people, they always get the same thing: chili, garlic bread, and brownies. My repertory is actually wider than that but the very idea of having ten people to dinner cuts off my creative juices!

But back to recipes: Occasionally, my sister-in-law will cut out a recipe from a magazine or make something she's eaten elsewhere and asked for the recipe, but I must say I've never seen her "cracking a book." Intrigued by this, I finally got around to asking her if she had any. And was bowled over to learn that she has *ninety-two* cookbooks in her Paris apartment, none of which she actually uses per se. She reads a few recipes, assimilates them, and then strikes out on her own. So that's why I never see her with a cookbook in hand—all she needs to know is in her head!

She's generous about giving recipes but there's one she swears she'll never give away. It is her grandmother's recipe for *haricots blancs*, white beans. I think they've been cooked with garlic and perhaps a tomato, and a bay leaf and thyme, salt and pepper. When you eat them with a *gigot d'agneau*, roasted leg of lamb, you're in heaven. They are, it is true, out of this world and I can't blame her for keeping that particular recipe a secret. This being said, I still sneak into the kitchen when she is making them in my endless effort to find out precisely what that special touch is!

Let's stop here for a reality check: in case I give the impression that all French women love to cook, I should say right here and now that it's entirely possible, even eminently possible, that my husband's French family is a special case. I know there are French women who can't stand to cook. I've even met a few. One told me that not only can she not boil an egg, but that she can't even make toast without burning it. Others have told me they do not relate in any way to what I am saying about the way my French family eats. And some French women, especially in the professional world or university milieu, are proud of the fact they don't cook and wear it as proudly as a badge.

No problem by me! I'm just glad I lucked into a French family where everyone loves to eat and cook.

Thinking in French

My sister-in-law reads recipes for inspiration. I read them for knowledge. Imagine having to suddenly think in kilos and grams and centiliters and deciliters instead of pounds and ounces. Imagine going to the market and trying to figure out how in the world you order oranges. By quantity? One, two, three? By kilos? After ordering *un livre* of oranges, which translates literally as a book of oranges, I learned that it was *une livre* and never made that mistake again. I gained confidence and was soon proudly ordering away in kilos and grams as if I'd been doing it my whole life long. I was on my way.

At least, I was on my way in France. Since I was always speaking in French, going to the market and shopping in French, and cooking in French, I never learned the English name of what I was buying. In other words, if I bought a fish at the market and it was a *raie* it never occurred to me to find out what the name of the *raie* was in English. In this way, I bought and prepared *bulots*, whelks or sea snails, *andouillettes*, chitterlings, and *lieu noir*, black cod, without the faintest idea of what they were in English. They just were. As long as what I was buying looked good and there was a recipe for it in a French cookbook or my mother-in-law could tell me how to make it, I didn't really care what its English name was. In the case of fish, I wouldn't have known the English name anyway since I grew up in the land of beef and chicken and the only fish I ever saw was frozen.

It was only when I started writing this book that I decided I really should become familiar with the English names of French products. I found a book of translations, which I regret not having when I first came here and all those years afterwards. Let me give a plug right here and now. It's called *The A–Z of French Food* and is published by

Scribo Editions. Before I bought it, I thumbed through it, telling myself that if there was no translation for *bulot* or *éperlan*, I wouldn't buy it. But there they were: "whelk" and "smelt," so I bought it and my life has changed (but the food tastes the same).

The first cookbook I received shortly after my marriage was an ingenious gift from a good friend. It was something along the lines of ten-minute meals and was, of course, in French. She knew me well. I figured that if you had to spend any more than ten minutes getting a meal on a table, it wasn't worth it. She figured that with my lack of knowledge, this way I'd at least get the basics.

After mastering the ten-minute meals, I decided the real problem of cooking was finding ideas for menus. So it was that I purchased a book called *Cuisine pour toute l'année*, which lists two menus a day for every day of the year. You will notice I am not mentioning Julia Child or the *New York Times Cookbook*. I figured since I was living in France, I would use cookbooks that would enable me to make the things the French eat every day as opposed to fancy dinner-party menus. In addition, recipes written in English with ingredients and quantities listed in English didn't do me much good.

My *Cuisine pour toute l'année* is still with me. I love to think that when I don't have an idea for what to make the second week in October, presto, I can open up the book and find a week of ideas. Of course, one has to be open-minded, for the menu for the second week of October starts out with sautéed veal heart. That was fine with me. I made sautéed veal heart! Somewhere along the way, though, I began to notice that the menus weren't always well balanced. Take, for example, this rather strange heart-unfriendly combination proposed as a Sunday night dinner: *saucisson sec, terrine de foie de volaille, emmenthal, and brioche à la confiture* (sausage, chicken liver terrine, emmenthal cheese and a buttery-bread loaf with jam).

I reflected, not for the first time, that the authors must not have any cholesterol problems or they died long ago from their own menus. I skipped days with life-threatening combinations like those, but for sentimental reasons the book is still on my kitchen shelf to help when I run out of ideas.

And some help from Robuchon

I also have French chef Joël Robuchon's books, *Le Meilleur et le plus simple de la Pomme de Terre* (The Best and the Simplest of the Potato) and *Le Meilleur et le plus simple de la France* (The Best and Simplest of France). The first gives recipes for potatoes, and the second gives recipes for regional specialties, from *la truffade*, a specialty of Auvergne and Limousin, to *pigeons à l'ail doux*, a pigeon-with-garlic specialty of the Perigord region. Do I use these recipes? Of course not! But I love to think that someday when I have time (I dare not say, when I have some counter space, because my French husband will say that I am a spoiled American . . .), I will. Actually, inspired by this passage, I did make Robuchon's *truffade*. His recipe calls for plenty of Tomme cheese, garlic, bacon, and pork fat with the potatoes, so it is not exactly "light," but I can tell you it is absolutely delicious.

Robuchon, one of France's most talented chefs, a model of creativity and plain hard work, always said he would quit his job as chef of the Robuchon restaurant at age fifty. No one believed this talented cook would do such a thing—but at age fifty, he did exactly what he said he would. I for one am glad because in addition to his cookbooks and the food columns he writes in various French newspapers, he now has a half-hour program on French television every

Monday through Friday in which he presents a visiting chef and dis-
cusses and demonstrates a recipe with him. Not only is it pleasant
and instructive to watch them shopping for the food at the market
and to hear the guest chef explaining to Robuchon why he does
what he does, but Robuchon gives useful tips as they talk. For example, I learned that you should always wash and dry your hands after
breaking eggs and especially before touching another ingredient
because of the germs that are on the eggshell. I suppose this may
seem obvious to germ-phobic Americans, but when I think of all the
years I have been breaking eggs and moving on to the next operation, hands unwashed . . . That tip alone was worth the whole program, which that day was a *flaugnarde aux poires*, an Auvergnat pear
pie. It was a good recipe and a simple one and I made it that very
night to the delight of my dessert-loving family. It reminded me of a
clafoutis Tante Françoise, my husband's aunt, made for us with cherries straight from her tree, and I vowed to make that soon as well. A
clafoutis or *flaugnarde*, by the way, could best be described as a custard
tart with fruit. It's delicious. Here's the recipe:

Françoise's Clafoutis aux cerises

3 eggs
½ cup of sugar
½ cup of butter
¾ cup of flour

A tablespoon of rum
½ pint of milk
1 pound of cherries, the
    darker the better

Break the eggs in a bowl and add the sugar.
Mix with the softened butter.
Add the flour. Mix well. Add rum and milk.
Set this mixture aside for a half hour.
During this time take off the stems and wash and
wipe the cherries (but leave in the pits!).
Heat the oven to 450°F.
Butter an 8-by-12-inch baking dish and
line it with the cherries.
Pour your batter right over the cherries.
Put in the oven 30 to 35 minutes or till it is golden.
Test with a knife to see if it is cooked through.

Take it out and let it cool. When it has cooled, dust the
surface with powdered sugar and serve it at room temperature. Serves 8.

A food note: Purists say that only cherries with their pit will do. Others say the pit poses too many problems. It seems to be a matter of taste—and practicality.

Famous authors and French food

When not reading cookbooks or recipes, I love to read about how food is referred to in French literature. If you've read the Belgian author Georges Simenon's whodunits about the French Inspector Jules Maigret, you'll see that the good inspector loves nothing more than to sit down to a delicious meal either in a restaurant or at home where a perfect Madame Maigret coddles Jules as she would a child, spending her days marketing and making his favorite dishes.

What does Maigret like? Simple robust fare, such as onion soup, quiche lorraine, beef stew with paprika, and *andouillettes*, tripe sausage. The late French food writer Robert Courtine went through all of Simenon's Maigret books and wrote a recipe book including citations from the passage in which the dish was referred to. In *Maigret and the Informer*, "Madame Maigret had prepared some young guinea fowl encased in pastry and the commissioner had gone to the cellar to get one of the last bottles of an old Château-Neuf du Pape which he had bought a case of at an auction one day when passing by the rue Drouot." Or, in *Maigret Gets Angry*, "At a regular rhythm, the peas fell into the enamel pan. Mme. Maigret, her knees apart, had them all over her apron, and there were two big baskets of them, picked that morning to can." We might note here that Simenon was known for being macho, and when you think that approximately half the women in France work outside the home these days, one mustn't take Madame Maigret as an example! I'd hate to disappoint anybody, but most busy working Frenchwomen buy their peas canned or frozen. Peas are indubitably better when fresh but most people don't find the time. (Fortunately, French canned peas are a cut above the ones found in the States!)

Many French authors, in addition to their fiction, were dedicated gourmets. At the age of sixty-seven, Alexandre Dumas, the author of *The Count of Monte Cristo* and *The Three Musketeers*, penned a learned *petit dictionnaire de cuisine*. In it, he defined the meaning of food terms starting with *abaisse* and ending with *zuchetti*. Honoré de Balzac was as well known for his gargantuan appetite as for his novels. At one meal, according to one of his publishers, he ate "one hundred oysters from Ostende, twelve lamb chops, a duck with turnips, a couple of partridges, and a Dover sole, not to mention the hors-d'œuvres, desserts, all this accompanied by the finest wines." Of course, crime doesn't pay: by the time he was forty, Balzac weighed more than 100 kilos (220 pounds) and was in failing health.

To keep him going, Balzac drank coffee all day long. He loved *pâté* and *rillettes*, a minced spread of pork or goose, and boiled eggs with *mouillettes*. Incidentally, I had never seen soft-boiled eggs eaten this way until I came to France. When I make a soft-boiled egg, I cut off the top of the egg, put on a dab of butter, salt and pepper, and then dig into it with a teaspoon. The majority of French people, or at least the ones in my husband's family and those in Balzac's day, cut off the top and then dip long slices of buttered bread, *les mouillettes*, into the yolk. Balzac describes this technique in his novel *Eugénie Grandet*: "The girl watched her cousin cutting his bread and butter into strips to dip into his egg, and was as happy in the sight as the most romantic shop-girl in Paris watching the triumph of innocence in a melodrama."

Checking out Le Cordon Bleu

After living in France for almost three decades and having at least learned the basics, I decided it was time to improve upon my repertory of ordinary French meals a bit and check out cooking classes.

Out of curiosity, I visited Le Cordon Bleu, which is a school for future chefs and mostly attended by foreigners. It's so much for foreigners, in fact—98 percent of the student body are non-French—that many French people have never heard of it. When I first mentioned it to my husband, his reaction was "What are you talking about?" It's normal that Le Cordon Bleu isn't a household name for the French as from its beginning in 1896, the emphasis of the school was on teaching French cuisine to the non-French. Julia Child, for example, earned her Chef's Toque from Le Cordon Bleu in Paris on the GI Bill; the Tokyo Le Cordon Bleu today is the largest employer of French chefs in Japan. French chefs take a different path. They are either apprentices with the great chefs or they get their diploma from nationally recognized French schools.

The day I visited the school, Chef Christian Guillut, who is on Le Cordon Bleu staff, was teaching a class on food from the Berry region. The students, mostly young Asians and Americans, watched intently as he composed a menu of *pâté de Pâques Maître Jean*, *pâté* wrapped in puff pastry, *coq en barbouille*, rooster cooked in red wine, and *poirat comme en Berry*, pear and cognac tart. A good-humored man, he deftly interspersed judicious remarks about cooking while preparing the food as the students furiously took notes or peered into the tilted mirrors for a close-up view. Commenting on *fond de veau*, veal stock, he remarked, to my great relief, that "most people don't use it in their homes." What he meant was that most people don't have a ready supply of homemade veal stock on hand. Like peas, they tend to buy it in a readymade version. I suppose there are people who do make their own, but I've never met any of them. (I'm sure I'll hear from them, though.) In restaurants, strict regulations require that veal stock be used the same day.

Once the students have watched the chef's three-hour demonstration, they're the ones under the gun, with three hours to prepare their dishes. After ten months of this grueling regime plus an internship in a restaurant, they receive their Cordon Bleu diploma and are ready to work. I positively salivate as I consult the brochure and see a list of "restaurant desserts" such as pistachio crème brulée; thin crisps with red berries, strawberry coulis; anise and raspberry almond macaroons. They sound even better in French: *crème brulée pistache; craquelin aux fruits rouges, coulis à la fraise; macarons anis framboise*. I drool over the Alsatian menu, which is composed of an onion-stuffed trout braised in Riesling wine, an Alsatian-style sauerkraut, and a frozen yellow plum parfait. In fact, I find myself wanting to make almost every menu presented: *suprême de bar à la peau et fenouil*, sea bass cooked in its skin with fennel, *cailles farcies au riz sauvage*, stuffed quails with wild rice, *pommes éclatées à la graisse d'oie*, potatoes fried in goose fat—ah, my mother-in-law does that!—*double de pomme au citron et cannelle*, apple stuffed with lemon and cinnamon flan mix.

I could go on but the truth of the matter is that I like the idea of eating this food better than making it. I don't know why I imagined chefs casually putting together meals like these: a peek into the kitchens showed me that these future cooks are running to get their work done well and on time. *La cuisine* is clearly a type A activity. A definite side benefit of attending the school and making the food is that the students get to take it home to eat. But as one student, Giselle Mamikunian, confessed: "After being around food all day, I can't stand to look at it anymore. I give it to the concierge and eat a yogurt." Lucky concierge!

Many of these students have never cooked before. Many intend to become chefs and open restaurants in their respective countries. Others want to be food critics and still others come just because they want to come (but they'd better be well-heeled because it's expensive). You don't have to be an aspiring chef or future food critic to go to Le Cordon Bleu, though. Courses on "chef's secrets," for example, are held throughout the year. For 150 French francs you can spend an instructive hour and a half watching one of the school's chefs demonstrating a couple of classic or modern recipes. The best part is that you get to taste afterwards. I attended a course in which I was fortunate once again to be instructed by Chef Guillut who was making a *crème de celeri au Roquefort*, celery-root soup with Roquefort, and a *côte de veau de lait aux champignons sauvages*, veal chop with wild mushrooms. There were about a dozen of us there, some French, some English speaking. We watched in silence as he effortlessly chopped and minced and mixed, all the while making comments which a talented young Franco-British translator put into excellent English. Although the menu called for the cream of celery soup, the chef took advantage of his celery root to make grated celery with mayonnaise and plain cream of celery soup as well as with roquefort so we could taste a bit of everything. Three dishes out of one celery root! Béatrice, a Frenchwoman with whom I'd struck up a conversation during the course, and I were happy he'd taken the initiative as we both definitely preferred the "plain" version of the soup. So did the chef, from what I gathered. We commented that the Roquefort obscured the taste of the celery and he agreed. "People today often don't know the taste of the basic ingredient," he said.

And did we learn secrets? You bet we did. Here are a few: never pepper things you're cooking until the last minute; when you serve sauce with meat, never put it directly on the meat which is cut because it will recook it; wipe mushrooms as opposed to washing them and *never* soak them; and make *rémoulades*, cold mayonnaise sauce, with a *lot* of mustard! But I won't tell you any more—you'll have to go see for yourself!

Even though Chef Guillut spends his days teaching students sophisticated sauces, he says that when he goes home his favorite dish is a simple *poulet rôti*, roasted chicken, and he's definitely in favor of simplicity in general. He laughs as he recalls going to a restaurant with a Japanese student. "She spent the entire meal analyzing every part of every dish we were served—and she hardly ate a thing!" he remarked, astounded. For Chef Guillut, "eating is a pleasure, not a scientific analysis." He told me he was amazed to see students who went through an entire course preparing a dish they never once tasted! "How can you cook if you don't taste what you're making?" he asks rhetorically. But he added, *toujours* optimistically: "Once you have the basics firmly in hand, you become the writer of your own cookbook."

Being around students from all over the world has given Guillut a chance to observe the way different nationalities view food and the making of it. Americans, for example: "Nothing stops them," exclaims Guillut, "because they don't have a long culinary past which weighs upon them heavily as it does for us French. The critique I would make here is that sometimes they try to create something without having made the original recipe. Sometimes this works and sometimes it doesn't. A person working from the basis of knowledge can do superb things—but they do have to have the basis before anything else."

That's the best-case scenario. What's the worst? Guillut laughs: "The person who worries me the most is the French gourmet who thinks he or she knows everything! A person who has no gastronomic culture and is humble will learn more in the end."

. . . and ADAC

After my expedition to Le Cordon Bleu, I decided to check out the cooking courses offered by the city of Paris. Since these courses are given only in French, I thought that I had stumbled onto something no other foreigner would ever have heard about. How wrong I was. At our first class, where nine people sat around a square orange table in a basement kitchen of ADAC (Association pour le Développement de l'Animation Culturelle de la Ville de Paris) headquarters in the fourteenth arrondissement, I discovered I was in the company of two Mexicans and an African lady. The rest were French who, I was astonished to learn, had little or no notion of cooking. And here I had thought all the French were born great chefs. Chef Dominique told me that the course is a veritable United Nations. "I've had Russians, Polish, Americans, and even an Englishwoman," he said. I need to reflect on that "even" a bit. . . .

The advantage of these courses is that they are moderately priced (970 French francs for eleven three-hour sessions which works out to roughly about 30 francs an hour) and you can eat the food you make. I wasn't so sure that would be an advantage until I found out that in fact the chef prepares the dishes and the students eat the food that he makes. The disadvantage is that you don't have a list of the menus in advance. All you know is that in the three-hour period you will make either a first course and a main dish or a main dish and a dessert. This can lead to odd or potentially disastrous situations such as the one in which I found myself the first night of the first course. As I took my place at the table and looked around the room, I saw that night's dishes posted on the bulletin board.

I read: *escalopes de veau aux champignons et à la crème*, veal scallops in a cream sauce with mushrooms, a dish I have made zillions of times even though I admit not as well as the chef did, and *tarte tatin* with *crème Chantilly*. Did you notice the word *crème* twice? I did! I said I made the *escalopes de veau à la crème* dish a lot, but I generally skip the cream. However, I pushed the idea of not eating these dishes aside for two reasons: one, you know how I feel about food phobias and spoiling other people's culinary pleasure. So what's a stomach-ache if you only indulge in cream from time to time? Two, I was delighted at the thought of making a *tarte tatin* for I have always loved this all-time classic carmelized upside-down apple pie invented out of a mistake the Tatin sisters made in their kitchen of the Hotel Tatin in Lamotte Beuvron, a village in the Loire Valley. I figured I wouldn't have to eat the *crème Chantilly*, which would be served on the side, as indeed it was.

The chef explained that because of a lack of time it would be impossible for each of us to participate. We would watch and take notes while he did the work. He then proceeded to put together the *tarte* so it would bake while he prepared the veal scallops, except they were turkey scallops, veal being very expensive. Meanwhile, as he worked, some of us chatted and it was then that I found out that most of my classmates could barely boil an egg! Most were younger than me and it seemed that none had children, a great way to learn how to cook. A convivial atmosphere developed as the chef toiled. When he'd finished, we all set the table and sat down to eat and everything was *vraiment très bon* or as the French would say, *pas mal du tout*. The only man in the course, Gérard, had brought some delicious bread, which we all pounced on and devoured in huge quantities with our meal.

"Do you like it?" queried Chef Dominique. The Mexican girl rolled her eyes with pleasure as the *tarte tatin* melted in her mouth. The rest of us were so busy eating the huge portions he had dished up for us that we could barely get our mouths open to say *"Oui."* But *"oui"* it was.

And of course I ate all the cream, including and especially with the *tarte tatin*. *Un délice!*

After that first class, I thought that perhaps with all those years of cooking behind me, I wasn't going to learn that much. Fortunately I was wrong. As the semester progressed, we learned how to make everything from a *poisson en croute de sel*, which is a fish coated in coarse salt, to a *charlotte aux framboises*, a fruit dessert with raspberries. The *filet de biche sauce grand veneur*, fillet of deer in a *grand veneur* sauce, was delicious even though the deer turned out to be a *sanglier*, boar, because the person doing the shopping that day couldn't find any deer. That was another thing I enjoyed about the course. We took turns dividing up the grocery list and doing the shopping. We set the table, and washed the dishes afterwards. The first time we sat down to our meal, we drank tap water because that was all that was there. By the time the second course rolled around, Gérard brought a bottle of wine with him. From that moment on, someone, generally Gérard, it seems, would bring a bottle of wine that we would share. One of us invariably brought bread as well, and if no one did, someone would volunteer to go see if a bakery was open. How can you eat a meal without wine and bread? One night as we sat sipping our wine and eating our delicious *sanglier* in its *grand veneur* sauce, we started talking about . . . what else, food, and somehow got on the topic of fish.

Chef Dominique, who is from Brittany, looked nostalgic as he said: "I like things like salmon rillettes (a fish spread he taught us to make) but what I really like most of all is *un bon plateau de fruits de mer*, a seafood plate, with spider crabs, large crab, prawn, oysters and mussels." His eyes lit up as he added: "I like it with a good bottle of cold white wine and some good country bread with salted butter."

I laughed to myself as I thought how funny it was to be sitting in a basement in Paris on a cold winter night eating boar in a red wine sauce and drinking red wine while dreaming with the chef about being by the seaside in Brittany on a summer day feasting on an enormous *plateau de fruits de mer* with sparkling cold white wine.

Aren't the French wonderful?

Enjoy!

My foray into the world of cooking courses convinced me of the importance of simple enjoyment and the capital importance of not viewing food as a foe.

I don't know if viewing food as the enemy is an American trait but a young French tourist guide I know told me that in her experience the difference between American tourists of a certain age and French of the same age is that the French, no matter what their health condition, consider food first and foremost a pleasure. The Americans, she observed, consider food as fuel. They check out menus like hawks to see whether or not there is meat if they're vegetarian, or fat if they're on a nonfat diet, or sugar if they're off sugar, or anything else that might be harmful or off their list. According to her, the French person of the same age who might even have equivalent restrictions says "hang it" and decides to have a good time!

I too have often noticed that the French either suspend whatever particular health regimes they may be on when they go out for dinner or simply don't talk about their dietary restrictions. Why? Very simply, because the French honor the notion of food as pleasure and even if they can't indulge in this or that, don't want to spoil anyone else's joy. If they have no particular problems, their watchword is "moderation." Good things, yes, but in small quantities. I think of my late father-in-law who ate and drank small amounts of everything, and my mother-in-law, now eighty-five, who eats and drinks a little of everything as well, but always with moderation. "Everything" includes a glass or two of wine with the meal, potatoes cooked in goose fat, vinaigrette made with plenty of good oil, cheese, an occasional dessert. It's important to note, though, that this is weekend eating with the family and that the quantities, by American standards, are miniscule.

Whether they're eight or eighty-five, the French love a good *fête* and are always ready to enjoy it. In the words of French author Cavanna: *"Tout le monde devenait vieux . . . et ne se privait pas de goûter les bons petits moments."* Everyone was getting old . . . and didn't deprive themselves of enjoying some nice times. Notice the word *goûter*, which means "enjoy," "relish," "appreciate," and "taste"!

INTERVIEW WITH PHILIPPE

HWR: I said that you think good cooking has nothing to do with the space you have to cook in. Is that true or am I misconstruing your thoughts?

PhR: You're not misconstruing my thoughts. You're typically American, i.e. capex-oriented.

HWR: What in the deuce does that mean?

PhR: It means that you think that in order to cook a decent meal, you need capital expenditure. But take a look at the delicious meals they eat on French nuclear submarines and those chefs are working out of microscopic kitchens. I hear they even bake fresh bread every day on those tubs!

HWR: And that's not capex?!

PhR: Yes, but it's for the glory of France.

HWR Et voilà!

4

Foraging for Food

Meandering through markets · La Mouffe · A stroll through a French hypermarket · Designer delicacies · The chocolate counter · The growing yogurt

Naturellement, in order to make food, you've first got to get it, and in France, shopping for food takes on a whole new meaning. Whereas in the States you can load up on everything for a week at your supermarket, in France you invariably end up shopping at the supermarket, the local market, and several other kinds of specialized stores as well. Invariably, you end up doing some kind of food shopping every day. The food you get is fresher and it's always fun to market, but sometimes it seems that the hunt for food is a never-ending quest.

In fact, sometimes it feels like this is how you're spending your *life*.

As the fictional engineer Norton points out in *The Chronicle of Engineer Norton, the Confidences of an American in Paris:* "The Frenchwoman's task is even more complicated because she shops in thirty-six different stores, for each retailer sells, and that's logical, only one item: the fruit salesman sells fruit and not fruit juice, the baker sells bread and not newspapers, the florist sells flowers but not boxes of chocolates, the pharmacist sells medicine but not sandwiches."

The famous American food writer, the late M. F. K. Fisher, described her first attempts at shopping in France in her book *Long Ago in France*.

> I learned a hundred things, all the hard way: I learned that les Halles were literally the only place to get fresh vegetables and that two heads of cauliflower and a kilo of potatoes and some endives weighed about forty pounds after I'd spent half an hour walking to market and an hour there and missed three crowded trams going home again . . . I learned always to take my own supply of old newspapers for wrapping things, and my own bowls and cans for cream and milk and such. I learned, with the tiredest feet of my life, that feeding people in a town like Dijon meant walking endless cobbled miles from one little shop to another . . . butter here, sausage there, bananas someplace else again, and rice and sugar and coffee in still other places.

She was writing about France in 1929. Things have changed enormously since her exhausting marketing expeditions. You no longer take newspapers to wrap things but you do take a basket or one of those rolling carts if you don't want your back to break. You can now find your rice and sugar and coffee all in one place—the supermarket. And the best thing that has happened since I moved to this country is that most of the major supermarkets now deliver. *Formidable!* However, shopping in France is still composed of many trips to many different places if you're not content to go to one of the huge supermarkets where you can buy absolutely everything.

The second challenge—after you buy all of this marvelous food—

is where to put it. I don't know about anyone else's fridge but mine is so small that once you get all those yogurts and *crème fraîche* and meat and vegetables back home, you need a degree in mechanical engineering to figure out how to shove them all in the *réfrigerateur*. Let's not even talk about the Thanksgiving turkey or the Christmas goose. What never ceases to amaze me, though, is how I can manage to lose, forget, overlook, not even *see* the food that's in that three-shelved wonder. Ah, that cucumber I bought two weeks ago and those rotting tomatoes . . . I wouldn't even want to think what would happen if I had one of those gigantic American fridges complete with an ice machine. That's hardly likely to happen, though, as those fridges are bigger than my kitchen!

Meandering through markets

Markets are fun and schlepping your bags of smelly cheese and ripe fruit on public transportation can be as well. One day on the rue Poncelet, a fine market street in the seventeenth arrondissement, I bought an exquisite melon that the vendor picked out especially so we could eat it that very night. I then boarded the number 43 bus back to Neuilly, carefully placing the bag with the melon at my feet. However, when the driver braked abruptly, said melon rolled out of the bag to an almost inaccessible corner somewhere underneath my seat. The *très chic* elderly lady next to me, who told me she had been a former Dior model in her youth, jumped up so that I'd have enough room to scratch around in the dark recesses underneath. I bent over and searched and searched blindly until I felt the rough contour of the melon. Five Spanish tourists watched these gymnastics with great fascination and by the time I had caught my prized fruit, everyone applauded and congratulated me for having picked a melon which by now had perfumed the entire bus! I wonder if they would have been as enthusiastic if I had lost a malodorous Munster cheese. . . .

One of the reasons I like markets is that they are probably one of the last places where people still talk to each other. There's a lot of bantering and teasing going on and it's fun to eavesdrop on people's conversations. At the Saturday morning market in Nogent-le-Roi, a town with a population of about seven thousand near our country house, I overheard a lady standing in line for fish tell the fellow selling them, the *poissonnier*, that she had cooked her *bulots*, whelk, for an hour and a half and that they were terrible, hard as rocks. She had returned to buy more, she said, but she needed to know what the problem was.

The mustachioed, black-haired, black-eyed fishmonger, luminously clad in an orange windbreaker, roared with laughter. "You were fossilizing the poor things!" he exclaimed as he handed her a new package of *bulots* which he advised her to plunge into boiling water . . . for ten minutes! Everyone laughed, the woman, her daughters, the *poissonnier*, Philippe and me. We laughed—but we didn't dare tell him our own story, which is that once we had bought whelk, not knowing how to prepare them. As the four of us sat at the table struggling to get them out of their shells, we became more and more horrified by the gelatinous mess we were creating and figured that we'd done something horribly wrong. An emergency call to my mother-in-law for some instant advice. "Cook them!" she said. Out of earshot of the *poissonnier* I shared my story with the lady in the line and we both got a good laugh out of our ill-fated *bulot* experiences.

The next Saturday Philippe and I returned to see the same *poissonnier* for I liked not only his fish but his tips on how to prepare them. (Even though I like reading recipes, I much prefer *hearing* how things are made). We hesitated between fresh tuna and salmon but spied a *raie*, which I can now tell you is a skate, and decided on it. I'd cooked one many years ago but needed a refresher course, which Mr. Mustache was only too happy to give.

"Bring a *court-bouillon* to a boil, put the skate in it for twenty minutes, turn down the flame. Take it out, gently peel off its skin, then serve it with melted butter, but not completely black as it's often hard to digest, capers, and a trickle of raspberry vinegar." My mouth watered just listening to this.

Thanks to his good advice and the fresh products we bought at the market, for lunch we started with radishes straight from the farmer's garden, proceeded to our skate with boiled potatoes, both doused with melted butter, and ended with a succulent melon.

The meal was even tastier because each item had been accompanied by a joke or friendly smile or some kind of human exchange. How different from buying exactly the same things in the cold silence of a supermarket.

La Mouffe

The very first market street I ever encountered and in fact lived right on top of was the rue Mouffetard, and I didn't even do it on purpose! When I moved there, I didn't know that it was one of, if not *the* most remarkably picturesque market streets in Paris. I must admit, for the cooking I did at the time, it was pretty much wasted on me other than the fresh fruit that I would buy and take back to savor in my studio (the one with the cops in the kitchen—at least the kitchen was used for *something*!).

One of the best things about the market and living on the rue

Mouffetard was the café next door. My friends and I spent many a happy hour there watching the crowds drift by. At the time it was one of those old-fashioned cafés that sold coal. Those cafés were called *bougnats* and were run by Auvergnats, hardworking people from the mountainous center of France. Philippe is an Auvergnat and I can vouch for the hardworking part. I returned to it about a year ago and found that other than the coal, which they no longer sell, the actual place hadn't changed that much. It's still dark inside, with black fake-leather banquettes, but the sandwiches are now served on Poilane bread. *Plus chic.* I asked the young people behind the counter how old they thought the café was.

"Oh, it's old," they said, "at least thirty years old!"

"That I know." I sighed (they themselves couldn't have been a day over twenty so for them anything thirty years old was ancient history). "I was here in 1967 and 1968 and they were even selling coal at the time!"

The young people were polite, but I could see that my story didn't impress them that much so I silently finished my espresso standing up at the bar and reflected that it's not very interesting to talk about the past. Then I took another look at the café. A bouquet of baby yellow and red roses adorned the counter, a radio with stupid songs played in the background, the help quietly ate their lunch. I walked out of the café to check out the door to my former apartment. It turned out not to be the seventeenth-century affair I remembered, but an ordinary old wooden door that now has a door code. Had the door been changed? Was it centuries old only in my imagination? Just as I'll never know how old that café is, I'll probably never know about the door. One of those things to be shelved in the "unsolved mysteries" category.

Aside from a few gentrified apartment buildings, la Mouffe, which traditionally was a working-class district, hasn't changed all that much in the thirty (oh, my Lord!) years since I lived there. The street is still narrow and cobbled and in spite of the crush during market hours, it has all the look of a sleepy village when at three in the afternoon the food vendors have gone off to eat or sleep, leaving their lemons and cauliflower and endives safely protected under gracefully draped green nets. I didn't remember the art gallery or the Moule au Gateau pastry shop or the Jeff De Bruges chocolate store or even the Café Marc from which a delicious smell of strong coffee was emanating, but I did recall and was happy to see the flower shop on the corner of the Square Vermenouze with its bounteous array of tulips, pansies, azaleas, and roses.

. . . and other markets

Each market has its own feel, its mores. You generally can only get a sense of this when you live in a neighborhood and shop at your local market a couple of times a week. Since we now live in Neuilly on the west side of the city, I sometimes go to the Marché des Sablons, which is about as far removed from la Mouffe as you can get, both geographically and sociologically. The Sablons was a vast expanse of sandy fields where Parmentier experimented with the *pomme de terre*, hitherto unknown to Parisians. It is said that King Louis XVI in a clever psychological ploy (too bad he wasn't as clever about other matters, he might have kept his head) put guards around the potato field, exciting the curiosity of the inhabitants who came to see what the hullabaloo was all about and pilfered as many of the coveted *pommes de terre* as they could. This was the beginning of the success of the potato in France—and Neuilly's claim to fame!

There's no stealing potatoes now. The clientele is well off, and the *marchands* seem to reflect that. There's little of that jovial loud shouting you hear in most markets. The products are excellent—and expensive. I go there when I want to make something special. One night we had friends for dinner and I wanted to make an *anguille en matelote*, eel in a wine sauce, so I of course headed to this market where I know that the fish is first-rate and my favorite *poissonnier* always gives me good ideas on how to make whatever I buy. Other than food, the Sablons market has an extraordinary array of clothes, wonderful shoes, flowers, silverware, jewelry, depending on the day. I love the idea that you can come home from the market with fresh fish, delicious cheese, a pair of shoes, and a shirt for your kid.

We have another market, a covered one, which is much closer to us, the Marché Windsor, which is open on Wednesday mornings and Sunday mornings. It's a *tomb* compared to Sablons and that's saying a lot. (Ever since I saw a lady in a fabulous fur coat doing her Sunday morning shopping, I've called it the "mink market." Actually, I think I really only saw that once, but it obviously made a big impression on me.) This is not the market to go to if you want a lot of buzzing conversation and funny remarks from the tradespeople. They're all perfectly pleasant and their products are quite good, of course. It doesn't offer, however, the fun I look for in a market.

I like markets where you hear the *marchands* touting their wares and cracking jokes. Otherwise, why go? As M. F. K. Fisher wrote about her experiences back in 1929: "I learned that the stallkeepers in the market were tough loud-mouthed people who loved to mock you and collect a little crowd, and that they were very friendly and kind too, if you did not mind their teasing." I don't get mocked or teased. However, every time I open my mouth, I'm asked if I'm English or American (and that after thirty years in France!). That accent will haunt me the rest of my days, I fear, but it's a great conversation opener.

A stroll through a French hypermarket

I mentioned that shopping in France can be a royal pain. I was referring to *hypermarchés*, those giant supermarkets where you can find everything under one roof, from food (of course!) to clothes, plates, silverware, cat litter, and TV sets. In fact, I love that term *hypermarket* because for me, even the idea of shopping in one of those places makes me hyper. After a *hypermarché* trip, I need about two weeks to recover.

However, when my children were young and I was condemned to regular shopping trips, I became so fascinated by these places that I would go even more often than necessary, ostensibly because we were out of food, but really to check out all the various wares. Although it no longer thrills me, and especially because the boys have grown and I have no more reason to stock up the way I did for a family of four, I still like to go from time to time. One reason for this is because everyone says that France is becoming like America and nowhere more than in these giant shopping meccas. This is somewhat true but believe me, you can still find typically French products from elaborate entrees by French chefs to absolutely heart-stoppingly good chocolate. The French are getting globalized, but peanut butter and taco chips continue to be placed in the exotic products along with chutney and English fruitcakes. These products from elsewhere are definitely not seen as "French."

Designer delicacies by French chefs

One thing you see in French grocery stores, the ordinary ones that would be our equivalent of Safeway, are gourmet dishes by such great French chefs as Paul Bocuse, Bernard Loiseau, and Joël Robuchon. For less than five dollars, you can buy Bocuse's *canard au poivre vert*, duck in a green peppercorn sauce, or his *sauté de porc à la graine de moutarde*, sautéed pork with mustard seed, or his *pavé de saumon au beurre d'échalote*, salmon in a shallot and butter sauce. The portions, for one, take three minutes to heat up in the microwave.

From Bernard Loiseau, you can get a *gratin savoyard au lard fumé*, Savoyard gratin with bacon, or a *coq au Gevrey-Chambertin et tagliatelles*, cockerel in a wine sauce with pasta. Joël Robuchon has a selection of six gourmet dishes, among them the "famous" *Parmentier au confit de canard*, potatoes with duck in its own fat, just over four dollars. I bought it and sat down to eat it one day for lunch. It was *pas mal*, as the French would say. Obviously, eating it alone in my kitchen lacked the charm of having it served on a specially designed plate in a restaurant but one can't compare a thirty-franc lunch to an eight-hundred-franc dinner!

The chocolate counter

Real chocolate is another thing you easily find in French grocery stores. In a supermarket in the U.S., I visited the chocolate aisle desperately looking for what I love most, real chocolate with a cocoa content that exceeds 50 percent. I found lots of candy: various kinds of M & Ms, Butterfingers (my absolute all-time favorite American candy bar), Milky Ways and Nestle's Crunches, but was fascinated to see that other than dark cooking chocolate, there was no good chocolate with much cocoa in it. As I examined the various wrappings, I scrutinized the list of ingredients and was amazed to see that although you can find out all you'd ever hope to know about the number of calories, fat, sodium, and carbohydrate, there is *no* mention of the amount of cocoa—the first thing we chocoholics look for! For example, I found Toblerone and Lindt but again, unlike in France, there was no indication of the amount of cocoa in the bars.

In France, attractive upmarket looking bars of chocolate proudly announce "55 percent" or "70 percent" cocoa right on the front of the wrapper. If the cocoa content isn't on the front, you can bet that chocolate connoisseurs like me turn the package over to check out just what's in the bar. *Quelle différence!*

Yogurt and cereal—growing, growing, getting sweeter

Yogurt: in the U.S. grocery store, I looked in vain for a yogurt that was 1) without gelatin in it, 2) what I consider a normal size, and 3) not nonfat or low-fat. Mission impossible! I did at one point spy a brand I know in France, Yoplait, whose yogurts in France are four ounces, which I consider a perfect size. In the U.S., though, the Yoplaits are six ounces. Oh, no! Size was one thing. Nonfat was another. After much searching, I finally came upon a *real* yogurt made with whole milk, the only one in the entire store. It was done by the Brown Cow Farm but was twice the size I wanted: eight ounces! Other than that, the entire yogurt counter consisted solely of nonfat yogurts with gelatin. I gave up on eating yogurt while in the States.

I had to go back to France to get the yogurt I was craving—and was surprised to discover that French yogurts are growing in size too. Why do I prefer the small size yogurt? Because I am convinced that when you purchase big things, you eat or drink them all, even if you didn't originally intend to, making you *fat* against your will. If the French keep their weight down, it is because they buy and eat small portions. When this ends, they too will have a fat problem on their hands.

Small portions are one thing: the diabolical inventions of new kinds of yogurts and industrial desserts is another. Every single time I go to the *supermarché* I see a new kind of dessert. I've tried many of them. They range from various kinds of *mousse au chocolate* to *crème caramel* to other variations of sweet desserts on the "cream theme." I can now say in all certainty that they have one thing in common: no matter what's in them, they all end up tasting alike and they all taste like . . . sugar. Every time I go to the supermarket in France, I'm amazed by the number of new products and wonder if the French realize that as they get more of everything, they're actually getting less. (Good-bye taste buds.) Globalization, my friends!

Another difference: cereal. The French may have the Americans beat in the yogurt department but as far as cereal goes, the U.S. is the world champion in terms of sheer variety. In my humble opinion, the American cereal counter exemplifies America's attitude toward food: a plethora of choice, pride in nonfat content, and enough sugar to rot the teeth of the entire nation.

In a Colorado grocery store, Philippe and I sauntered down the cereal aisle and did an informal survey. (I'd been living in France for so long that I had forgotten what my choice might be should I have a craving for breakfast cereal.) And here's what we found: Kix, Cocoa Puffs, Cocoa Crunchies, Cocoa Pebbles, Cocoa Krispies,

Cocoa Frosted Flakes, Magic Stars (sweetened oat cereal with marshmallows), Lucky Charms, Oreo's Cereal, Reese's Peanut Butter Puffs, Cap'n Crunch's Peanut Butter Crunch, Cinnamon Toast Crunch, French Toast Crunch (hey!), Cookie Crisp, Golden Grahams, Apple Jacks, Trix, Fruity Pebbles, Corn Pops, to mention the most exciting ones, and then some more classic, but healthier, ones: Cheerios, Shredded Wheat, Corn Flakes, Special K, Rice Chex, Grape Nuts, Enriched Bran Flakes, and Raisin Bran.

In France there's much more of a choice of cereal than there used to be, which isn't hard. Until perhaps ten years ago, the French didn't eat cereal for breakfast. But cereal eating, like so many other things, is part and parcel of globalization. Compared to the U.S., though, the choice (Special K, Kellogg's Chocos, Kellogg's Smacks, Kellogg's Nutfeast, Kellogg's Country Store, Kellogg's Extra All Bran Petales—hey, does Kellogg's have the corner on this market or was it the store I was in?) is modest in France. And no one has had the idea—yet, thank the Lord—to transfer cookie or candy type foods such as Reese's Peanut Butter Cups or Oreos into cereal. Anyway, it wouldn't make it. How could one possibly down a bowl of Reese's Peanut Butter Puffs or Magic Stars and then go on to a two-, three-, or four-course noon and night meal the way the French do? The French diet is already tending to be a bit schizophrenic but if they ever mix things up to that point, *bonjour l'obésité!*

Big sizes, big smiles

On our voyage through the Colorado store, Philippe was astounded by the size and variety of products: a twenty-ounce onion, a sixty-four-ounce squeeze container of tomato catsup, zillions of kinds of

barbecue and steak sauce, an eighty-ounce container of peanut butter, not to mention a one-gallon jar of Miracle Whip. He couldn't
believe the variety of salad dressing: thousand island, ranch, Italian,
Italian classic Caesar, parmesan Italian, creamy Italian, Italian ranch,
ranch with bacon, peppercorn ranch, cucumber ranch, French onion
ranch, and I've left out at least a dozen more. What really got him,
though, was the reduced-fat peanut butter (isn't this a contradiction
in terms?) and the five-quart container of vanilla ice cream. When
Americans ask "how can the French eat all that food and remain so
slim?" I instantly think of the sheer size of those containers. Even a
family of ten would have a hard time getting through those babies
without taking fairly substantial portions.

On the plus side, in the U.S. grocery store I shop at when I visit
my relatives in Tucson, the smiles are as big as the quarts of mayonnaise, my groceries are bagged in record time, and I am asked if I
would like to have them taken to my car. Not only that, but once
the store people spontaneously offered to save me money.

"Do you have a super savings card?" asked the smiling blond
cashier.

"No, I'm visiting." I replied.

"No problem—does your brother or sister have a card? Just give
me the phone number."

I gave it to her and saved 5 percent on my goods. I had the feeling the U.S. store would do anything to get and keep me as a customer. In French grocery stores, I rarely get that feeling, but then,
France has never been known for its customer service.

In the French grocery store, I can find my precious yogurts but
checkout time is, on the whole, a *cauchemar*, a nightmare. But before
I go any further, I should distinguish between a hypermarket or
supermarket in Paris and a medium-size grocery store in the small

town of Nogent-le-Roi. There's no comparison. In the store in Nogent, the cashiers are relaxed and friendly. There's no crush, so you can find your way easily around the aisles, and everything you would possibly need is there. If you forget something, the cashier patiently waits for you to go get it.

. . . and bagging machines instead of baggers

In Paris, the rush is on. It used to be—and still is the case in many stores—that you had to bag everything yourself. This is not only boring, but a huge waste of everyone's time. Now many grocery stores have ingenious bagging machines that enable the cashier to ring up the item and place it in a bag until it's full. At this point he or she pushes a button, which gets the bag going on its way to you, the customer. All you have to do is pick it up. This is good for the customer—and it's especially good for the owner of the store. The machine replaces all those human beings, those part-time workers! In France, this is vital since social charges for all employees, including part-time workers, are so high. Meanwhile, unemployment (at this writing) hovers at around 10 percent and the French sneer at the Americans who hire people part-time and fire them just as fast. No job security, they say!

The Socialist government has put into place the thirty-five-hour work week, which is supposed to create jobs, but since the charges are so high, clever stores find machines to replace workers. I'm not an economist, and my political sympathies tend more to the left than the right, but it seems to me there's something missing in this picture. The fact of the matter, and forgive me if I sound like your local curmudgeon, is that you can probably count on the fingers of one hand the number of government ministers who have actually ever worked in a company. This is as true of the left as it is of the right. How can these decision makers possibly be expected to know anything about the economy when they've all been professors, lawyers, or professional politicians their whole lives? Sorry for the rant, but I think about this every time I see a bagging machine.

So where would I rather shop, in an American supermarket or a French one? I think I'd opt for a compromise: the wide, wide aisles and the general cleanliness of most U.S. grocery stores (is that because there are so many part-time workers cleaning up?) and the *human* baggers (part-time workers again). Oh, yes, and those friendly branch banks you find in some U.S. grocery stores. From the French stores, I'd take the typically French products such as *boudin*, blood sausage, and the right-sized full-fat yogurt and the friendly butcher at the meat counter at Franprix, a really *sympathique* guy who tells you how to prepare whatever you're buying from him, and the *fromage* counter at Monoprix which, for a store like this, has an astounding variety of delicious cheese.

En somme, a bit of both, but I'd especially root for the French market, whether it's the lively rue Mouffetard or the upscale Marché des Sablons. Something for everyone, I say. May this diversity not be killed by globalization. The day I no longer find my four-ounce yogurt with *fat*, and cheese that is runny and smelly, I'm out of here.

INTERVIEW WITH PHILIPPE

HWR: What do you think about the French substituting breakfast cereal for their morning croissant?

PhR: This is globalization raising its ugly head.

HWR: And peanut butter?

PhR: Unspeakable.

HWR: Catsup?

PhR: Okay as long as it goes on hamburgers and not on *entrecôte sauce Bordelaise*.

HWR: Is that the worst thing that could happen?

PhR: No. The worst would be to have what you call French dressing invading France.

When I get back from the hypermarket, I am generally very hyper and generally invaded by conflicting sentiments: I either want to make all kinds of good things with what I bought—or I can't bear the idea of cooking. When that's the case, I make either one of the following salads.

Easy endive salad

Endives (1 medium-sized
  per person)
Roquefort cheese

Walnuts
Bacon
Apples

Chop endives into pieces
(be sure to cut out the bitter part of the endive
at its stem).
Add Roquefort in little pieces,
walnuts in bite-size pieces.
Fry some small pieces of bacon and add
to all of this.
If you like, you can add peeled apples
chopped in small pieces.
If you add a bit of the bacon fat (but not too much)
it will be even better.
Then you mix it all up and add a good vinaigrette,
salt, and pepper.

Easy salade frisée, curly lettuce salad, with bacon and duck gizzards

Frisée, curly lettuce
Bacon
Preserved duck gizzards
Shallots
Garlic

Tomatoes, any kind as long
as they're not the
cardboard hothouse
variety
Vinaigrette, see page 44

Fry some bacon and sauté some duck gizzards
(in France you can find wonderful gizzards either in
cans or vacuum packed. If you can't find them in
the States, you can use chicken livers, which give
a different taste but which are also good—
be sparing with them though).
Cut up some shallots and crush some garlic.
Get out some of your tasty tomatoes.
Put all this together in a huge bowl with the lettuce
and add the vinaigrette.
Croutons are good in it, although certainly
not necessary.

(Cont.)

Easy to make, tasty, and takes only a few minutes to assemble. This is a first course, not a meal, though, so you'll have to find something to serve after it! If you don't like the idea of duck gizzards, leave them out, but it's too bad because they give this salad its taste!

5

À la campagne

La maison de campagne · The Fête de St. Lô · An American connection · Good times and good food · A family tradition · A typical Sunday lunch in the country · Making mirabelle alcohol · Some dental work at lunch · How do they eat like this and not get fat? Or . . . no doggy bags.

On Sunday mornings at my in-laws' house in the country, the ritual was always the same. At 8:00 A.M. or thereabouts, my father-in-law would arise and disappear into the kitchen. Smells of strong coffee would soon emanate from that region of the house, and he would emerge with a tray carrying the coffee and dozens of slices of buttered *pain d'épices* (a spice bread) and head back to the pretty pink bedroom.

In the bed was my mother-in-law invariably surrounded by one, two, three, or four grandchildren who had seen the door open and had rushed to dive under the warm covers with Mamie.

The rest of the day my mother-in-law was definitely the one in charge of the cuisine (on Sunday she would serve two major, and I mean *major* meals to any number of people from two to twenty), but I remember with fondness the pleasure my father-in-law took in offering her breakfast in bed.

La maison de campagne

The Rochefort country home is in a small village called Bréchamps, population three hundred. Located in the Eure-et-Loir, an hour's drive from Paris and only twenty miles from Chartres, Bréchamps isn't really all that far from the capital. But it must have seemed very far when my father-in-law bought the property in 1943. Since no one could take a car out of Paris because of the war, he biked the seventy kilometers every weekend to rejoin his wife, her parents, and his children.

As the years went by, the house, built in 1860, went through various changes to turn into what it is today, a sprawling pretty vine-covered brick home with a large sloping roof of ancient tiles, a spacious terrace looking over a landscaped garden with huge pine trees and the river Eure flowing by. The land goes all the way back along the river to behind the cemetery and the church three houses away. The house looks bigger from the outside than it really is: inside it's a homey place with small rooms with low ceilings and dark wooden beams and plenty of little corners and places to go.

It's also a place in which a lot of good food has been produced, starting with my mother-in-law's mother, Jeanne, who raised snails and stuffed them personally. The story goes that although she was a devout Catholic, she preferred to stay home to cook on Sunday morning. Some Sundays the priest, a jovial short and stout *bon vivant*, was invited. When he arrived, she would look him in the eye and say "I didn't steal and I didn't kill. For the rest, you'll have to ask me." The two of them would then take a walk outside in the garden along the river and when they came back, her confession had been made.

As for my diminutive white-haired, blue-eyed mother-in-law, to this day, my husband's friends still speak in awe of her *boeuf bourguignon* and her perfectly executed *crème caramel*. Now it's my sister-in-law's turn and she finds no greater pleasure than cooking all weekend long for the various family members and friends. I admire this greatly, especially because I would rather stick my head in a book! The *crème caramel*, by the way, looks and is easy to do but like many French recipes, it requires a *tour de main* that you only get by doing it a lot. Here's the way you make it:

Crème caramel à la Bréchamps

16 sugar cubes   A vanilla bean
½ cup of water   8 eggs
1 quart of whole milk   1¼ cup of sugar

In a 7-inch mold you can put on the flame and
in the oven, make a caramel with
sugar cubes and water.
Cover the bottom and sides of the mold
by swirling the caramel around.
Set aside.

(Cont.)

In a pan, boil the milk and the vanilla bean.
Let it cool and take the vanilla bean out.
In a separate bowl, mix the eggs and the sugar.
Add the cooled milk slowly while stirring constantly.
Filter this mixture and pour into the caramelized mold.
Bake in a bain-marie 30 minutes at 325°.
Carefully dip a clean knife into it to make sure it is completely cooked.
Let cool.
Put in the refrigerator to chill before unmolding it.

You can make it a day ahead of time. If you do this right, you'll have plenty of delicious caramel. Serves six.

Le Village

The name, Bréchamps, according to local historian Lucienne Jouan, comes from the Latin *brocoe*, campus or land among the woods. It was called Brochantellus in 1028, Borchant in 1250, Brichamps around 1570, Bréchampt around 1620, and Bréchams in the middle of the eighteenth century. Located on the edge of the Beauce, a flat agricultural region best known for Chartres and its magnificent cathedral, Bréchamps lies between the two valleys of the Maltorne and the Beaudeval. The Eure River flows through the lower part of the village where the church and cemetery and the town hall (*la mairie*) are all huddled. Over the years it became a place Parisians favored for their country homes.

The *en haut* or high part of the village consists solely of houses, some of which command a superb view over the valley. Even in such a small village, there's a climatic difference between the two parts, with the drier air *en haut* and humid air *en bas*. The advent of television and the closing of the town school brought changes to this rural village. TV drove people inside and the laughter of children coming and going to and from the communal school, which was located in the same building as *la mairie*, no longer fills the streets. Since the school closed in the '60s, the few children who live in the village are bused to neighboring communities. In the '80s the village church of St. Lô, built in the thirteenth century, lost its priest and no replacement was sent. Masses in the church are held once a month and the rest of the time those who wish to attend services have to go to the cathedral in the nearby town of Nogent-le-Roi.

But things are picking up. In 1999 for the first time the village participated in the annual Heritage Day, Fête du Patrimoine, in which historical buildings all over France are opened to the public. It was on Heritage Day and while visiting the church that I learned all kinds of things I didn't know, from details on some of the figures in the stained glass windows to the fact that up until recently pews were bought by families and reserved for their use. As we ambled through the church, my sister-in-law proudly showed me the Rochefort family bench (as you can surmise, I hadn't spent much time in that church!) and the tiny twelfth-century crypt she remembers the parishioners using for Mass on days it was too bitterly cold to stay in the sanctuary.

The Fête de St. Lô

The *mairie* also makes sure that village celebrations such as the Fête de St. Lo, the village's patron saint, are still held every fall. Had a stranger walked into the village this year, he would have no problem finding the *fête*. The smell of an entire pig roasting permeated the air and as you approached the Salle des Fêtes, there it was: the fated animal turning, turning, on its skewer. At seven it was already dark but the town hall was gaily lit. Yellow and blue cloths and a vase of fresh flowers adorned each table. We didn't do it on purpose but we ended up, fittingly, sitting underneath an oil painting my father-in-law, a talented Sunday painter and for many years a city councilman in Bréchamps, had donated to the *mairie*. I sat next to a friend who, for the first time, I noted, bore a striking resemblance to the French actress Stephane Audran. When I voiced that, her husband's reply was: "I'd rather she looked like Julia Roberts!"

For some reason, we got into a conversation about how rude some restaurant owners can be. Our friend told us a story about an incident in Provence in which he looked up from the menu on which he had seen *lapin farci*, stuffed rabbit, and asked what it was stuffed with. "With stuffing!" replied the owner indignantly. We all laughed appreciatively as we tore into our food, a first course of *cervelas*, pork sausage accompanied by potato salad, and a main course of wonderful grilled pork straight from the pig outside, along with some *semoule*, crushed wheat stuffing (at least *we* know what the animal was filled with!). As we awaited the cheese course, the noise level of the hall revved up to a dull roar and it became time for music and dance. There's always one couple brave enough to get out on the floor and then as the evening progresses more and more people shed their inhibitions. Unfortunately for me, my Cartesian husband finds dancing a strange activity . . . and anyway, we had to get back to Paris so we bade a discreet farewell to the people we knew and sneaked away. We'll have to leave the dancing for next year's *fête*.

An American Connection

In the late afternoon of June 23, 1944, my mother-in-law was at her next-door neighbor's house when she heard a loud sound. She looked up to see an American fighter plane rapidly falling almost directly over her house. The villagers watched in horror as the plane continued its fall, shaved the roof of the Virgin's Chapel of the church, and landed on some tombs in the cemetery. When they discovered that the pilot was dead (he had died before landing), my mother-in-law's mother ran to the house to find a sheet to cover his body.

I had heard the story of the pilot ever since I had first started coming to Bréchamps but the events of that day never became clear to me until a ceremony in May 1994 when a solemn commemorative service attended by the mayor of the village, a high official from the French government, a representative from the American embassy and many villagers, was held at the Monument to the Dead. (Each French village has its monument to the dead on which is inscribed the names of the men in the town who died in World War I, World War II,

Indochina, and Algeria. It is always a moving experience to see these names, especially when so many were brothers, uncles, or cousins.)

We observed a minute of silence as the name of the American pilot was added to the other names on the monument. Now when you walk past it you can see the official recognition of the French government for this American hero. The marble plaque reads:

Weins Lloyd C.
Pilote Américan Mort pour la Liberté
23 juillet 1944

Weins Lloyd C.
American Pilot Who Died for Freedom
July 23, 1944

Good times and good food

When I go to my husband's family house, the cooking is no longer my chore. Too many cooks spoil the broth, I tell myself somewhat hypocritically, so I'm content to take a back seat for a meal or two to my mother-in-law and sister-in-law, who are fine cooks and the soul of hospitality.

When my father-in-law was still alive, he would head out the door right after the bells began chiming for Mass. Whoever wanted to go with him was welcome but this tolerant man never insisted on anyone's coming. While he attended church, my mother-in-law was in the kitchen preparing lunch for any number of people. What I remember best about those days is how we would tease her when the chicken was being passed. She would always take the worst piece, the neck, with no meat on it, and swear to anyone who wanted to hear that she loved it. She slaved over the food but the best pieces naturally were reserved for everyone else!

Fortunately for all of us, my mother-in-law passed on her considerable *savoir-faire* to her daughter who is now at the helm. Martine loves to cook and does it effortlessly. There's always plenty to eat and it's always good. Because of her, I was under the mistaken impression that all French families pass on their knowledge of cooking from mother to daughter. This turned out to be wrong but it took me years to figure that one out! I do consider myself lucky to have landed in a family where there is a true appreciation of good food and of the mealtime moment.

There is one thing I should tell you though. In my very traditional *belle-famille*, you do not skip meals. You may not be hungry and you may not eat very much of what is served but you are at the table. There's no question of each person "doing his thing" as mealtime rolls around. If you don't want to participate in the family meal, then you don't go out there for the weekend!

A family tradition

Cooking and love of food run through the veins of the Rochefort family. Tante Françoise, my mother-in-law's sister, was a wonderful cook, concocting jars and jars of delicious homemade pickles and jellies (orange, cherry, mirabelles), homemade soups, long-simmering stews, and huge vats of her specialty, couscous in a miniscule six-by-ten-foot kitchen with no dishwasher and hardly any counter space.

As for Tante Andrée, this racy statuesque former top model from

Burgundy turned out to-die-for meals in a kitchen that was even smaller than Françoise's! I have a vision of her standing in that kitchen ready to serve a formal dinner for eight. I was quite young at the time, not yet married to Philippe, and my French wasn't good enough to understand all the quick repartee taking place at the table. In addition, I was in utter awe of this extremely elegant woman dramatically dressed in black with huge gold jewelry . . . who was also a terrific cook. I will never forget her chocolate chestnut cake and as an American could not for the life of me figure out how she could even take a bite of it and not put on forty pounds. It was so good that years after she passed away, every time someone would speak of the cake, there would be a minute of respectful silence as we all conjured up separate images of it. Apparently she also turned out a mean *baba au rhum*, one that was not appreciated to its full measure by either my husband or his sister because they were too young to like the taste of the alcohol.

Somehow the recipe for the chocolate chestnut cake got lost and although we all spent a lot of time trying to reconstruct it and had earnest conversations about making it, none of us ever quite got around to it. And who knows? Perhaps only she could have done it with such panache.

A typical Sunday lunch in the country

On a hot Sunday in August, my son Benjamin, his cousin Sophie, my in-laws, and I are all on the terrace eating a typical Sunday lunch. Martine would be embarrassed that I am reporting on what she would consider an ordinary meal but that's the point. This is the kind of ordinary Sunday meal we eat in the country.

To start with, she serves a tasty colorful medley of green, red, and yellow peppers which have been marinated in olive oil and garlic (I *must* find out how Martine makes this but haven't asked yet out of sheer laziness—something about having to get the skin off of all those peppers . . .). There is also a sweet lovely-smelling melon cut into slices.

This is followed by a variety of various meats, blood sausage or *boudin*, spicy sausages called *merguez*, nonspicy sausages called *chipolatas*, and lamb chops, all of which have been grilled on the barbecue. She serves the meats with some delicious potatoes from the island of Noirmoutier sautéed in butter and served with their skins on. (This is one of the rare times in France I have eaten potatoes with their skins on—normally they're taken off.)

Then comes a cheese plate composed of a Chèvre, Camembert, Pont l'Evêque, and a Chaource. *J'adore.*

Dessert consists of a fruit pie Philippe and I bought at the bakery as our contribution. This is not "cheating"—why make it when the *pâtissier* can do it as well or better? Besides, this was relief for my sister-in-law who had been trying out various ways of making apricot pies, one a day for almost two weeks. After the fruit pie is gone, she brings out an appetizing bowl of other fruit, apricots, nectarines, and greengage plums, in case anyone is still hungry.

We had a glass of sparkling Saumur before the meal. During the meal there was a choice of red wine and rosé and water. Coffee is served *after* all this as a separate course.

Another typical day we had melon and ham and cucumbers with cream to start with, steak tartare (raw meat bought fresh from the butchers and served an hour later) and *frites* (real ones, not frozen, *bien sûr*!!), a pecan pie (store bought and the American touch to this very French meal!), and homemade mirabelle sherbet.

It is my hope that by listing these menus American visitors reading this book won't do what I and other neophytes did when first in France—eat gigantic portions of the first course thinking it was the meal!

Making mirabelle alcohol

In late August, everything we eat is with mirabelles. The mirabelle is a small golden yellow plum that grows abundantly in Lorraine but also for some reason in the Eure-et-Loir. The season doesn't last that long—only three weeks—so you have to take advantage of it. You make pies, you make stewed fruit, you make homemade sherbet. Master chef Joël Robuchon gives a recipe for a *soufflé aux mirabelles* in his book on the best and simplest cuisine of France and notes that "the flesh of the fruit is exquisitely sweet." So true. And mirabelles make a fabulous *eau-de-vie* as we well know since the Rochefort family makes it every year either with pears or mirabelles. (It's a community effort for the Rochefort family—but to be scrupulously fair, I'd have to say that the 98 percent of the work is done by my energetic brother-in-law.)

Transforming mirabelles from their status as pretty round fruit to liquid in a bottle is a time-consuming process. It starts with the shaking down of the mirabelles from the trees onto a large white sheet. They are gathered up and then put into a large oak barrel where they spend the winter rotting and fermenting and making bubbles. By June the delicate golden plums have become a disgusting brown juice and are ready for a visit from the government certified distiller who will transform the cloudy goo into a lovely clear delicious *eau-de-vie*. (To fight against alcoholism, the government in 1954 proclaimed that only those people already making alcohol could continue but that nobody new could do so. That was called the privilege of the *bouilleur de cru*. Home brewers have the right to make twenty-four liters a year and no more.)

For me, the smell of mirabelle or pear alcohol that has been made in Bréchamps is a sheer delight and even though I am far from consuming even a tenth of our twelve liters a year, I love to dip a cube of sugar in a glass of it (that's called a *canard*), while sitting in front of the fireplace and taking a deep breath of our *eau-de-vie faite maison*. One reason I am so moderate is that early on I once drank some of our production of pear alcohol as if it were water. It does indeed look like water and it is indeed delicious. Still, it's stronger than gin and drinking great quantities of it is *not* recommended. A friend of mine did likewise and swore off alcohol for the next three years. Perhaps we should start thinking about offering our production as a cure for alcoholism.

Some dental work at lunch

On one of the days we had been transferring the finished *eau-de-vie* into bottles, its delicious odor perfuming the air (and most undoubtedly altering our brain cells permanently), my brother-in-law, Alain, a dental surgeon who has looked after our family's teeth for years with rapidity and competence, looked across the table at Philippe quizzically:

"Didn't you tell me you were going to come to the office to get your tooth replaced in a couple of weeks?"

"Yes," replied Philippe.

"Well, do you have it with you?" Alain queried, pursuing his idea.

French Fried

"Yes," answered Philippe, who always walks around with a spare tooth on him. One never knows . . .

Alain jumped up from the table, pulled out a chair, and beckoned for Philippe to sit on it. "Let's do this right now," he said, getting out his various dental tools.

He deftly cleaned the area, mixed some glue, and skillfully placed the tooth in its hole. Meanwhile, Martine had arrived with a bicycle pump which she enthusiastically aimed at the tooth to dry it after Alain had applied the glue.

"*Serre,*" bite down, he instructed.

"It's going to taste horrible," he continued. "You'd better have a *coup de gnole.*" *Gnole* is a familiar word translating to homemade brew. Philippe declined. The smell of the *eau-de-vie* was sufficient.

The patient was satisfied. The doctor was satisfied. The dental assistant manning the bicycle pump was satisfied and my mother-in-law and I had a good laugh. The tooth, however, fell out a week later in spite of all the good will and Philippe still had to trek out to Alain's office. But the dental work did give a certain *élan* to an otherwise ordinary family meal.

In case you're thinking that dental work and family meals is something we combine frequently, well, not really. The only other occasion happened many years ago when Alain took out three of my wisdom teeth (without any anesthesia) in his office and then drove me back to our mother-in-law's apartment where we sat down to a heavy meal including the famous Rochefort *haricots blancs.* Suffice it to say that even with my healthy constitution, this was all a bit too much and the *haricots* never had a chance of remaining in my stomach. We decided after that, with the exception of this latest incursion into Philippe's mouth, not to combine "business" with pleasure. It really can ruin a good meal.

How do they eat like this and not get fat? Or . . . no doggy bags

By now I'm sure you're asking yourself 1) If my French in-laws are crazy, to which I will answer "No" but they're a lot of fun! And 2) How can people spend all this time at the table, eat all this food, and not get fat, especially when I tell you that my mother-in-law is from the Périgord in southwestern France, a region where the fat used to cook is duck or goose fat. My mother-in-law would no more cook with butter than cut off her hand. The potatoes in her delicious potato omelette are *of course* cooked in goose fat. Traditions die hard, fortunately for us and the Rochefort omelette.

Here's what I've observed. The French don't snack all day long and they eat hardly anything with their before dinner drinks. A few peanuts, a cracker or two. The reason for this is simple: they are anticipating the meal and they're happy to wait for it. This is a major difference with the U.S. where we tend to eat so much before dinner we're barely hungry for it by the time we get to the table. The French know they're going to have to wade through all those courses during the meal so they pace themselves. And, an important point, French servings are about half the size of American servings. This means you can eat small portions of a lot of courses without even coming near the amount you'd get on the average American plate!

In spite of the incredible number of dogs in this country, there are no doggy bags here!

INTERVIEW WITH PHILIPPE

HWR: What would you do on Sunday if you didn't spend three hours sitting at the table for lunch?

PhR: What else can you do in the country? I'd be chopping down trees and it would be even worse.

À la ville

*Give us this day our daily meals . . . twice a day . . . and in
courses, please*

From my husband's family I learned not only to cook but to at
least make the effort to turn out two sit-down meals a day. It
is an effort for me because sometimes I think there are better
things to do than spend all that time at the table, not to mention the before and after, but when I see the pleasure it gives, I
know it is worth it.

Chaos reigns!

This being said, I always thought it ironic that it was in France,
land of the pleasurable meal, that chaos reigned at my family's
mealtimes. As I mentioned earlier, in my youth my dad came
home at 6:00 P.M. and we were all together at the table at 6:30 P.M.
like clockwork. I fear my mother must have been shocked when
she came to my place in France and saw how the Rochefort dinner hour went.

There was always, shall we say, a certain tension in the air due to the fact that Philippe arrived home so late (8:30 or 9:30 P.M.) and as a result dinner was up for grabs. My two rambunctious youngsters could hardly wait until that late hour so I generally ended up feeding them first. There were several variations on the theme: some days the boys would eat first and I would await Philippe. On other days, the boys would eat first, then I would eat, and then Philippe. And on yet other days, I would eat with the boys and Philippe would eat alone. We often ate totally different things as well. It wasn't until my kids were grown and it was too late that I *finally* figured out the solution to my problem: a *plat unique*, a one-dish meal, which could be served to all the different shifts at different times. Oh, well, maybe in another life.

. . . when you try so hard to be French!

Here's an example of a typical anarchic meal *chez nous*. I'd like to tell you how perfectly organized and smoothly running this place is—but in truth it resembles that adage "the road to hell is paved with good intentions." On this particular day, I had been to the market on the rue de Poncelet where I bought some magnificent looking *coquilles St. Jacques*, scallops, and some *filets de grenadier* (I liked the name, which appears to be untranslatable, but they are in fact whitefish fillets). I had a wonderful recipe by Joël Robuchon for the *coquilles* and figured I'd wing it with the *filets*. Then reality set in. By the time I got home it was too late to marinate the *coquilles*. Instead, I sautéed them. I had some lamb I had asked my son to eat at noon so that it would be finished and we could have the fish. He hadn't eaten the lamb for lunch so it was still there and still good—but it wouldn't be the next day and I hate to toss food. Exit the idea of fish.

So now our meal was the sautéed coquilles, and lamb for David but not us, first of all because there wasn't enough, and second of all because Philippe was recovering from the flu and not feeling like eating anything. This was compounded by another reason: he had had a business lunch at the Royal Monceau Hotel where he had eaten . . . *coquilles St. Jacques!*

You might think that after a mammoth business lunch my other half would not be hungry. That is, in fact, what he often announces when he makes it back home around 9:00 P.M. saying that "today we had a business lunch at . . ." Les Muses or Divellec or the Carré des Feuillants or Ducasse—take your pick. He negligently tosses out the names of these fabulous restaurants as I stare at him in sheer envy.

But don't think that when he says he's not hungry he doesn't want to eat. The guy is French, right? Not being hungry means he doesn't want *much* to eat but of course we will sit down to a real meal with a starter, a main course, and cheese or dessert. As I said, we do not skip meals in this family. I should perhaps add here that this is not simply because my husband is traditionally French but because for me skipping a meal is an abomination. It is just something I would never even consider.

If I multiply the fated *coquilles St. Jacques* dinner by 365 days of the year, you'll get an idea of the ambiant schizophrenia. Lots of good intentions downed by the realities of daily life, too many good ideas, too little time. Sometimes I entertain the dark thought that if I had daughters, they'd be out there in the kitchen helping me, but when I look around at most of the daughters of friends of people I know, that illusion is quickly dashed.

Why, oh, why, don't I just give them all hot dogs or hamburgers? (Answer: because I believe in assimilation! When in Rome . . .) I heard once on the news the story of a French mother who turned out marvelous meals for her family, who sat there, never talked, and watched the tube. Fed up, one day she served them cat food. *That* got a reaction. But don't get me wrong: we're not there yet. I'm relating this story to tell you what happens when you make a daily effort to give people something other than a sandwich or tell them to go to the fridge and help themselves.

The positive part of all this is that as the boys grew older we finally did manage to sit down together instead of eating in shifts. Dinner wasn't always that calm moment I dreamed of (that's an understatement) but at least we were all together, sitting at the same table. The boys coped with our good moods and our bad ones and we coped with theirs as well. We actually got them to do civilized things like setting and clearing the table (I kept hoping one of them would want to be a chef and try out his creations on us but no such luck). The moments we all remember best were the funny ones, and there were many of them. It was time-consuming indeed but if we are close as a family, it is in large part due to those family meals. So, yes, it would have been easier if we had all dipped into the fridge when the spirit moved us but it wouldn't have been the same. Not the same at all.

Lunchtime at home

Dinner's one thing. Lunch is another. I thought the *cantine* or school lunch was the best thing the French school system ever invented. I stuck my eldest in it at age four, if I recall. Perhaps it was a wee bit early, for when he was ten, he decided to quit going. With all those years of school lunch behind him, he somehow *knew* it would be much more fun to spend his lunch hour at home. I wasn't overly enthusiastic about this idea because there was no reason to have to go into major lunch mode just for myself. It turned out that Benjamin was not going to be satisfied with the sandwich I tried to foist off on him. No, the kid had very French genes (in spite of rumors to the effect that he is a Coca-Cola addict) and expected a real meal with salad or *pâté* or sausage or sardines to start with and meat and potatoes or something hot in the middle and yogurt at the end.

And that is what I did.

I have to admit that it gave us an opportunity to talk (sometimes shout at each other when we didn't agree) and I don't regret it at all. I'm not the only mother who appreciated this precious moment. Stephanie Stolin Moreno, another American wife of a Frenchman, says she spent ten years "food shopping, peeling, preparing, cooking, and cleaning up afterwards for the whole family. Both girls came home for lunch . . . and the husband came home often with colleagues (no advance notice)." Stephanie says that in spite of the juggling, "something special happened at those kitchen meals. We talked to each other."

When my youngest also decided to abandon the school lunch program and come home at noon (Would I *never* be free?), I was ready to make the same effort for him but he turned out to be my little American. He would, he assured me, take care of lunch himself. He then proceeded to cook himself pasta or make a sandwich or heat soup, in short, do his own thing. It was a load off my back but I found I missed the conversations and camaraderie one can have when sitting down to a meal together.

Lunchtime at *la cantine*

By the way, even in an age where French kids are munching on sandwiches and drinking Cokes, French school lunches still reflect the traditional French way of eating. I had wondered if this would change and saw that it had not when I recently passed by my son's former elementary school. Not only had nothing changed but things had improved. When my sons were young, I often made them the same thing for dinner that they had had for lunch because I hadn't looked at the school lunch menu for the day. The menus are still posted but there's been an addition: now you are given suggestions of what you can make the kids for the evening meal in case you need any ideas!

Here's an example, just to show that the French haven't been globalized in this respect: on one typical day, a school lunch will consist of a hard-boiled egg with mayonnaise to start with, *steak haché* (a hamburger without the bun), mashed potatoes, Camembert, and a fruit. For the evening meal, they suggest radishes to start with, moussaka, and a *petit suisse*, a small soft cheese enriched with cream and, in my case at least, eaten with a lot of sugar. Another typical day: *cervelas* (cold pork sausage with vinaigrette), spaghetti Bolognese, cheese, and fruit. Suggested menu for the evening: a leek-potato soup, *salsifi* (salsify), fruit. Guess what they *don't* eat, *never* eat, at school lunch in France: sandwiches!

Granted, the school lunch version of French favorites such as *quiche lorraine*, *paupiette de veau*, and *bœuf bourguignon*, all of which figure on the menus, may not, for economical reasons be as good as what Maman or Mamie might cook at home. *Blanquette de veau*, for example, might occasionally be *blanquette de volaille*, chicken. What is interesting, though, is that in this age of globalization these French classics are still very much part and parcel of what a child will be given and be expected to eat. Some French nutritionists are now saying that children should be given a *plat unique*, and that they shouldn't be expected to sit at the table for so long. I tend to agree but can't help but think that one reason my kids learned the virtue of patience is that they were forced to sit through seemingly interminable meals which actually "only" lasted about forty-five minutes.

The nonexistent *petit déjeuner* and cold hake for lunch

In my family, breakfast is each to his own and always has been. My sons learned early on that their mother was off limits in the morning, which in the end was very good for them because they had to get up, shower, dress, and get ready to get to school on time on their own steam. This taught them autonomy, of course, but naturally I regret having given them such atrocious habits about breakfast, i.e., no habits.

Even on the weekend, breakfast is the only meal we don't sit down to together. Lunch, on the other hand, is four courses, something to start with, for example, a tomato salad or *pâté*, followed by meat or fish and a vegetable, cheese if anyone wants it, and dessert, which is generally a yogurt or fruit. On Sunday this differs and we have a wonderful cake or *tarte*, which is a treat and reserved for this once-a-week occasion—once a week because if we ate all the delicious cakes you see in French bakeries on a daily basis we would be blimps! Many times we have a *plat unique* such as a rice salad that is very simple to make but copious.

Sometimes we'll have cold fish or something that requires homemade mayonnaise. The cold fish is not hard to make but requires a great deal of manipulation and attention. Philippe and I generally go to the market and buy a *colin*, hake, which we then cook for ten minutes in a special fish cooker in which you first put a glass or two of water, then a rack with the fish on it so that it will be steam cooked. The trick here is that once it's cooked, you have to take off the skin very carefully. Once you've done that, you've got to get the fish out of the cooker onto the plate, and that, I can assure you, is a definite challenge and invariably the start of a bit of Gallic yelling. (On joint efforts like this, Philippe and I cooperate, but, generally speaking, whoever is in the kitchen wants the other person out of it.) Once you manage to get that beautiful creature, complete with head, on an appropriate serving plate, you're on your way to dressing it up and making it pretty with slices of tomatoes and hard-boiled eggs and parsley for color. We serve it with Philippe's homemade mayonnaise, which is simple but absolutely delicious. It is, however, not for those who have a cholesterol problem. That is why it is called Philippe's Homemade Heart Attack Mayonnaise. The recipe for it and the rice salad are below. *Bon courage!*

Philippe's Homemade Heart Attack Mayonnaise

All ingredients should be at room temperature:
1 raw egg yolk
A teaspoonful of Dijon mustard
Salt and pepper, not too much and not too little

Oil (light cooking)—no way to tell you how much—quit adding when your mayonnaise has formed
A tablespoon of red wine vinegar

Put the egg yolk in a mixing bowl and mix with the
mustard and salt and pepper.
Now slowly, very slowly, pour a constant thin
stream of oil while beating the yolk continually. You
can do this either with a fork (the tried and true
old-fashioned way) or with a mixer.
Unless you're totally out of luck,
the mayonnaise will start to form.
When you've got the quantity you want, stop
pouring the oil, add vinegar and mix together.

Author's comment: Sure, you can buy mayonnaise in a
jar or a tube but homemade is so much better, *n'est-ce
pas?* Be sure not to look at how much oil is going into
it, though, or your blood will freeze in your veins.

Philippe and Harriet's It-Goes-a-Long-Way Rice Salad

This is so simple that it's embarrassing to put it in recipe form. That said, everyone always loves it and it's perfect for a crowd. It could also be called the Kitchen Sink Salad because the more things you put in it, the better it is. The keys to its success are the French cornichons and the French vinaigrette made with French mustard!

Here goes:

Rice	*Dill pickles*
Canned tuna fish, water- *packed*	*Anchovies*
	Capers
Hard-boiled eggs	*Swiss cheese*
Green peppers	*Black olives*
Tomatoes	

Boil rice (1 cup per person) and don't let it get mushy! Let it cool.

Put the rice in a bowl. Drain a can of water-packed tuna and add to rice along with some hard-boiled eggs, green peppers cut up, tomatoes cut up, pickles (dill, or French cornichons if you can find them), onions, capers, anchovies, Swiss cheese cut in bite-size cubes, black olives, and anything else you can find that looks like it would be good.
Make a vinaigrette with real French mustard. Gently combine all these ingredients, add the vinaigrette and mix.

If you put on more rice, you'll need more tuna and more of everything else, but that's easy to see! The advantage of this miraculous rice salad it that it seems to *grow* and expand. It can feed *thousands*.

A giant cultural gap

And a final remark: What my family eats and when, is, I concede, not the most fascinating topic in the world but there's a point to all this and it's called "cultural differences." Talking to a couple of young Americans one day, I described how we do sit-down meals in my home and all over France. They both gazed at me as if I were from outer space, as if the idea had never occurred to them. One of them thought for a while before volunteering: "My family *never* eats at home. Sometimes we'll all go to McDonald's together for a burger." The other one said: "We *try* to have a family meal once a month." I did my best to think of the French families I know with children who *never* eat together and couldn't come up with any. *Voilà une différence—et vive la différence!*

 INTERVIEW WITH PHILIPPE

ℌWℝ: How can you make and eat such delicious but life-threatening things and be so slim, so vibrant, in such perfect health with no cholesterol or heart problems? What is your secret?

Phℝ: It's easy. No sports!

ℌWℝ: No, seriously, Americans are always wondering how the French can eat all that good food and drink all that wine and not have the obesity problem we have in the States.

Phℝ: You Americans take food very seriously, more than normally, and you do something we French don't do. Whenever you're hungry, no matter what time it is or where you are, you eat. We wait for mealtime even if we're starving.

(Cont.)

HWR: So what's your advice to visiting Americans who are terrified at the pounds they are going to gain from all that great *pâté* and all that wonderful cheese and all that wine.

PhR: Americans associate food with guilt. The French associate food with pleasure. My advice is: just enjoy it! The Puritans already ruined your joy for sex. Don't let health freaks ruin your joy for food.

7

Body Parts or: Is offal awful?

The French eat everything in the animal · *A butcher store and
a rabbit head* · *A horsemeat surprise* · *Making blood sausage
· Brains in the microwave* · Le porc

The thing I love about France (and animal lovers will now
wince) is that most of the time what you see is what you
get. In a humorous description of an American in France, the fictitious engineer Norton, in *Les chroniques de l'Ingénieur Norton,
Confidences d'un Américain à Paris*, recounts his reaction to what
he sees at the market or in stores: "You see the heads of pigs cut
off at the base of the neck, or stuffed feet, all these things coldly
called by their name. They eat the entire animal, from the ears to
the genitals, without feeling the need to euphemize them, to cut
them up or cover them up like we do. I can't look at their black
sausage (coagulated pig's blood) without wanting to vomit."

It doesn't make me want to vomit really but it is always a
shock to see rabbits, pheasants, partridges, hanging, head down,
with their fur still on. At the market in Neuilly one day I saw
rabbits hanging upside down, with aluminum on their heads.
"Why are their heads covered?" I asked, and learned that they
are hooded because blood from their eyes might drip on the

counter. How unaesthetic! On another day I strolled past a *triperie*, a stall selling organ meats at the market in Nogent-le-Roi. I noticed a small table near the stand and on that small table a perfectly monstrous head that kind of reminded me of Ernest Borgnine.

"What *is* it?" I asked the man behind the counter.

"A boar's head," he replied, as normally as if he had said "A pair of shoes."

"A boar's head," I repeated, attempting to conceal my disgust and revulsion. "What do you do with it?"

At this, he waxed eloquent. "Well, you can make a *civet de joue* (red wine stew using the blood) or you can cook the whole head in wine, take the flesh off the bones and make a *pâté* out of it."

I immediately thought of another use, one that would probably be illegal, which would be to put it in one of those nice ready-made packages the French *poste* sells, and to send it to my worst enemy. Wouldn't that be a sensation—and after all, the whole head was on sale for only thirty francs!

The French eat everything in the animal

After the initial thrill, my sons no longer eat McDonald's burgers anymore. One son has very French taste buds and will eat blood sausage and *tripes à la mode de Caen*, a Norman specialty of beef tripe prepared with carrots, onions, leeks, all cooked slowly in water, cider, and Calvados, apple brandy. The other wouldn't even consider such a thing. You can forgive him. Many French people don't go for organ foods either and it's not something you would serve at a dinner party unless you hate your guests and hope they'll never come back. No, tripes are only for deserving tripe-lovers—and I am one—but only if they are of excellent quality. Philippe's favorite treat is a *ril-lon*. Also called *grattons* or *grillons* depending on the region, it is a pork belly piece sautéed in lard. I don't know how she knows, but the butcher's wife in Nogent almost always offers him a *rillon* when we're in the store. "Good for the cholesterol," she jokes. Philippe is into pork fat in a big way: I remember watching with wonder the first time he spread pork fat on a piece of bread and wolfed it down for an (exceptional, it must be said) afternoon snack. Well, I suppose it's no worse than a Mars bar, in the end. I console myself by thinking that perhaps he is among those who benefit from the French paradox and that somehow all the red wine he drinks dissolves the fat!

When you live in France, you are in for some surprises on the gut front. Eileen Bastianelli, an American who married a Frenchman, told me of a conversation she had with her two-year-old daughter Lola who had returned from a trip to her French grandmother's house. "Grandma gave me tripes," she said, as Eileen responded with a hypocritically enthusiastic "Super!" trying not to gag. "Another time we had tongue," Lola continued. "And on it went," said Eileen. "In a five-minute talk, we found she'd ingested every horse, brain, and ball on the planet." Eileen says that she grew up in a cosmopolitan household where she had tasted snails as a tot. But at age twelve, "I suddenly realized what I was eating and was utterly disgusted." Unfortunately her epiphany occurred at an important business dinner her father was hosting at Lasserre, one of France's most prestigious restaurants. The snail was already in her mouth when she realized it was nothing but a gooey gastropod. To her father's horror, she bolted from the table to the ladies' room. ("I'd been taught to be polite so at least I kept it in my mouth and didn't spit it out on the plate," she recalls.) That was the end of Eileen's eating of body parts days. Obviously Lola's got her beat in that department—until the day she too realizes what she's eating.

Actually, we Americans used to eat what was euphemistically called "variety meats" in the States. Meta Given's *Modern Encyclopedia of Cooking*, 1952, supplies recipes for brains à la Newburg, scrambled brains, heart chop suey (how gross!), and deviled kidneys. How times have changed.

A butcher store and a rabbit head

After living in France for all these years, I thought I'd seen just about everything, but how wrong I was. On a perfect September day in the country, I went to the butcher store in Nogent-le-Roi to get a rabbit to make for dinner.

"Shall I cut it in pieces for you?" the butcher asked.

"Yes," I replied, and then asked how long it would take to cook the rabbit.

"An hour and a half," he said, not looking up from the rabbit he was skillfully carving into pieces, "and not twenty minutes, which is what the cookbooks tell you." A customer waiting for her order joined in the conversation and we all agreed on the joys of eating food that has gently simmered and is flavorful.

Back home, I unwrapped the package . . . and found myself staring eyeball to eyeball with the rabbit's head, yes, eyes and all! It had been so long since I had bought a rabbit that I had forgotten about the head!! Quick, a call to my mother-in-law!

"Do people *really* eat the head?" I asked.

"Some do, some don't," she replied. The reason for putting the head in the package is not only because people might want to eat it but to show them that they are buying a rabbit and not a cat.

"*What?*" I exclaimed.

During the war, she told me, this often happened. You would order a rabbit but rabbits and cats look very much alike. After all, there's only a couple bones of difference between the two. You never knew what you were getting. To this day, my mother-in-law doesn't eat rabbit. However, her neighbor in the country taught her how to cut the eyes out should she ever need to. (She thankfully didn't offer to share her expertise with me.)

"Why would people eat the head?" I continued.

"For the cheeks and the brain, which, though small, is very good," she told me.

"Hmmm," I mused, as I recalled a conversation with a French friend who had told me that his mother ate both the cheeks and the eyes, which she adored, and gave him the brain, which he loved.

After thinking it over for about two seconds (Did I *really* want to cook that head and did I *really* want to ask my mother-in-law for a *cours supérieur* on how to get the eyes out of it?), I disposed of it.

I cooked the headless beast on a low flame for an hour and a half in a lovely wine sauce with bacon and mushrooms and it was very good. And at least I knew I wasn't eating a cat!

A horsemeat surprise

My first experience with horsemeat was with a French family in Mexico. Invited to lunch, I was served a portion of what looked like a steak and heartily ate it, just as I heartily eat almost anything that is put before me unless it is awful looking or stinky or lukewarm when it should be hot.

After lunch, my hosts looked at me and asked me in a suspiciously teasing tone what I thought the meat I had eaten was.

"Cow, what else?" I replied innocently.

"No, *cheval!*" they chortled with delight.

Fortunately for them, I'm a good sport and, as I said, not turned off by very much. We have remained friends to this day, although I haven't tried horsemeat again on my own. (My son David however quite likes it and keeps asking me to buy it for him. He's out of luck, for this meat, which was very popular up until the '50s and even considered more hygienic and tastier than cow meat, can now only be found in a few supermarkets and on some stands at outdoor or covered markets.)

All of this is to say that when it comes to the insides of animals, even friendly animals like horses or rabbits, I do not flinch. *Au contraire.*

Making blood sausage

I've always liked *boudin*, blood sausage, but as with most foods like this, I try not to think too much about what it is composed of. One Sunday though at the Foire de Maintenon, a kind of a huge citywide garage sale, I stopped in my tracks as I saw a big mustachioed fellow with a white apron with blood spattered on it and his hands. On the table in front of him were two small bowls with the *boyaux*, the intestines and stomach linings of pigs. Closer to him was a huge basin in which he prepared the *boudin*: Out of a vat behind him, which was under the table so you didn't see it, he scooped up a ladle of *pig's blood*, then poured it through a siphon at the end of which the intestine was attached. As the blood ran through, the intestine filled up and formed a perfect coil. This wasn't the end of the operation. He then tied it up neatly and plunged the *boudin* into boiling water, where it coagulated and lost its red color and turned black, the way you see it when it is sold. "What stops it from running through?" my husband asked. "The onion," replied the fellow. He then offered his arm, not his hand, to a friend. The French shake hands on almost every occasion but if the hand is occupied, or in this case, bloody, they offer the arm instead.

"I'm American," I ventured, "and I don't think most of my compatriots would eat your *boudin*, especially after seeing how it's made." Hardly discouraged by my comment, which once out of my mouth I found pretty dumb, he didn't miss a beat: *"Ah, il y a un marché à prendre!"* There's a market over there! And he then told me he had an American student who was, in fact, learning the tricks of his trade.

This exchange took place barely an hour from Paris, forty minutes by train from the Gare Montparnasse, and on the day of a major food fight between the U.S. and France. The U.S. was banning Roquefort and *foie gras* (not that most Americans would suffer from the lack of these two products) in retaliation for the French refusal to import hormone-treated beef from the States. The French refusal was part and parcel of a general resistance to what the French call the *mal bouffe* (bad eating). In the meantime, here was a fellow calmly making his *boudins* in front of the supermarket where he works and selling the finished product to people who were delighted to buy the real thing fresh. And, *en plus*, he had an American follower!

At the same fair, we bought several kinds of sausages, including two kinds of *andouilles*, Guémené and Vire, the names of the places where they are produced. *Andouille*, by the way, is a cooked sausage generally served cold while *andouillette* is served hot, fried or grilled or with a sauce. I thought back to a fair we had attended in Steamboat Springs, Colorado, only two months earlier: There had been every kind of food imaginable from Greek to Italian to American (but no blood sausage!) and people sat all over the place eating at picnic benches or on the grass or walking along. Although there were food stands at the French fair as well, my husband pointed out that "most of the people are going to go home at noon and come back after lunch." Which is why some were buying the fresh *boudin*, probably.

By the way, if you're into learning French slang, a *boudin* is a pejorative term for an unattractive girl, as in "she's a real *boudin*." It's rather old-fashioned now. Kids my sons' age say *thon*, tuna. And if you call someone an *andouille* it means they are stupid. Well, whatever. I wouldn't use any of those terms if I were you, but they're always interesting to know.

Brains in the microwave

What I love about the French is their ability to adapt traditional typically French dishes to modern life. We bought a new microwave after our old one conked out; with it came a book of instructions and gourmet recipes. I learned, for example, that in my microwave I can make *andouillettes à la moutarde*, chitterlings in a mustard sauce (twelve minutes), *cervelles d'agneau aux câpres*, lamb brains with capers (seven minutes), and *rognons de veau au madère*, veal kidneys in a Madeira wine sauce (six minutes). So if you come to my house, watch out. I may serve you a microwaved brain.

Le porc

The famous eighteenth-century French gastronomic critic Balthazar Grimod de la Reynière could have bragged about a number of things—but the thing he was most proud of in life was his ancestors who were *charcutiers*, pork butchers. The story goes that his fellow boarder was a pig with whom he shared his room and that one of his servants had as a special task the bathing, brushing, and rubbing down of the pig with oil on a regular basis. Not only were pigs highly thought of but they were the animal par excellence because there's no waste. Wrote Grimod de la Reynière: "The pig is the encyclopedic animal, a veritable meal on paws. You throw nothing of it away, up to the feet, you eat everything." As the saying goes, *tout est bon dans le cochon*, everything in the pig is good. In his *Petit dictionnaire de cuisine*, Alexandre Dumas has twenty different items, including pig's brains, pig's tongue, pig's ears, and pig's tail *à la purée*.

I have always been proud of my open-mindedness about body parts but I discover daily the number of dishes I have not yet tasted. A pig's ear is one of them. An American friend of mine who has lived in France for many years told me that she was served a pig's ear at what she called "a raucous women's luncheon" in a Paris restaurant to celebrate Beaujolais nouveau. The ear was the first course. It was followed by stuffed cabbage, and a pudding with black currant liqueur. "The pig's ear was gigantic—it took up the whole plate so you could hardly shove it aside. When we finally got around to asking the waitress how you eat a pig's ear and she told us that you only eat the fatty part, it was too late. I had already eaten the cartilage. Horrible!"

If you go into a *charcuterie*, check out the number of dishes made out of the pig. *Museau*, pig snout, anyone? It's actually very good with onions and vinaigrette. Just don't tell your unsuspecting guests what it is they're eating.

 INTERVIEW WITH PHILIPPE

HWR: Why do the French eat the guts of animals and the Americans don't?

PhR: Guts don't go on barbecues.

HWR: Don't you think eating calf snout and pig's ears is disgusting?

PhR: If you think snout and ears are bad, just think of ancient Rome when the delicacy was swan's tongue and sow's vulva.

HWR: No need to be *dégoûtant*.

Food note

Tripe can be found at the supermarket, but it's best to get it in a special store or stall at the market called a *triperie*. To prepare it, all you have to do is heat it slowly in a pan on a low flame. As it heats, the "block" it comes in dissolves into its parts with a sauce. You serve the tripe with boiled potatoes, sprinkled with parsley to be pretty, and that's all there is to it! As for the *boudin*, you buy it either in a *charcuterie* or, again, the supermarket. Generally you grill it ten minutes on each side (prick it with a fork so it doesn't explode) and serve it with cooked apples and/or mashed potatoes.

8

Le pain, le vin et le fromage

Long comme un jour sans pain · *Harriet gets some help on
wine* · *Champagne tasting at the Ritz* · *A conversation with
George Lepré* · *A Brie in the States* · *Cheese meals and
cheese cravings* · *Meeting a fromager*

One night as ten of us were sitting around the table in Bréchamps savoring the Rochefort potato omelette prepared
by Philippe, I started thinking about what was "typically French"
on the table and in our way of eating. It was simple: everything!

The omelette, of course, the bottle of red wine, several baguettes (no question of not having enough bread), and a huge bowl
of a fresh lettuce salad with a simple vinaigrette to eat either with
the omelette or after it, depending on one's preference. Cheese
and dessert were waiting in the wings (or, to be more accurate, on
a side table).

There were a few things on the table, I thought, that really
were indispensable not only to this meal but to all meals in
France: the bread, for even though we were eating potatoes, we
needed the bread for all kinds of purposes: to gently push things
around, to eat with the omelette, the salad, and the cheese, even
to mop up the remains of the vinaigrette in the salad (hoping

that no one would be looking). The bread is a security blanket, a must. There is no *way* that any meal would occur without bread and the fact that there are other starches in the meal has nothing to do with bread being there. I learned that many years ago when I forgot to buy bread and pointed out to Philippe that it wasn't important because we were eating spaghetti. It was then that he explained to me that whether we're having spaghetti or noodles or rice has absolutely nothing to do with the bread. The bread has to be there no matter *what* we are eating. Perhaps because bread is such an integral part of the meal, it has no special plate. Other than at formal dinners, the bread's place is right on the tablecloth!

As far as the wine is concerned, it too has to be there for it is the perfect accompaniment to everything, especially the cheese. It's there—but don't think that the children at the table, for example, are serving themselves out of the bottle. Nor are the women. It's considered quite uncouth for women to pick up a bottle, even of water, and serve themselves. In fact, except *en famille* it's considered quite gauche for anyone else but the host to serve the drinks. Philippe allowed our sons to taste wine when they were about eleven or twelve—but tasting means tasting, not drinking. He served them and they sipped and talked a little bit about where the wine came from and the different wine regions. (Benjamin puckered up his lips and decided he didn't like wine. He turned into a beer drinker instead.) David was more interested and so from age sixteen on, Philippe would offer him a glass of wine from time to time. The inclusion of wine with the family meal means that it is something normal, not a taboo; a direct result of this is that you rarely see young people in France indulging in the binge drinking one sees in the U.S.

Whether the cheese "needs" to be there or not is a moot question. We're in France! What's the point of living in a country with four hundred or so different kinds of cheeses if you don't have at least a sampling of three or four of them on your table?

All of this, of course, I now take for granted. But my little reflection session got me thinking. I realized that in spite of all my years in this country and the thousands of French meals I had both made and eaten, I really didn't know that much about the Holy Trinity of France: bread, wine, and cheese.

It was time to investigate these three worlds, see the people who make and bake the bread, live in the world of wine, and age and sell the country's cheese.

But before I go any further, here's the way to make the Rochefort omelette.

The Rochefort *omelette de pommes de terre*

A favorite family meal! You'll need plenty of bread to complement the omelette and eat with the good cheese plate you'll serve afterwards. And you'll need some good red wine to go along with it all.

2 pounds of potatoes (red potatoes or any type of boiling potato)
6 tablespoons of goose fat

eggs
A tablespoon of milk
A clove of garlic
Salt and pepper to taste
Parsley

Peel the potatoes, cut in thin slices, wash, and dry with a clean cloth.
Sauté the potatoes very slowly with goose fat. Cover until tender. This can take as long as an hour. Check them!
Add the eggs, which have been beaten with salt and pepper, a tablespoon of milk, and seasoned

**with a finely chopped clove of garlic.
Right before the eggs are cooked, sprinkle on some
finely chopped parsley.**

The trick of this simple recipe is to get the potatoes perfectly cooked—not burned, not undercooked, not reduced to mush—and to get the omelette onto a big serving plate without it falling on the counter or floor or turning into a mess of scrambled eggs. Philippe does it perfectly but practice is recommended for beginners. Serve the omelette with a lettuce salad (not iceberg!) seasoned with a vinaigrette. Serves six.

Long comme un jour sans pain (as long as a day without bread)

If you have any doubts as to the importance of bread on the French table, look at the long lines outside the bakeries as lunchtime or dinnertime rolls around. Or, better still, invite some French guests to dinner and either forget to serve them bread or underestimate how much they'll eat. The French generally count three people to a baguette, an excellent formula that almost always works. All you have to do is correctly estimate the appetites of your guests. In general women eat less than men, and the Americans and most other non-French eat less than the French. If you're serving a stew or any kind of *plat en sauce*, although it's not polite to "mop," you'll need more bread. *Et voilà!*

Bread in fact is so important, so vital, that on French nuclear submarines where of necessity the men have to eat frozen food, there's an onboard baker who turns out fresh baked bread and croissants every day!

When an official at the Ministry of the Marine told me of the onboard baker, I expressed astonishment. And he expressed astonishment at my astonishment. "Can you imagine a Frenchman without his daily bread?" he asked me. A strictly rhetorical question.

Bread expressions pepper the language. *Long comme un jour sans pain*, as long as a day without bread or *se vendre comme des petits pains*, sell like crazy, are but two. Bread can also refer to money as in *gagner son pain*, earn one's living. *Avoir du pain sur la planche*, to have bread on the board, means you've got a lot of work to do and *je ne mange pas de ce pain-là* means I don't buy that story. *Un pain*, I only recently learned, can be a blow as in *j'avais envie de lui donner un pain*, I felt like hitting him, probably because the skin that is struck rises like dough.

Part and parcel of life in France, bread is a necessity and not an "extra." One of the greatest pleasures I have every single day of my life is going to the bakery, once before lunch, once before dinner, and buying a freshly baked baguette, one end of which is generally demolished by the time I get home. I am incapable of walking from the bakery to home without taking a bite off my baguette, especially if it's still warm from the oven, and I'm always pleased to cross fellow bread eaters in the street who are doing likewise.

La baguette

Even though they want and need their daily bread—and 10 million baguettes are sold daily to a population of 60 million—the French consume much less than they used to. In the nineteenth century, they consumed more than sixteen ounces of bread (not baguettes as they didn't exist then) a day; that's now down to five.

This may be due to a concern for diet or it may be linked to the declining quality of the baguette, one of the most popular breads in France. Who can think of a Frenchman (the stereotyped image, to be sure) without his beret, bottle of wine, and baguette?

Created in the 1930s in Paris, the baguette for many Frenchmen has always been considered a typically Parisian phenomenon. And while the baguette may have been good in the '30s, as the years went by bakers started producing a bad baguette, with a cottonlike inside and a paper-thin crust, the antithesis of what a good baguette should be. And what should it be? Writes Jérôme Assire in the authoritative *Le livre du pain*: "The real baguette, the good baguette, is in reality a little treat, and has nothing to do, fortunately, with that which is too often sold. In actual fact the authentic baguette requires the conscientious work of a veritable craftsman: quality flour, little yeast, no additives like the flour of beans or ascorbic acid, a slow kneading, and a fermentation of at least four or five hours. Then one obtains at one and the same time the crustiest and the most tender of breads which should be eaten fresh."

To stop the onslaught of the bad baguette, in May 1998 the government passed a law that stipulates that only bakers who actually make their dough and bake their bread at their workplace have the right to call themselves *artisans boulangers* (there are 35,000 of them). Watch for the sign! The bakeries that don't have this sign are called *dépots de pain*, literally places where bread has been "deposited" but not made.

The baguette is still very much around and is good or bad depending on where you buy it; alongside it one now finds a variety of other delicious breads, sometimes with exotic names. The most unusually named bread I've come across I found at my local Monoprix, a kind of a chic Woolworth's. I don't know who named it but whoever it is should get a prize for pulling together an image of health and the good old days in only three words (four in the English translation): *bio intégrale médievale*, integral medieval biological bread!

Back to the past

About the time I started getting fed up with the horrid baguette I was buying and throwing away every day, I discovered a "new-old" baguette called the Retrodor, a clever name evoking a golden past. The Rétrodor (pronounced Ray-troh-door) is new because it was invented a couple of years ago and old because its inspiration is the baguette of the '30s. The Rétrodor is one of the many different kinds of baguettes bakers are now coming out with. One reason for all this creativity, cynics say, is that the price of the normal baguette is fixed by the government so bakers don't put much effort into it. Who knows? All I know is that I and many other people have been so disappointed by the basic baguette that we are only too happy to try something that tastes better—and pay the price.

I remember the first time our bakery started carrying the Rétrodor. I bought one and bit into it: it was crusty on the outside and dense but not too dense inside. I liked it because if we didn't finish it for dinner, it could be for breakfast, slightly toasted, something you can't generally do with a normal baguette. I became positively enamored of my Rétrodor and curious to learn more about it, found the name of the man who invented it, picked up the phone, and set up a meeting with his son at their bakery in the eighteenth arrondissement. Before lunch at a nearby Moroccan restaurant where we were served couscous and, you guessed it, Rétrodor, thirty-five-year-old dark-haired, dark-eyed Alexandre Viron led me to the downstairs of the bakery where three young bakers were watching over their production like anxious parents over a baby. I had expected something rather elaborate but instead found only the essentials: flour, water, salt, and yeast. "That's all you need," said Viron, who then showed me how the dough is formed into separate pieces which will then go into a machine for elongation. A final touch from the baker to give it its shape and personality, and *voilà*!

Upstairs, in a small room right behind the bakery, he took a freshly baked loaf and a bread knife and cut it in two lengthwise. "Now you can see how good bread should look," he said, turning it so I could see the bottom or the *sole*. This should be smooth, he said, and the top should be puffed up and caramel colored. The inside should be the color of cream, not white, he noted, holding it up against a white cupboard so I could see the difference. There should be little holes in the inside, *la mie*. When I complimented him on inventing the Rétrodor, he commented that the invention was in the simplicity. "Our innovation was going back to the source. Rather than add more and more products to bread, we went back to time-honored methods where less is better."

Bio bread

Once relegated to the eccentric category for health freaks, what the French call *bio* or organic products, foodstuffs from grains to vegetables that have been grown without harmful sprays and pesticides, have become enormously successful as people become more frightened by mad cow disease and in general of pollution and health dangers lurking in food. Today when you walk in any French grocery store, you're almost sure to find a counter of *bio* products.

It wasn't always so.

"Ten years ago they told me I was crazy when I decided to make only biological bread," says Michel Moison, a baker and owner of three *bio* bakeries in Paris that supply stores such as Hédiard and Lafayette Gourmet, cafés such as the Café Flore, and restaurants such as La Ferme St. Simon and Ma Bourgogne. Opened three years ago, his fourth store, on the avenue Général Leclerc, is already saturated with twelve hundred to thirteen hundred clients a day and he's planning to open another bakery soon.

The son of bakers in Normandy, Moison says he was *"né dans le pétrin,"* born in the kneading trough, and remained there. White-haired Moison is dressed in baker's white—a white T-shirt, white pants, and apron—and although he is seated behind his desk for our meeting, it's obviously a way station. The real activity is going on some three floors below where he's been baking bread since three in the morning. After we chat a bit, he takes me down the narrow stairs and shows me sacks of the biological flour that composes the bread and then down another floor to where his bakers make and roll the dough and bake the bread. I watch as a baker skillfully traces knife cuts in the *fougasse*, a flat latticelike bread with olives, anchovies, herbs, or onions that one often associates with Provence.

On the lower level where the bread is baked, a young *boulanger*, floured right to his eyelashes, takes a handful of dough and rolls it out with expertise. Michel Moisan joins him, picking up the dough and automatically rolling it and shaping it into what will be its final form. "So what does it take to be a baker?" I ask him, wondering how long it would take a neophyte to master his movement. "You need to have a feel for the dough," says Moison, as he continues his expert treatment. "After all the theory is over, you need to be able to judge the different flours and the baking time. You need experience to adapt yourself to the different flours and products."

I left him to his business and walked out to the rue Daguerre, a bustling market street that abounds in shops and stalls proffering tasty food. I walked into a fish shop and bought three *filets de sandre*, a perchlike fish, for our lunch; then I wandered down the street and into a *charcuterie* where I bought a *brandade parmentière*, salt cod and garlic purée, a *salade au chou*, cabbage salad, and some huge white beans in a tomato sauce. Generally when I get going like this, I hit the cheese shop, and the fruit and vegetables, but since I didn't have my rolling cart or even a basket, I decided to call it a day. On my way back to the car, I passed in front of Moison's bakery again and entered. I knew the bread I wanted: a round golden flat loaf flaked with basil called *pain au basilic*, basil bread. Once I was in the car I decided I couldn't wait to have a bite. By the time I got back home forty minutes later, half of it was gone. Now *that's* good bread!

The Holy Trinity

But what's bread without cheese, and cheese without wine? For most Frenchmen, bread, cheese, and wine are the Holy Trinity, an indivisible threesome. Before writing this chapter, I asked myself which I would rather be—a cheesemaker or baker or a wine producer. It didn't take long to decide. I eliminated baker because of the early hours and cheese maker because of the smell, which I love at the end of a good meal but wouldn't care to work in all day long.

That left wine, which fascinates me. Like many people who do not come from a wine culture, my fascination is tinged with intimidation so in a quest to educate my tastebuds and learn a bit I started reading about wine. In doing so, I came to the important realization that if you have been fortunate to travel in the many regions of France you already know more than you think you do simply by osmosis. By traveling, you know, for example, that an Entre-deux-mers is from Bordeaux and not the Loire-Atlantique, and that a Côte-rôtie is a red Côte du Rhone and not a white wine from the Jura. Those were two of the questions asked in a multiple-choice quiz in a special supplement on wine in the French weekly magazine *L'Express*. I took it for fun and was surprised to see that in spite of my gargantuan ignorance, I knew more than I thought simply from having been in or near the places some of the wines are produced. Why? Because you drink the wines in the places that produce them and forever after that associate specific wines with specific places. For some traditionalists, the soil is the unique factor that determines the taste and character of wine. And the soil, one wine expert told me, can change from one vineyard to the next even if they're only one kilometer away from each other.

Harriet gets some help on wine

In spite of nuggets of information such as these, I still needed major help. I immediately thought of a young wine steward I had seen on a French TV documentary featuring the Ducasse restaurants. His name is Gerard Margeon and he is the chief wine steward at six-star chef Alain Ducasse's Paris restaurants.

Margeon says he was literally born into the world of wine in the now-extinct maternity ward of the Hospices of Beaune, that beautiful fifteenth-century hospital in the center of Beaune, which is the site of a famous international wine auction held each year on the third Sunday in November.

Other than that auspicious beginning, Margeon didn't come from a family of winemakers nor did he taste wine early on at the family table. It was only when he was fifteen that he tasted it one day at school. But that one day was enough. Wine would be his life.

At the Hotel Meridien Montparnasse in Paris where he was employed as head wine steward, he received a phone call from superchef Alain Ducasse. "Ducasse said he was looking for his *chef sommelier* in Monaco and asked if I could come to see him at his restaurant there. I told him I had other plans, and he said, 'Too bad because I already have your ticket.' That was in October 1993 and I didn't start working for him until March 1994 but he kept calling me."

Working for a hyperactive, hard-driven, high-energy boss like Ducasse would be exhausting for anyone other than Margeon, who himself is a speed demon. Of Ducasse, Margeon says: "He likes to have the answer before the question." Both men talk fast, work fast, move fast. In fact, Margeon's not an easy interview because he can't sit still that long and you literally have to run alongside him to catch what he's saying.

Of course there's a reason for the running: every single day, Margeon has a wine tasting. He travels in Europe but also to New Zealand, Australia, and the States. He's responsible for the wine menu at the Bar & Boeuf in Monaco as well as for all the Ducasse restaurants in Paris. And we're talking volume here: in the wine cellars in Issy-les-Moulineaux outside Paris there are 45,000 bottles of wine uniquely for the Alain Ducasse restaurant in Paris. The most expensive bottle of wine he has ever sold: a Pétrus 1945 for 50,000 francs ($7,000) at the Ducasse restaurant in Monaco.

This was the man I called up on the phone and asked to meet. At that point I had no idea of how my request for an interview would be received. Would it be fifteen minutes, in and out? Or would he understand that I really did want to learn about what the *chef sommelier* of one of the top restaurants in Paris does and how he works? No way to know.

Every once in a while you really do get lucky and knock at the right door and this turned out to be one of those times. I was afraid he would be haughty and closed. He was down to earth and open. I was afraid he'd laugh at my monumental nescience—instead he included me in tastings so that I could see how wines are chosen for the restaurant. Do I sound like a groupie? Perhaps, but this is because I truly find the world of wine to be a fascinating one and admire the knowledge of the people for whom it is life (as much as I abhor show-off wine snobs).

I asked Margeon incredibly naive questions (well, how else are you going to learn?) which he more than politely answered. In fact, I showed up at our first meeting at Ducasse's restaurant on the avenue Raymond Poincaré with a few books on wine I'd been reading and asked him what he thought of them. "This is okay," he said, thumbing through one. And looking at another: "You could do better than this." But throughout our interview—and this is important—he didn't make me feel like a fool for not knowing. Diplomacy is what one needs as a *sommelier*. Diplomacy and instinct born from experience.

Margeon, who, incidentally, is also a certified ski instructor, told me that even before he goes to see the clients at their table he has already sized them up as they arrive in the restaurant. "At first glance I can tell who is going to be easy to deal with, who is going to be difficult, and especially, who is going to be going for very expensive wines and who will be choosing less expensive ones." This is an important, a crucial, point, says Margeon, and "we can't afford to make a mistake. If you propose wines that are out of line with a person's budget, the next time he comes and says 'give me the wine list, I'll choose by myself,' you know you've lost him." Fortunately, this doesn't happen very often. "My second and I 'feel' the client the minute he enters the room."

Since 60 percent of the clientele of Ducasse's restaurant is composed of foreigners, I couldn't resist asking him which nationality he preferred.

"The Belgians," he replied, without a minute's hesitation. "The Belgians, because they don't have vineyards in their country and so they are simple and objective." The English, he says, are "very technical and very often real wine connoisseurs." The Americans, or at least the ones who go to Ducasse's, are "worldly wise, well traveled and sophisticated, and big spenders." Bring out the Petrus!

And the French? "The problem with the French," Margeon said, "is that they come from a country in which almost every region has a vineyard so most Frenchmen have plenty to say when it comes to wine—and most of it, or at least a large part of it, is off base or wrong!"

My interview with Margeon took place in the *cave du jour* underneath Ducasse's restaurant in the chic sixteenth arrondissement. You could mistake this teeny office space for the cockpit of a plane were it not for the neatly arranged and labeled bottles on shelves. On the small high table on which I was writing were eight or nine bottles of different wines from different countries which he had been tasting—including a Petrus. All of them of course had been spat out—including the Petrus. I indulged myself in thinking what it would be like to have a job in which one of your duties was to taste and spit out some of the world's most expensive wines.

But thanks to Margeon I was soon going to be able to begin to imagine it for he had a splendid idea: would I like to join him at a wine tasting at the Ritz, and then a few days later, one at Spoon, Ducasse's trendy restaurant off the Champs Elysées?

Would I? And how.

Champagne tasting at the Ritz

On a gray November day, I joined Margeon at the Ritz for a very special tasting of Champagnes from the best houses in France. With its plush sofas, antiques, gilded ceilings and chandeliers, the ambiance at the Ritz was warm and the Champagne was cold and flowing in abundance. The people attending this event were professionals: restaurant owners, wine salespeople, wine stewards, journalists specialized in food and wine and one very nonspecialized but interested party—me.

As we walked into the room, Margeon told me that he would be going through rapidly so as to taste everything but that of course I could stay on as long as I liked. In truth my main objective was to stick to him like a shadow. I knew nothing about tastings. I was such a greenhorn that I didn't know you had one glass for the entire tasting and kept putting mine down and losing it. Seeing this, Margeon kindly pointed out that I must keep the same glass with me. As we walked from table to table, I was justifiably impressed as I watched the ease with which the experts swirled the bubbly in their glass, sniffed and resniffed, checked out the color, asked questions about the composition, the *dégorgement*, disgorgement or the removal of yeast deposits, which is the final step in the Champagne process, in terms I had never heard before in my life.

Being at the side of a top wine steward at a top tasting is a bit like going to the moon as a guest of an astronaut. And it was as strange as the moon to me, this world of people who make the wine, the people who live by it and in it every day. If I'd asked for a dream initiation into the world of Champagne, I couldn't have done better than this tasting where the best houses, large and small, had brought their finest vintage Champagnes: Dom Perignon, Gosset, Krug, Lanson, Jacquesson & Fils, Bruno Paillard, Charles Heidsieck, Delamotte Deutz, De Vonge, to name but a few of the prestigious houses that were in attendance at the Ritz that day.

I don't know why but I thought Margeon would taste a few and call it a day. Somehow along the way I forgot that this was his *job* and he was at work. He told me that since he doesn't have time to visit every Champagne house, this was a unique occasion to do a lot all at the same time, tasting Champagnes that he hadn't tasted before. And he did. He tasted every single Champagne there, surveying, sniffing, swirling, spitting, and asking a few pointed questions. Since I was at the level of "I like it a lot" or "I like it but not as much," I was happy to simply listen to the way the connoisseurs speak about wine.

Again and again I was impressed by the vocabulary Margeon and his peers employed to describe the odors and aspect of the Champagnes. For example, as we tasted a Rosé Ruinart 1986, Margeon told me that rosé Champagnes are very difficult to make and that it is often said that rosés are very full-bodied. This one, he said, after thoughtfully savoring it, was, on the contrary, "very elegant." His description of the Gosset Grande Réserve was *"pointu, vif, nerveux, frais,"* sharp, lively, nervous, fresh. My description was: "delicious"!

Inexperienced as I was, I found myself swirling and spitting (not all that elegantly) with the best of them. But I think I knew enough to appreciate that we were tasting what Margeon described as the "quintessence of Champagne."

Champagne . . . One thinks of it in terms of festive occasions, but one winemaker I talked to at the Ritz that day told me he'd actually seen a funeral at which a bottle was opened. Well, why not?

At the end of our tasting, I was ready to head home to rest, but Margeon announced he had to run as he had two more appointments before returning to Ducasse for the evening. He told me he's been running like this since he was twenty-two years old and that at age thirty-nine he's one of the oldest *sommeliers* in the profession.

I had of course had Champagne many times before in my life. But tasting Champagne with the experts opened up a whole new world. Thanks to that glimpse, I even began distinguishing the various tastes! I have to agree with Baudelaire: "If wine disappeared from human production, I believe it would cause an emptiness, an absence, a defection, for intellect and for health, much more dreadful than all the excesses for which wine has been made responsible."

A wine tasting at Spoon

A week later I showed up to meet Margeon at Spoon. The other wine stewards had arrived but Margeon wasn't there yet so I took the extra time to look around. The decor: pure New York and not at all French. Next, I checked out the menu and almost passed out when I saw, are you ready for this, *iceberg lettuce* and *bubble gum ice cream, glace malabar.* Is this some kind of hokey joke? There's also a chocolate pizza for dessert and a BLT (for 85 French Francs or about $12.50). That's the American influence (also the menu is written in English first, French second) but there's also a bow to Asia with chopsticks on each table.

Ducasse is no fool—the French love it. As I stood next to the manager, who had a floor plan of the tables in front of him, the phone rang . . . and rang. . . . and rang, and the answer was invariably the same. "No, I'm sorry, we're full," he replied. In fact, he told me, you have to reserve ahead one week for lunch and three for dinner. "What do they love about it?" I asked. "The fact that it's new, that they can compose their own menu, combining different tastes." You can love Spoon or hate it but Ducasse is onto something here—the wave of the future? How appropriate to open this world cuisine restaurant at the close of the twentieth century.

Along with the iceberg lettuce, macaroni and cheese gratin, and BLT comes some very good non-French wine. The French touch is offered via the cheese—that month, a Saint-Nectaire Fermier and a Comté, proposed with a wine either from Australia or South Africa. Each month Margeon assembles the *sommeliers* of all his restaurants for a wine-tasting session to select the wines for Spoon. I had never tasted wine at 10:00 A.M. and thought perhaps I would only observe but I was fast finding out that with Margeon you don't stand around and watch. I found myself standing up at the bar on which a few dozen tulip-shaped wineglasses were lined up like good soldiers. Along with the *sommeliers*, I waited for the proceedings to begin.

Two young men who had been standing aside and chatting with the *sommeliers* stepped up to present each wine (the wines that day were from New Zealand, South Africa, and Australia) one by one, giving the name of the winemaker, the region in which the grapes were grown, and the composition of the wine. Next the wine was poured and each *sommelier* solemnly peered at its "robe," sniffed for its "nose," swirled it again in the glass, tasted again, and then spat it out in one of the three large *crachoirs*, spitting basins, placed on the bar. I lost count but I think we went through fourteen wines this way, ten white and four red. Impressed, I didn't say a word but observed the others. It was clear that Margeon was the boss. He was the only one to make a final comment on each wine after tasting and his word is the one that counts.

Laurent, his second, told me that "we're here to be open to wines of the world, not to compare a wine from South Africa to a wine from Australia." This policy goes well with the open spirit of the restaurant and later Margeon told me that the kinds of wines chosen are expressly to go with the casual atmosphere and exotic food served at Spoon. There's no way that any of the wines proposed for Spoon would end up on a table at the Alain Ducasse restaurant in the sixteenth arrondissement, for example.

In general I was impressed by the experts' knowledge and ability to recall other wines, but on this day I was impressed by the incisiveness and rapidity of Margeon's comments.

On the first wine, a Sauvignon blanc from South Africa: "It's good but not very biting, *mordant*, it lacks the structure and acidity

I'm looking for." We then moved on to a New Zealand Sauvignon blanc that he liked better. It notably had a *"robe lumineuse,"* luminous robe. A Chilean wine inspired an even more detailed, if measured, reaction: *"Très vif, c'est propre, un peu court, rien à dire,"* "Very lively, clean, a bit abrupt, nothing to say," judges Margeon, who takes the opportunity to get a message across to his assembled troops. "Remember, you always have to take into account the *rapport plaisir-prix,* relationship of pleasure to price. One must situate these wines in their parameters. One *must* talk about price. For these prices, there's hardly anything left in France."

But time is passing and Margeon wants to keep things going. *"Allez, tire bouchon, Monsieur, action!"* "Let's go, sir, corkscrew, action!" he prods a young *sommelier* next to him who he has been teasing because he doesn't look quite awake.

My initiation period over, I congratulated myself for having chosen such a good mentor. I'll take a course on my own now but I'll remember the useful word of warning Margeon left me with on the subject of wine courses: people should take them if they are interested, but they should only do them for their personal enjoyment. He said: "Take courses to enjoy wine, not to become a technician. Wine should always remain a pleasure."

A conversation with Georges Lepré

For the next step in my wine education, I went to see Georges Lepré who is the former head wine steward of the Hotel Ritz and now the quality manager of the Savour Club where he also gives wine-tasting courses. The son of Italian immigrants, Lepré grew up in the southwest of France, which is known for its good food, good wine, and the proclivity of the people there to eat such robust fare as *confit de canard* and *foie gras* while drinking red wine and still living long, healthy lives. Lepré said that his mother-in-law, who died at the age of 105, drank a glass of red wine for lunch and for dinner every single day of her life. "Moderation is the secret," he said.

At the Ritz, Lepré served the rich and famous. The story he loves best to tell is the day he served a magnum of Petrus worth $6,000 to a couple of Texans. What fascinated him even as much as the fact that they drank the entire magnum *à deux* was that they didn't order any food with it! In spite of the glitzy life he led as *sommelier* in a glittering world, he himself has remained down-to-earth and open-minded, the very opposite of the stereotyped intimidating *sommelier*.

"After thirty years on the floor," he told me as we sat chatting in his office at the Savour Club in the sixteenth arrondissement, "I've found that you can say everything to a customer as long as you say it nicely. For example, a famous American actress said to me: "Georges, you're going to be mad but I'd like to have an ice cube in my Champagne." I replied: 'Oh, that's too bad for the ice cube,' and we both laughed."

For Lepré, the wine you choose depends on the situation—the season, the decor, the ambiance, who you're with, whether it's lunch or dinner, a big party or a small one. "You have to respect your taste—it's yours. I'm against hard-and-fast rules and absolutes when it comes to saying what wine goes with what food." On the other hand, he said, "Wine resembles the person who makes it and the person who drinks it. You get the wine you deserve. Some people buy a label to show off. On the other hand I have seen people so moved by the wine they were drinking that they were almost crying. These people got the mesage that they were ready to receive something great and they did. A masterpiece must be respected. You must be ready to accept it."

What, I asked him, is the worst thing that ever happened to him in his career as a top *sommelier?* "A couple of Japanese ordered a bottle of Château Latour 1945, one of the best years for Bordeaux, and when I presented the wine to Monsieur, he never reacted, not a nod, not a look, not a smile throughout the entire meal. Even though he apparently liked it and gave me a big tip, it was the worst moment I ever had experienced," answered Lepré for whom the connection with the customer remains the most important part of his profession.

"It was in America that I learned to respect the customer because a restaurant can't exist without them. You first respect them and then you bring the customer to your field."

And what a field. "The world today is so fast but there is one thing that isn't frozen or vacuum-packed. Wine is alive, fragile, dynamic, and dying."

Les fromages

After the generous and uncomplicated welcome I was given into the down-to-earth vital basic world of bread and the sparkling mysterious otherworldly world of wine, I thought that getting a handle on cheese would be a cinch.

Wrong.

One well-known *fromager* set up an appointment and simply wasn't there when I arrived—and never called to apologize. Others I contacted seemed distinctly unenthusiastic about meeting me and asked me to call back after the Christmas holidays, obviously hoping I'd drop dead in between. Yet another, when I praised her wonderful cheese and said that we don't have anything like it in the U.S., embarked on a long harangue about how pasteurization kills taste and how there are more listeria cases from hot dogs than from a Camembert.

"Wait a minute," I told her, with a smile plastered on my face. *"Vous prêchez à une convertie!"* "You're preaching to the converted!"

A Brie in the States

Let me say that I was disappointed not to be welcomed with open arms by the cheese people because I *adore* and champion French cheese. I eat every single kind of French cheese I can find. Whenever I am in the States, French cheese is what I end up missing most. I have uncontrollable yearnings for cheese and am always hovering around the cheese counter which, sorry to say, doesn't make it, thanks to stringent U.S. government sanitary requirements which forbid unpasteurized cheese. The pasteurized Camembert and Brie we get in the States has nothing to do, sadly, with the real thing.

Here's what I read on a package of Brie I picked up in a U.S. supermarket:

BELMONT BRIE PRÉSIDENT, SOFT RIPENED CHEESE.
Nutrition Facts:
Serv. Size 1 oz (28 grams) Servings varied. Amount/Serving: Calories 90, Fat Cal. 70, Total Fat 8g (12% DV), Sat. Fat 3g (15% DV), Cholst. 15 mg (5% DV), Sodium 170mg (7% DV),

Total carb O g (0% DV), Fiber Og (0% DV), Sugars Og, Protein 5g (11% DV), Vitamin A (4% DV), Vitamin C (0% DV), Calcium (87% DV), Iron (2% DV), Percent Daily Values (DV) are based on a 2,000 calorie diet. Ingredients: Pasteurized cow's milk, cheese cultures, salt, enzymes, All natural. Keep refrigerated.

My reaction to that label was: 1) I was depressed just looking at it, 2) I didn't want to buy cheese wrapped in plastic, 3) I didn't want to put the cheese in the fridge because the cold would kill the taste if it has any left—I turned out to be wrong on this point as you will see further along in this chapter, 4) I certainly didn't want to know how many calories it has or how much fat it contains!!!

As I turned it over in my hand to read the label, I thought back longingly to the Marché des Sablons where I regularly chat with the cheese person about which cheese I should take and what is in season. "Would you like your goat cheese dry or not so dry?" I'm asked. (I like it dry.) The cheeses are all aligned right there in front of me, arranged on attractive mats of straw. They look friendly, they smell strong. Some even smell downright ferocious! That's fine: it means they're alive! I want to eat each and every one of them.

The Brie I held in my hands looked dead and cold. No one was there to tell me where it came from, who made it, how long it had been aged. This supermarket cheese had no history, no story behind it. No odor pervaded the atmosphere as the poor cheese's development had been stopped in its tracks. Whereas the Brie in France may *run*, the congealed Brie we have in the States will never do so. Man, that cheese is *dead*!

The importance of mold

Some vital statistics: Each year in France 460,000 tons of soft *pâté*, 31,000 tons of *pâté persillée*, 21,000 tons of Tomme de Savoie and Saint-Nectaire, and 10,000 tons of Reblochon are produced.

But "without the help of some of the two hundred thousand types of molds which have been indexed, the cheese industry would have a hard time garnishing a cheese plate at the end of a meal" writes Jean-François Augereau in the French daily newspaper *Le Monde*. In other words, cheese lives! Camembert, Brie, Coulommiers, Neufchâtel and the Carré de l'Est are all cheeses that benefit from the work of Penicillium candidum whereas Penicillium album frequents goat cheeses and not surprisingly Penicillium roqueferti works on Roquefort. Saint-Nectaire and Tomme de Savoie are inhabited by Penicillium nalgiovense. Vive le mold!

Cheese expressions

My favorite cheese expression is *entre la poire et le fromage*, between the pear and the cheese, which refers to the moment in the meal when you can relax and bring up certain subjects you may not have wished to talk about before that point. For French business people, business talk usually gets serious between the *poire et le fromage*. One big cultural difference that makes foreign business people think the French aren't "serious" is that since the French honor food, when they go out for a business lunch, they often talk about everything else under the sun except the deal at hand until they get to the cheese course! (I hear that's changing—too bad!).

I also like the expressions *en faire tout un fromage*, to make a big deal out of something, and *il a trouvé un fromage*, which means he found a really cushy job.

The French don't call someone important a *grand fromage*, a big cheese, as we do in the U.S. They call a VIP *une grosse légume*, a big vegetable (and not *un gros légume*, which would be grammatically correct). And when they want you to smile for a picture, they don't say "Cheese." They say *ouistiti sexe*. Ouistiti is a little monkey and pronouncing it (oui-stee-tee) makes you stretch your lips into a smile. As for the sex part of it, that's supposed to give you happy thoughts. At least that's the idea!

Cheese meals and cheese cravings

In spite of my love for cheese, I have never had a cheese meal in a restaurant. It's something I intend to do someday but just never seem to get around to and I admit it's not high on my list of priorities. I don't crave a meal in which cheese is incorporated into every course—a soufflé, a steak *sauce Roquefort*. However, I do like the idea of eating a meal which is nothing but cheese. A cheese party, however, is something Philippe does not like to do for two reasons: one, very frankly, he doesn't appreciate cheese as much or as often as I do, and two, for him, when you invite people in the evening, it is for dinner and dinner for him is not cheese and wine. To compromise, I try to make a meal that is very light so that we can have a sumptuous cheese plate. I love to invite people to my home and let the cheese be the star. Nothing pleases me more than to set out eight to ten totally different cheeses and watch my friends taste each one. I also like to find cheeses my non-French guests aren't familiar with, such as Gaperon and various sheep cheeses, *fromages de brebis*. These are cheeses we can't get in the States and so are even more appreciated by visiting Americans.

My favorite French cheeses? I truly like them all, but I must say that a Mont d'Or or Vacherin which you find in winter in its characteristic wooden box—they say you should not remove it even when serving—is one of my absolute favorites. I love a good Brie and a good Camembert, when you can find one, which is becoming rare. I love *vieille* Mimolette because of its distinctive orange color and crumbly texture. It is wonderful to eat with an apple. I love Reblochon and Beaufort from the Savoy region. I love Gaperon and Langres and Epoisses and Munster and even the strong Boulette d'Avesnes. I love all blue cheeses—the Bleu d'Auvergne, the Bleu des Causses, Bleu de Bresse, Bleu de Termignon—and those are only a few of them. I love Cantal from the mountains of Auvergne. (On a trip to Auvergne, Philippe once purchased a huge assortment of Auvergnat cheeses which he took back with him on the plane—and forgot there. We often joked about the fate of those cheeses—and the crew—as they ripened and perfumed the cabin.) I love . . . the list is too long and I haven't even tasted all of France's wonderful cheese. They say there are five hundred different varieties. It will probably take me the rest of my life to taste them all—but what fun along the way! I figure if I'm lucky enough to live another thirty years and can taste sixteen or seventeen different cheeses a year, I may someday reach what now seems an unattainable goal.

Meeting a fromager

I finally did contact a cheese maker and briefly ran my woeful tale of rejection by his peers past him. *"Ce n'est pas bien,"* was his comment. By the time I told him, though, my peeve was of no further importance for I had spent almost two hours discussing cheese with dynamic forty-year-old Breton Philippe Alléosse, whose father, Roger, recently retired, founded one of the best cheese stores in Paris. How, I wondered, did someone from Brittany, a region known for crepes and cider and outstanding seafood but not for its cheese, end up as a *fromager*?

"My father loved good wine but was always frustrated because he could never find good cheese to go with it and was disappointed at the end of every meal. So when we moved to Paris, he decided to buy a cheese shop and specialize in the *affinage* of cheeses," Philippe told me.

The tiny shop in the tenth arrondissement steadily grew with Roger's reputation for finding and cultivating the best cheeses. It was at this point that Philippe Alléosse decided to join the family business.

"I was twenty-six and I had a lot of ideas about new things to do which no one took account of at first. My father made it clear that I didn't know anything about this trade. He told me to take two weeks to read books like Androuët and to come back to see him when I'd finished and we'd see if it was going to work out or not."

It did—and little by little Philippe introduced modern management techniques. When Roger retired, Philippe took over the reins of the *fromagerie*, which supplies top restaurants (L'Ambroisie, Laurent, Bernard Loiseau, Pierre Gagnaire, and the Pré-Catelan to name but a few) and top food stores like Hédiard.

Success wasn't automatic. "We spent ten years explaining to our clients that we aren't here to sell any old product but that we want to satisfy their tastes. We also want to explain to them the importance of the aging of cheese. So we listen to them and they listen to us. Now, when our clients go on vacation and discover a good cheese, they come back with the name and address of the producer!"

Philippe works closely with some eighty cheese producers scattered all over France. "Sometimes there are *coups de gueule* (blowups)," he says. "When I get a cheese that is inferior to what I want or not as good as the last time, I want an explanation."

The thing he is the most proud of are his cellars where the cheeses arriving from the various regions of France are carefully aged and then sent out to his store or to various restaurants. "It's a pleasure to see how we bring an ordinary product to a *pièce unique*."

Underground

I had only a vague idea of what "bringing an ordinary product to a unique piece" meant. To show me, Alléosse took me down to visit the caves in the seventeenth arrondissement where "we work with between a hundred eighty and two hundred fifty different kinds of cheeses yearly." (I asked him how many cheeses there are in France, citing De Gaulle's apocryphal statement 'How can you govern a country which has three hundred kinds of cheeses?' and he told me that there are actually many more than that, "five hundred or six hundred.")

The shop where the cheese is sold, he explained, is "fifty percent of our work. The other fifty percent—the most important part—takes place here." "Here" is 2500 square feet of caves right in the middle of Paris. Before we went down, he handed me a warm vest which he said I'd probably appreciate given the difference in temperature, which varies between 39°F and 59°F depending on which room you are in.

The first thing he showed me after we had descended a flight of steep stairs was without any doubt the most important: the motors that keep the caves constantly humid, disseminating one thousand liters of water in fine particles every day. We contemplated them with the respect they were due—if caves aren't humid, there's no mold, hence no cheese—and then proceeded to the first room where all the pressed hard cheeses are kept.

A powerful smell of ammonia pervaded my nostrils. Alléosse laughed. "That's normal," he explained. "It's from the fermentation. The cheese is breathing." I was as well, but just barely. However, I forgot the fumes as I became absorbed in the view of, on either side of me, thick, high Cantals, concave-shaped Beauforts, a round Comté weighing thirty-five kilos. He took a knife-shaped instrument and told me he'd do a "carotte," the term cheese makers use when they refer to testing cheeses to see how they are maturing. He carefully inserted the small sharp instrument into the huge Cantal and brought out a piece, which we each tasted. Superb. Then, carefully with his finger, he filled in the tiny hole the knife had made. Across from the Cantal were some Mimolettes, one of my favorite cheeses. He held one up for inspection, showing me the dusty rind—literally dusty, as small bacteria called cirons eat away at it and have to be brushed off regularly. "They determine the taste of the cheese," Alléosse told me, as he handed me a carotte of Mimolette. "It's delicious with sherry for the aperitif," he commented. I can't wait to try! We move on to a huge round wheel of Gruyère, which, he explained, does not have holes (what we call Swiss cheese with holes is Emmenthal). Once again, he plunged his instrument into the cheese and we savored its taste. "It's buttery, and the *pâte* is fine," was his verdict.

The second room was filled with soft cheeses with white molds—Brie de Meaux, St. Marcellin, St. Felicien; the third room with croutes lavées, cheeses washed with salted water, Maroilles, Munsters, Vacherins de Chèvre, Langre, Reblochons, Livarots, and Soumaintrains. As we chatted, he sprayed an Epoisses with some *vieux marc* from Burgundy and pointed out a square-shaped cheese I had never heard of—vieux Lille, also called *le puant de Lille* "the stinky from Lille," which he says is "one of the strongest cheeses in France." I remind myself to try it. He picked up a white, hard Reblochon. "This is how it came to us. In another three weeks or one month—it's up to us to decide—it will be ready and will look like this"—and he picked up another Reblochon, which had a yellow crust and no longer resisted when he pressed it with his fingers.

One last door and we were in a room devoted entirely to goat cheeses, fifty to sixty, of every shape and form and color. Here, every two days, three or four *fromagers* turn each and every cheese *by hand* until they are ready to go to the store. This can take anywhere from three to six weeks depending on the variety of the goat cheese.

By the end of our tour, my understanding of what a cheese is before it gets to a cheese shop had been revolutionized. This is not a simple business! Alléosse introduced me to his brother-in-law, Olivier, who is the chief *caviste*, responsible for knowing absolutely everything about every one of the two hundred or so cheeses in the caves. "It took Olivier seven years to acquire the expertise he has today, to know about every cheese. Each product is different and the *affinage* is different. You need much time to understand cheese. This is a profession of patience."

What to put on a cheese plate

Our time was almost up—a group of Japanese were waiting to see him (yes, the Japanese love good cheese, he told me)—so I hastened to ask my burning question: what to include on a cheese plate for special occasions. Here's his suggestion (quantities depend on the number of people and their appetite):

- two or three kinds of goat cheese, one creamy, one slightly nutty, one with more taste and character but not too strong
- a Camembert, Coulommiers, Brie, or Fougerus
- a Reblochon
- a Pont l'Evêque, a Livarot, or a Pavé d'Auge
- a blue cow cheese, such as Fourme, Gex, or Termignon (which is only made in the French Alps and which is a natural *bleu* as opposed to one made by the addition of penicillin), or
- a blue sheep cheese, Roquefort
- a Brillat-Savarin, St. Marcellin, or St. Felicien
- and one can add a Beaufort, Gruyère or Comté for those who don't really like cheese.

He suggests starting with the softer-tasting cheeses, eating the blue or Roquefort in the middle, and ending with the goat cheeses.

How to keep cheese—some do's and don'ts

While we were discussing the composition of the cheese plate, he gave me a few tips on how to preserve cheese. This was a real education for it turned out that in spite of my love of cheese I had been doing almost everything wrong. I always thought that putting cheeses in the fridge killed their taste, and it turned out that this is not so.

Yes, they can and should go in the fridge and remain in the vegetable bin between 46°F and 54°F. Cheeses should not be kept outdoors for the temperature will modify their development. They should remain wrapped in the paper the *fromager* has put them in for it is made especially for the good conservation of the cheese. Aluminium foil should never be used, except for blues or Roquefort, as it will make the cheese sweat. Never put them in plastic containers—it will also make the cheese sweat and create mold.

So when should they be taken out of the fridge? "People always say 'an hour before the dinner' but if the dinner lasts three hours, your cheese may be long gone. Use common sense and take them out so that they don't change too rapidly before you get them to the table," Alléosse advised.

What cheese—what wine?

I showed Alléosse an article in a well-known women's magazine in which a top wine steward had set down his ideas for which wines to drink with which cheeses. After looking at the wine steward's list, I figured I'd have to take a pen and pencil to the table with me as I would never remember what wine went with what cheese. But to my great relief, Alléosse responded to the article with a commonsense answer: "With a cheese plate, we need to remain festive and open-minded and convivial. Invite your friends and have each one bring a bottle. Try different combinations and be ready for surprises, both good and bad. Go to the regions where the cheese is made and see how the people eat them there and what they drink and look at how they eat with gusto and pleasure. The main thing with cheese is not to follow a rule book but to *passer un bon moment*."

I certainly had had *un bon moment*, and believe me, as a result, if you come to my house, you'll get cheese but it won't have been in plastic or wrapped in aluminum foil!

 INTERVIEW WITH PHILIPPE

HWR: Why do you have to have bread with everything, even when the meal includes other starches? Isn't one enough?

PhR: Bread is the staff of life. And your choice of the word "starches" is funny. It's like that American guest of ours who said she'd like "protein" for breakfast. We're not running a chemical factory.

HWR: That's the truth. Speaking of bread, tell me again about that afternoon treat your Auvergnat grandfather would make for you—the piece of bread rubbed with garlic and pork fat. Wasn't he worried about cholesterol?

PhR: Are you kidding? He was worried about whether he was giving me something with taste; he ate raw onion for breakfast and pork fat every day of his life and he died at age ninety-four.

9

Sweets

Le pain d'épices · *A course at Lenôtre* · *Les artistes du chocolat* · *Real chocolate versus candy*

I have a dream: someday I will go into a French pastry shop and help myself to one of each of the following: a *mille feuilles*, an *éclair au chocolat*, a *tarte aux fraises*, a *tarte au citron*, an *opéra*, a *baba au rhum*, and anything else I might fancy and eat them all on the spot!

Actually when I was pregnant with my first son, I almost made that dream come true. I had a craving for chocolate so went into a pastry shop to buy and devour several, and I mean several, of the chocolate pastries that seemed to be waiting there especially for me. That didn't last long. Alas, being pregnant is nothing more than a nine-month excuse, and my attachment to sweets ("only the best," of course) hasn't waned; I often find myself attracted like a magnet to the tastefully decorated windows of French pastry shops where I gaze wistfully at the gorgeously presented creations and then (usually) turn away.

Recently I stopped in front of an ordinary-looking pastry shop and started writing down what I saw: a *tarte citron meringuée*, a *feuille automne* (chocolate), a *baba au rhum*, a

Tropézienne, an *éclair*, a *Paris-Brest*, a *trois frères*, a *religieuse*, an *amandine*, an *opéra*, a *café noix*, a *sacher*, *pommes de terre ou figue*, *barquette marrons*, *hérisson*, *tarte pomme amande*, each one as pretty as it could be. No wonder I want to taste each and every one of them!

Not only am I fascinated by how pretty they look but I am fascinated by the names and histories of these pastries starting with the St. Honore, a Parisian cake dedicated to the patron saint of bakers and pastry cooks, and the Paris-Brest, created in 1891 for the first bike race. Does it look like the wheel of a bicycle? It's supposed to! The *puit d'amour*, well of love, is said to have been created by a baker who saw someone commit suicide in a nearby well after a tragic love affair (I learned this tale at a dinner party at which the *puit d'amour* was the dessert). My favorite name, though, is *la religieuse*. The *religieuse*, or nun, is a puff pastry filled with *crème patissière*, a pastry cream, and glazed with either chocolate or coffee icing. In both cases, the top or what I call the head of the nun is decorated with a white "collar." When we have cakes at home, I always take the head of the nun, leaving her body to whoever else wants it. There are always takers.

Le pain d'épices

It doesn't really qualify as a "pastry" but I adore *pain d'épices*, a simple spice bread made of honey. M. F. K, Fisher writes of her discovery of *pain d'épices* in Dijon in her book *Long Ago in France*: "We smelled Dijon cassis in the autumn, and stained our mouths with its metallic purple, but all year and everywhere we smelled the Dijon gingerbread, that *pain d'épices* which came perhaps from Asia with a tired Crusader. Its flat strange odor, honey, cow dung, clove, something unnameable but unmistakeable, blew all over the town. . . . The smells were heavenly." I wouldn't quite call the odor that of cow dung (!) but it's true it smells heavenly and when it's good it's wonderful. However, finding good *pain d'épices* is a real quest. The industrial ones are too dry and the artisanal ones are uneven. For years I've been searching for one that will satisfy me.

A course at Lenôtre

I decided to make a leap from admiring and tasting pastries to seeing how they are made. Why "seeing how they are made" rather than "making them"? A combination of instinct and laziness led me to think that it might be beneficial to watch the experts before taking the plunge.

Why not aim for the top? thought I, and signed up for a course at the Ecole des Amateurs Gastronomes Lenôtre. Gaston Lenôtre, now retired, was one of the best chefs in Paris. The Lenôtre stores feature food that pleases both the eye and the palate: if you are lucky enough to attend an event catered by Lenôtre, I can assure you that you can both taste and see *la différence* between what you are served there and the banal cocktail fare one usually gets.

The cake that would be demonstrated on the day I attended a workshop was the famous *opéra*, created in the late nineteenth century by a pastry chef whose shop was located in front of the Opéra-Comique. Look at any *opéra* and you'll see a gold leaf on it. The story goes that the gold leaf was put on the cake to evoke the beauty and glitter of evenings at the opera.

Whether you want to make an *opéra* or a *mille feuilles* or any of the other wonderful French pastries, if you speak French and want to see some of France's best-trained chefs work wonders firsthand,

Lenôtre's courses for amateurs are tops. (Besides pastry, you can also learn how to make choucroute, terrines, bouillabaisse, savory tarts, and other typically French dishes.) Located at the Lenôtre pastry shop on the avenue Victor Hugo in the upscale sixteenth arrondissement, the courses are given in a specially equipped kitchen at the back of the shop, separated from the store by a wrought-iron bread shelf. Given this setup, the chef's comments are often mixed in with the singsong of mothers coming in after school to order their *pain au chocolat* for their children. Hearing the voices of mothers and children brought back vivid memories of the days when I would pick up my children at school, *pain au chocolate* in hand, as they couldn't even wait to get to the bakery for it.

The kitchen was immaculate, with red-and-white tiles and a central counter area around which a maximum of seven students can be seated. The first thing I noticed was a tempting dish of *petits fours* Lenôtre placed in the middle of the counter, perhaps to get us in the spirit of things, and in any case, a lovely gesture. In the beginning they stayed there untouched. I was wondering who would be the first to make the move and finally to my great relief someone else did. By the end of the four hours all but two had disappeared. An American student didn't take any because she said she was on a diet. "You're on a diet and you come to a course on the *opéra?*" Chef Alain Blanchard teased her gently.

It is indeed astounding to think that one could attend such a course and make this pastry without eating it but I guess some people have more will power than others. The attractive, slim, thirtyish Frenchwoman next to me, for example, told me that she had lost fifteen kilos (thirty-three pounds) and would be on a strict diet for the rest of her life because of a thyroid problem.

"What are you doing here then?" I asked, amazed.

"Life isn't only about eating," she said philosophically. "I like to make food for others and I just don't eat it." I listened to this, totally fascinated, for I am the kind of person who is incapable of making brownies without licking the bowl, and as for chocolate chip and oatmeal cookies, the only reason I *make* them is to eat the dough. And I have a really hard time making food and not participating in the eating of it.

After these two encounters, for a fleeting moment I thought I might have fallen into some kind of weird sect of food-making noneaters and that I was perhaps the only person there interested in actually consuming the afternoon's results. This of course turned out to be far from the truth.

But first it was time to get down to business: Chef Blanchard, a young dark-haired, dark-eyed man in a white apron and white chef's toque, passed out the recipe. As I scanned it, I saw names I didn't know in French. That afternoon I learned, for example, that a *tant pour tant* is a mixture of 50 percent powdered sugar and 50 percent almond powder, *poudre d'amande*. Never knew that before! I also learned that weighing ingredients is essential. Being a somewhat slapdash and instinctive cook, I have a tendency to "estimate." This is definitely not the thing to do when you are making pastry. Having the right mixer, thermometer, and scales is essential. I learned that for cakes like the *opéra* you work, like a painter, within a frame. I learned that to make the *opéra* you prepare 1) a *biscuit Joconde* 2) *punch café* 3) a *crème au beurre café* 4) a *ganache chocolat* and 5) a *glaçage opéra*. These five parts are done separately and the cake is assembled at the end. In sum, I learned that the entire process bears no resemblance to any pastry I had ever attempted in my life!

The course on the *opéra* was an education in itself. About a half hour into it, I realized that I had no notions at all about how pastry

on this level is done (I'm talking the summum of pastry, not chocolate chip cookies.) I had always entertained the idea that pastry
requires special techniques but had not a clue as to how highly technical it is. In my defense, I must reiterate that the cake being done
that day is not one of the simplest: the *opéra* as I mentioned, is a
layer cake requiring five different operations which it took the chef
four hours to assemble. After watching him do it with all his skill
and in a kitchen with all the equipment one would ever need, I esti-
mated that it would take me at least four days, if not four years, to
make one of my own.

We jotted down notes (I ended up with *thirteen pages* of almost
indecipherable scribbling), jumped up to help the chef, and in general participated as much as we could. We even attempted to ice the
cake as smoothly as we had seen it done by the chef. At the end of
the class, we divvied up the cake into slices and then we each took a
turn decorating our pieces with the golden leaves and arabesques
that are placed on the real thing. We also wrote *opéra* on the icing
with varying degrees of success. It's not as easy as it looks. My hand-
writing looked like a five-year-old's.

I called my sister-in-law right after the course. When she learned
that the course was on an *opéra*, her only comment was: "That's a
cake you *buy!*"

A qui le dis-tu? You're telling me? I replied.

The whole experience was worth it, though. Never again in my
life will I ignorantly think that this cake, especially if it's done by
Lenôtre, is too expensive. The work and the expertise that goes into
it represents hours of a chef's training. For example, the *coup de
main.* When Chef Blanchard applied the final icing, the surface was
so smooth it looked like a shiny chocolate mirror. This alone would
take any amateur several courses to master and it got me to wonder-

ing if the French expression *ce n'est pas de la tarte* which literally translated means "it's not a piece of pie" and figuratively means "it's not easy" wasn't first coined by someone who had tried to make an *opéra*! It also made me more appreciative of the following phrase by Carême, the famous eighteenth-century chef and author of twelve volumes on French gastronomy, who wrote that "Pastry is the principal branch of architecture."

In pastry the expression "anything goes" is not true. There are rules, there are exact measurements, there are age-old recipes (there are new ones as well, veritable creations), and there is always, always the concern for artful presentation. That is why I laughed when I read a passage in M. F. K. Fisher's *Two Towns in Provence* in which she describes going into a *patisserie* where she is a regular customer and asking the *patissier* to make a birthday cake for her youngest daughter following a drawing her oldest daughter had designed.

Madame looked openly shocked by the picture, and called the head chef. . . . He looked sadly at us, and shrugged, and made the cake, but Madame told us coldly that it was the first time such a thing had ever been requested. . . . The result was a reptilian masterpiece, carefully carved in an artful sponge cake and then covered, coil by coil, in a thick layer of green almond paste. There were skin markings of glaze, I remember. A delicate pink fork of sugar protruded between tiny white teeth. The eyes were fierce. A miasma of Alsatian kirsch hovered over and around it." And she says "We never saw the chef again. . . . The episode was never mentioned by the wee lady, so smartly dressed and coiffed, who ran the pastry shop.

Les artistes du chocolat—Robert Linxe and Christian Constant

He's now in the beginning of his seventh decade and at the head of a Maison du Chocolat empire with shops in Paris, Tokyo, San Francisco, Hawaii, and New York and sixty thousand square feet of laboratories in the west of Paris.

But when Robert Linxe started out in the world of chocolate, it was in an eight-hundred-square-foot former wine cellar on the Faubourg-St. Honoré where he was a one-man show. "I even dipped the chocolates by hand, one by one," he recalls. By that time, he was forty-seven years old and knew he was taking a huge risk by opening his own shop and going out on his own. But Robert Linxe had an obsession, an idea that wouldn't leave him and that was "to rehabilitate chocolate in all its noblesse." Thus it was that he had one of his best friends, Arnaud Saez, take over the decoration and the image of his chocolate house. Some might find it a trifle severe or foreboding but his idea was to make it a place for "cultivated, refined, and demanding" clients. Hence it was that they chose the decor which is still there today: Brazilian granite floors, cinnamon-colored walls, nougatine colors for the marble of the counters.

No chocolates in pink satin wrapping here. "Some people found the environment a bit stark for a sweet as amiable as chocolate. But my idea was to impose the image of a different chocolate, pure and noble, and rid of all its creamy and sugary affectation," Linxe writes in his book *La Maison du Chocolat*, unfortunately not translated into English. Everything is thought out, right down to the logo, a stone *metate* mortar on which the Aztecs ground the chocolate beans with a round stone pestle called the *metlapilli*.

As I sat chatting with Mr. Linxe at a small marble table in the shop on the rue François I (the only table that day since they had been taken out for the Christmas rush), I reflected on his incredible one-man success story. Even he can't believe how far he's come from his poor childhood in the southwest of France. Poor, but happy. His father was one of nine children and was a self-taught man who loved music. The family home was one in which "everyone sang, it was very gay." From that atmosphere of music, Linxe grew up with an appreciation for opera and classical music and played the violin for many years.

The passion for music extends to his passion for chocolate, which is why many of his creations have musically related names, such as the Bohème and the Rigoletto, and many of La Maison du Chocolat's aficionados are musicians like Daniel Barenboim and the late Yehudi Menuhin who would come straight from giving a concert at the Salle Pleyel to stock up at his boutique. From his father, who had "more taste than money," he inherited his penchant for good things in small quantities. "My father loved good wines and since we couldn't afford to have many, we really learned how to taste and appreciate what we had."

Linxe learned even more about taste and the unctuousness of chocolate when he enrolled in a prestigious hotel school in Basle, Switzerland. He stayed on to work as an apprentice before moving to Paris, where he opened his first store near the Parc Monceau. Keeping in mind that "there's never room for the last person," he endured five hard years reabsorbing the deficit followed by five years making money at last. It was after that experience that he opened the boutique on the rue Faubourg-St. Honoré.

This continuing emphasis on taste and the palate he cultivates and respects is one of the reasons for his success in the field of chocolate. "I don't smoke and I don't drink," Mr. Linxe told me. "When I wake up in the morning, I drink a thyme herb tea and then I'm ready, and my palate is ready, to taste."

And taste he does. For him "the palate and taste is culture. It's not enough to have recipes. To arrive at refinement, you have to have the palate."

He had decided that it was time for me to taste some of his creations and excused himself to go behind the counter to personally pick out a variety of chocolates. He presented them on a small plate with a small sharp knife and then cut a fingernail sized slice from the first one and presented it to me. He didn't tell me until afterward, but I understood that we were tasting the chocolates in order: "a crescendo," he said, from the purest to the ones with the more unusual flavors. The first one, Quito, a pure black chocolate, melted in my mouth. It was delicious. The next was the Bacchus, made with smyrnah raisins, flambéed with alcohol. It was out of this world. We went on to the Romeo, a milk chocolate moccha from Ethiopia, to Sylvia, which had the taste of caramel, but a caramel from the chocolate and not from any caramel that has been added. And on to the Garrigue, ginger taste; Andalousie, a zest of lemon; and Zagora, an astonishing mint tea taste that reminded me of Morocco. By this time, I was seriously cogitating. How long does it take you to create these different chocolates? I asked. "One or two years," replied Linxe. "But that doesn't count our busy periods when we're in the store." It also doesn't count losing sleep at night, as he told me he did, thinking, thinking, thinking about how to perfect a taste and get it just right.

Later, I took a look at the book Mr. Linxe had generously offered me. I particularly liked the description of the Quito, the chocolate he prefers and which took him a year to create. After describing its composition, he notes its inspiration: Ecuadoreans he knows who he writes "were very pious and faithful, very handsome as well, with a sober and natural elegance that I wanted to reinstate with the Quito, which expresses at one and the same time refinement and power."

Who could disagree with the late French writer Jean-Paul Aron that "it was Robert Linxe who brought *le luxe* to chocolate." I would add not only luxury but deep reflection and respect.

Linxe is rightly proud of his accomplishments but hardly one to rest on his laurels. "I respect people who work. If you are offhand about your work, you are not respecting your client."

There's certainly no risk of that at La Maison du Chocolat.

Dressed in black from head to toe (like chocolate!), Christian Constant, one of the best chocolate and pastry chefs in Paris, greeted me in his office before running out to take care of a huge order for a party Clinique was throwing to launch a new product. His office above the shop on the rue d'Assas is a tiny cubicle stuffed with books and papers. There's barely enough room for the two of us. In spite of his busy schedule, he's ready to talk but I find that like most food artists, he's more at ease talking about his art than his life. The son and grandson of wine makers, Constant didn't discover his passion for chocolate—and it is a passion—until he started working with the great chef Gaston Lenôtre. "Gastronomy in general interested and interests me but it was then that chocolate became the great passion of my life," he told me.

For some reason I volunteered that I had developed a theory about wine people, cheese people, and bread people, which was that bread people are down to earth, wine people are outgoing and outward looking, and cheese people are hard to get to know. He sat back in his chair and looked at me.

"And I have a theory about people who love chocolate," he pronounced. "They're *sympathique*. And I think one should be wary of people who don't like chocolate. They're hiding something and they don't like pleasure. They're sad and lugubrious." We both laughed but he really wasn't kidding and neither was I. After our meeting, I tested out his theory on a chocolate addict friend of mine. "He's right," she exclaimed, "and did he mention sex? I'm *sure* people who don't like chocolate don't like sex." Yet another theory to test.

But back to the serious matter at hand. Christian Constant has spent most of his adult life engaged in the enviable pursuit of creating both desserts and mouthwatering top-quality chocolate collections. For him, gastronomy is an art and pastry is an exact science. "From the time you've perfected a recipe you have to respect it absolutely. This isn't the same as in cooking where you add a dash of this and a dash of that. What's marvelous in cooking is that you can always create." What interests him in all this, he emphasizes, is the invention and the creation. "Pastry is frustrating and the pleasure I get from it is from creating recipes. I take no pleasure in making pastry once I've created the recipe. Someone else can do it."

All chocolate doesn't taste alike and if you don't believe it, taste some of his creations. "Chocolate is like wine. There are totally different tastes depending on the country, the way the beans are grown." I have to confess that while I'm writing these lines recapping my talk with him I am dipping, oh so carefully, into a lovely box of Christian Constant chocolates. I take one from the flowers and perfume selection. It is redolent with roses and corinthian raisins. I let it melt in my mouth and indeed . . . taste a rose! I can't resist a Yemen jasmine and green tea chocolate (after all, this is research, right?) and last but not least dip into a beehive-shaped jewel of pine nuts and honey. Research or not, this has got to *stop*. Good-bye, chocolate paradise.

Real chocolate vs. candy

Up until now French chocolate makers have operated under very strict rules stating that chocolate is only chocolate when it is composed of cocoa beans and the butter from them (cocoa and cocoa butter). Some sugar and soy lecithin can be added in very specific proportions—and that is it. The French can put noncocoa fats in their chocolate, as many northern European countries do, but in that case the finished product can no longer be sold as chocolate. For the moment real chocolate occupies an enviable place in the French panoply of gastronomic products. It is not and never has been considered candy the way, for example, we consider it in the States. Even in a normal French grocery store, real chocolate has an elevated status.

This status will change now that the European Parliament has voted a law that will enable chocolate manufacturers all over Europe to replace cocoa butter with noncocoa fats and still call their product chocolate. Why this abysmal decision? The great leveling of Europe! And greater sales. How else can one explain that the French Chocolate Manufacturers Union was not against this law? As you can imagine, French chocolate connoisseurs and the French "chocolate artists" like Christian Constant and Robert Linxe were appalled by the decision.

"It's not worth refusing beef with hormones or talking about mad cows if we accept chocolate that isn't chocolate," Christian Constant told me (our interview took place shortly before the law went through). "If we head that way, we'll soon have wine made out of cherries instead of grapes!"

Sadly, though, the law was passed and as a result there is no longer any way for the average consumer of a chocolate bar purchased in a

French grocery store to know what the exact contents are, for the manufacturers are not obliged to put the exact ingredients on the package.

Serious chocolate lovers now have only one alternative and this is to flock to the specialty stores, which will continue to uphold the tradition of the *vrais chocolatiers*. I personally will lead a one-woman boycott against the chocolate "candy" that will inundate French grocery stores. Never again!

You've guessed my opinion on all this. Chocolate *is* noble. People like Robert Linxe and Christian Constant and others of their ilk are artists. *Vive les artistes*.

 INTERVIEW WITH PHILIPPE

HWR: The European Union recently decided to allow noncocoa fat in chocolate. What do you think about this?

PhR: Europe, influenced by certains nations I don't want to mention here in the interest of not alienating readers, is lowering standards.

HWR: Will the European Union wreck everything?

PhR: There are two things it can't destroy: things that are too subtle and things that are too gross.

(Cont.)

HWR: What do you mean?

PhR: As long as the French have *petits fours* and *mille feuilles* and even have Americans like you eating pig's feet, there's hope for a civilized Europe.

Martine's Chocolate Mousse

One of my favorite chocolate desserts is that great French classic, the *mousse au chocolat*. Like onion soup, there are many ways to make it. The best one I have ever tasted is my sister-in-law's. She was kind enough to give me (and you!) her recipe:

6 eggs
10 ounces of black
   chocolate
¼ cup of butter
1 tablespoon of instant
   coffee

⅓ *cup of sugar*
A small glass of Cointreau
   or rum

Break the eggs and separate the whites
from the yolks.
Beat the egg whites until they are very stiff.
During this time, melt the chocolate and
the butter in a bain-marie.
When it is thoroughly melted, add the liquor and
the coffee.
When the chocolate mixture has cooled, add
the egg yolks. Stir well.
Pour the sugar into the egg whites, beat
them for one minute.
Very delicately incorporate the chocolate
mixture into the egg whites.

Put the mousse in the refrigerator to chill before serving. Serves 6.

10

Get Thee to a Spa

Thalassotherapie · Get me out of here · Try, try again ·
Saint-Jean-de-Luz · Weighing in · Flavor sans fat; or, eating
light, eating well · My kingdom for a cook

I once read somewhere in a magazine that it is useless to weigh
yourself every day because there is so much variation between
one day and the next. It is much better (and less depressing), the
article said, to weigh yourself once a week.

I had an even better idea. I would no longer weigh myself at all.
I decided that the skirt would be the judge. If there was a slack, so
much the better. If the waistband got tight, time to watch out.
Throw out the scales! (Fortunately, I didn't go that far.)

A couple of months later, I was feeling quite constricted
(euphemism) in my "reference skirt" and couldn't take the sus-
pense any longer. Gingerly, I crept up to the scale, emitted a
hearty sigh, and then stood on it watching the bright red digits
flash their verdict.

And I freaked.

I hate and despise diets (what the French call *régimes*) but it
was obvious that something had to be done to get rid of what I
had not very affectionately begun to call "the pumpkin." After

all, I didn't want to end up looking like the Michelin Bibendum (the funny Michelin Tire Company emblem who looks appropriately like . . . a rubber tire). To make things worse, as spring approached, French women's magazines had only one story and one picture on their covers: the story was how to lose 5 million pounds in two days with no effort. The picture was of a lithe, slim young wisp of a thing with a very, very flat belly.

I wanted to strangle her.

At the same time, a powerful desire began to form in my mind and that was to get rid of the surplus weight quickly and with as little effort as possible. It was then that I had my brilliant idea.

Get thee to a spa! A French spa, being French, is not a vulgar fat farm. Many French people don't even go to spas or *thalassotherapie*, hydrotherapy centers, to lose weight. They go to relax and feel better and be coddled and pampered and taken care of, things which generally don't happen in normal daily life. And while they are getting coddled and pampered, they eat the most fantastic gastronomic food you can imagine. All part of the fun.

Some people go, though, for the express reason of losing weight, not as much fun but since you are kept busy running from seawater baths to massages to aquagym classes to Turkish baths and saunas, there's hardly any time left to think about the most important thing in life: *Food*.

Thalassotherapie

France has some fifty *thalassotherapie* institutes scattered along its coasts. One of the first centers was founded in Quiberon on the coast of Brittany in the 1960s by Louison Bobet, an injured Tour de France champion who was healed by seawater therapy. He was convinced that sea water, pumped into oceanside institutes, could cure certain illnesses in the same way that mineral water had traditionally done. He decided to promote the concept and now, it would seem, hydrotherapy centers are all the rage, offering everything from treatments for losing weight, improving your back, improving your beauty (a week of facials, anyone?), to relaxing after having had a baby. French Social Security will reimburse people who seek treatment for some very specific medical problems at certain thermal-water spas but will not reimburse any of the treatments at hydrotherapy centers. You're on your own!

This hasn't stopped people from going—on the contrary. Each year 200,000 people, mostly women (70 percent), flock to these centers. "Some women," Emmanuel Henry, Director of the Hélianthal Hydrotherapy Center in Saint-Jean-de-Luz told me, "have taken two cures a year for fifteen years." The average age of the clientèle is between forty and fifty-five and many retired couples come to these centers to maintain their form. According to Henry, "People come in a preventive way. They consider that a week of being taken care of and doing everything to feel better is a vacation as well as an investment in better health." An important note here: the average French worker has five weeks of vacation a year so a week or even two at a hydrotherapy center does not represent, as it would in the States, the entire yearly vacation.

Get me out of here

Confession time: *thalassotherapie* was not unknown to me. I had spent a brief weekend at a seawater therapy place on the coast of Brittany a few years ago and found the scene so snobbish and the whole idea so unreal that I vowed at the time I would never go back. Philippe and I took one look at the unfriendly-looking (hey, does anybody smile around here?) self-absorbed *curistes* padding around in their white sandals and white robes and decided they looked and acted more like inmates than people having a good time. Maybe they *weren't* having a good time. It certainly didn't look like it.

"Let's get out of here," Philippe suggested, and it took me about two seconds to acquiesce. We fled to the nearest bar on the port to drink a cold glass of white wine to celebrate our "liberation." Definitely not our thing. At least at that time.

However, it was because of that earlier, negative experience that when I began searching for a place to go to relax and get rid of my extra pounds, I tried to choose what appeared to be a convivial place, not some factory where my flesh would be treated with haughty indifference. After all, this is my *bod* we're talking about!

Try, try again

In the end, I chose the Hélianthal Hydrotherapy Center at Saint-Jean-de-Luz, a seaside resort of twelve thousand in the heart of the Basque country in the southwest corner of France. The name, Hélianthal, which I had a hard time turning around my tongue, is derived from Helios, Greek for sun, and Thalassa, for sea, I read in the brochure. The hydrotherapy center at Saint-Jean had many advantages: it was in the south of France, near the Spanish border, and I felt like going south; it was both on the beach and in the town so I could cut out of there when I'd had enough; it was relatively small, with one hundred and sixty *curistes* a day as opposed to some of these places which run through six hundred or more people a day.

In addition, I had already visited Saint-Jean-de-Luz many years ago and had a good memory of it.

Before going, I met with Jacques Courtillé, the director of the center, Fabienne Lae, the nutritionist, and Emmanuel Henry, the manager of hydrotherapy, at the Paris Salon des Thermalies (Paris Spa Show). They explained to me that the approach of their institute is not to starve their clients but to serve carefully planned light meals and especially to help people go away from their cure with better habits and some good recipes for "light" cooking in hand. "Our policy," says Henry, "is to give nutritional pleasure to people who want to learn to eat lightly. Many people call us and say they want to lose five kilos (eleven pounds) in a week. We tell them it isn't possible." I took one look at Fabienne, a pert, brown-eyed brunette, and decided that if that is what you look like when you eat healthy, light food on a regular basis, it would definitely be worth a try.

Another reason I opted for Saint-Jean-de-Luz is that it is on the direct very fast TGV (pronounced Tay Zhay Vay) train line from Paris. On I hopped at four in the afternoon and off I hopped at nine. Each TGV has its personality, I have observed. My ride down was a "happy" train with a conductor who had a friendly word and joke for each person as he punched our tickets. A group of tall, hulking rugby players from the southwest, which produces the best rugby teams in France, kept going back and forth through the car I was in. They spent most of their time on the platform between cars telling jokes and singing songs. Since I love to hear people laugh, I felt it was an auspicious beginning.

Saint-Jean-de-Luz

The atmosphere on the train might have been gay and lively but Saint-Jean-de-Luz on a March night was not. As I walked from the train station up the pedestrian street trailing my bag behind me (clack-clack-clack-clack its wheels resounded on the stone pavement), I had the feeling I was waking up the entire town.

Saint-Jean-de-Luz has two major claims to fame: the first is that it is in the town's church that the Sun King married Maria-Theresa, the Spanish infanta. The door they entered for the royal wedding has been walled and a plaque placed upon it. The second is that composer Maurice Ravel was born there. The hydrotherapy center is, poetically, I thought, located on the Place Maurice Ravel. People in this region speak with the singsong accent of the southwest. Many speak Basque. I learned that there are Basque schools and that people can even take their school-leaving exam (the Baccalaureat) in Basque. The white houses are brightened up with red and blue shutters and red and pink tiled roofs. The town has many park benches both overlooking the sea and in the pedestrian area. As I strolled down the main shopping street, I observed an old man sitting down to enjoy a cigarette, young women pushing baby strollers, and salespeople stepping out of their stores to greet friends. It seemed—and I know this since I grew up in a small town—that almost everyone knew everyone else. This is the way it is until July and August, when the population swells from twelve thousand to about fifty thousand and then those deserted streets I described above are so crowded you can hardly walk through them.

At one time Saint-Jean-de-Luz was a major whaling port; later, its fishermen concentrated on cod and tuna. Fish still dominates. At one *poissonnerie* I saw marinated anchovies, mussels in cream, oysters of all kinds, dried cod, shrimp, winkles, mottled combshell, clams, and cockles—and that was just what was outside. I passed by a bodega with a sign for *bocadillos*, the Spanish name for sandwich, which I can now add to my collection of French "fast food." At the town's oldest pastry shop, Adam, founded in 1660, I actually saw a brownie next to a cake called the Beret Basque.

But the brownie would seem to be the only concession this proud people has made to globalization. At the tourist office I expressed an interest in the local cuisine and was given a list of recipes for: *piper-ade, marmitako, ttoro* (pronounced tio, I was told—it is kind of a basque bouillabaisse), the *gateau basque* called Etcheko pastiza in Basque, and the *hachoa*, a veal dish with *piments doux*, sweet peppers that you can buy in the region. By the way, the lady at the tourist office told me, if you see something on a menu *à la basquaise*, it means that the sauce is made with tomatoes and onions and peppers. The Basques eat well: their cuisine is colorful and savory and spiced up with the *piment d'Espelette*, a mildly hot chili pepper from the village of Espelette in the foothills of the Pyrenees.

Weighing in

On my first morning at the spa, I met with one of the center's doctors, who weighed me. I silently awarded her the prize for diplomacy when she asked me if that was my "winter weight." I must say that the beer and olives and peanuts I had bolted in the hotel lobby the night before didn't help my score, but hey, the day *before* your cure, you really have to let loose, *n'est-ce pas?*

I only stayed four days, which is not at all recommended (so unrecommended that I was not weighed at the end). The minimum time to spend at a hydrotherapy center, no matter what the cure, is six days and more if you can. I couldn't take that much time but I played the game as if I were remaining for the whole cure. I met with the doctor, and I saw Fabienne, the nutritionist. She asked me to tell her what and how I normally eat—always a funny thing to do because as you recount it, even while arranging the truth so it doesn't sound too awful, you are generally horrified by your bad habits. Fabienne assured me she had heard worse. She said we'd meet again at the end of my cure and she would have some recommendations on how I could change some of my bad habits. *Fantastique!*

The cure

Every morning I opted for breakfast with a newspaper in my spacious room, which looked over the rooftops of Saint-Jean-de-Luz. I was pleased to see that the "dietetic" breakfast was more interesting and varied than the "traditional" breakfast so at least I didn't wake up in a bad mood. After lolling in bed for a time, I threw on my regulation white bathrobe and white sandals and sauntered down the corridor to the elevator, which whisked me directly down to the hydrotherapy center. Each *curiste* has four treatments a day, depending on the person's state. My "state" must have been stressed for many of my treatments consisted of massages and relaxation. One treatment was a *douche sous marine*, an underwater shower, in which an attendant takes a hose and applies water to your legs, feet, hands, shoulders, and back as you lie down in a huge tub. Another treatment was cold green algae on the legs. Very good for circulation. The one I didn't like but is surely good for you was being covered in gruesome green algae and left alone wrapped up in plastic and a blanket. I felt like a living corpse, and my sole desire was to get up and get out of there, an impossibility unless you want to run around looking like a Martian. Maybe a lot of people feel as claustrophobic as I did because there was a bell on the wall. And so it went, four treatments either in the morning or in the afternoon. Some people love being taken in hand; others, like me, have a hard time not being in control. In the end, though, you're so waterlogged you don't remember what control is all about. Every once in a while I'd glance in the mirror and say "Who is that wet rag?" and realize it was me.

Flavor *sans* fat; or, eating light, eating well

We took our meals in a huge, light dining room looking directly out over the ocean. On one wall was an enormous colorful mural of travelers on an ocean liner dressed in 1930s garb. Some are talking, some are playing shuffleboard, and some are looking over the railings out to sea. The art deco hotel was designed by Robert Mallet-Stevens; sometimes, sitting there in the dining room, I had the feeling I was on a huge ocean liner and that we were either already out at sea or "our ship" might push out at any moment. There was no segregation: you could be at the same table as people eating "normal" food—and miraculously not suffer as you watched them drinking wine, eating cheese, and indulging in bread. We "light eaters" had no wine, no cheese, and were encouraged to go easy on the bread except for breakfast.

Being France, the food was aesthetically pleasing, served at the table, and in three courses. Here's a typical lunch: a first course of a vegetable canneloni with soy sauce and a yogurt sauce with dill (four delicate cannelonis wrapped in a thin pancake with rocket lettuce in the middle and a pretty sauce around them—a feast for the eyes). The main course was an attractively wrapped-up chicken torte served with a delicious low-fat sauce. We finished the meal with a *fondant de chocolat à l'orange*, a light, sweet chocolate-orange dessert. I was at the table with Annie from Albi (I call her that because I never learned her last name, par for the course in France—it's miraculous even to learn someone's first name!) whose coffee for some odd reason arrived before she had finished dessert. She couldn't have been more surprised if the waiter had undressed in front of her. "I hate having my coffee with dessert!" she exclaimed. Her reaction is the greatest proof I've seen that the French are quite attached to their coffee as a separate course, a cultural difference par excellence.

If I managed to eat light food for ten meals and not rush out to gorge on a *gateau basque* or the famous *tourons*, a ground-almond, egg-white confection that is extremely tempting, it is largely due to the talent of chef Scott Serrato. Half American, half Italian, Scott speaks fluent Spanish and French (but tells me that, paradoxically, he doesn't speak either English or Italian!). He started cooking at age fifteen and has worked in many prestigious places in France and Spain, among them the Palace Hotel in Biarritz and the Burgos Palace in Spain. He fell in love with the Basque country and didn't want to leave it. "It's convival, the people are friendly, and they love their traditions and *fêtes*," he told me. "When you are accepted by them, they are very warm."

When he was contacted by the director of Hélianthal in 1996, he said he knew nothing about light cooking. The director said: "No problem, you'll learn," and Scott accepted the challenge. "I make a lot of sauces based on fruits and vegetable juice and the juice of shellfish. You add the herb that goes with it and you have a light sauce with a savory taste." For Scott, "a cook who makes good food is one who respects the seasons. Making a good recipe with a bad product is nonsense."

My time at the spa included a cooking course. At the lesson, five of us gathered around Scott as he showed us a few of his tricks, many of which consisted of skillfully dicing vegetables and fruits both for an artful presentation and to get the most out of the flavors. He worked rapidly, cutting the various carrots, zucchini, leeks and celery with precision. As I watched him cut, I decided that he could offer a course solely on chopping vegetables.

"Would anyone like to try?" he asked, holding up a grapefruit whose skin he had sliced off in a gesture worthy of a surgeon. Annie from Albi volunteered and everyone marveled as she followed his instructions. It seemed as if she had been cutting out grapefruit segments for her entire natural life. (Doing it fast and not messily is not as easy as it looks.) Serrato gave us recipes for a fake mayonnaise and fake vinaigrette, which I will share with all of you who do not wish to eat Philippe's Heart Attack Mayonnaise or his classic vinaigrette.

Scott Serrato's false mayonnaise

The yolk of a hard-boiled egg
½ teaspoon of French mustard
1 teaspoon of lemon juice

5 tablespoons of fromage blanc (Fromage blanc is a smooth white lowfat cheese which can be found in specialty stores in the U.S.)
Salt, pepper
Shallots or herbs or tomato or pickle (dill)

**Crush the yolk with the mustard and lemon juice.
Beat the *fromage blanc* and slowly add it
to this mixture.
Season it with salt and pepper and the ingredients
you have chosen (shallots, herbs, etc.).**

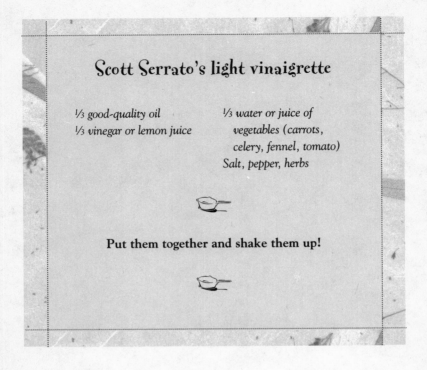

Scott Serrato's light vinaigrette

⅓ good-quality oil
⅓ vinegar or lemon juice

⅓ water or juice of
vegetables (carrots,
celery, fennel, tomato)
Salt, pepper, herbs

Put them together and shake them up!

His next demonstration was a delicious filet of sea bream grilled in its skin and cooked on top of a bed of coarse salt. He served it with what he called *une sauce simple* (simple for him!) and shredded vegetables. We watched, entranced. I could almost see bubbles above people's heads with the question: "Will I be able to do that when I get back home?"

My kingdom for a cook

Serrato may work in a hydrotherapy center but he doesn't take himself for anything but what he is: a chef. "I'm not a doctor or a nutritionist. I am a cook. What is important is not to stress people out. We want them to take pleasure in eating light. If not, when they leave here, they'll go home to stuff themselves and that's not the point."

When I weighed myself on Saturday morning *chez moi*, I saw that two kilos (4.4 pounds) had come off. Those weren't miracle kilos and the center does *not* promise dramatic weight loss. They dropped off mainly because I was drinking only water (no booze— too fattening), eating healthy but noncaloric food, sweating off my weight in the Turkish baths, and walking it off on the beach. And here's what I wasn't doing: thinking about what to buy for dinner, grocery shopping, getting up from the computer to visit the fridge. It's called, in short, R and R (and getting out of your house!).

After a week of hydrotherapy, I arrived at several conclusions. The first two are realistic, the third is wishful thinking. One is that the French are really onto something here. Two is that I'm definitely going to make a hydrotherapy cure a yearly outing. And three and most important is that what I need in my life is a Scott Serrato in my kitchen. . . . I think a few other *curistes* felt the same way.

Well, it never hurts to dream. . . .

INTERVIEW WITH PHILIPPE

HWR: Did you see any visible difference between when I left for Saint-Jean-de-Luz and when I came back?

PhR: Yes, you were in a better mood.

HWR: Didn't you notice I shed a couple of kilos?

PhR: No, but then you didn't really need to.

HWR (*to readers*): That's why I married a gallant Frenchman. . . .

11

The Parisian Waiter

*Some good views of waiters . . . and some not so good • A
cultural misunderstanding • My days as a waitress • A ballet
• Coke in a carafe • What waiters find funny or frustrating*

If there is one instantly recognizable character in France, it is
the Parisian waiter. Terms traditionally used to describe
him—and I say "him" on purpose because to my knowledge
hardly anyone talks about the Parisian waitress—are rarely com-
plimentary. "Haughty," "snotty," "arrogant" are but three adjec-
tives that come to mind.

Some good views of Parisian waiters

At least this used to be the case. I'm now starting to hear things
like "amazingly friendly," "helpful," and "spoke English," instead
of the former pejorative trilogy. Even travel writer Bill Bryson,
who can't be accused of being too kind to the French or any
other nationality in his hilarious book *Neither Here Nor There,
Travels in Europe*, has to admit he's foiled by the "new politeness"
of French service people in general and the waiter in particular:

It took me two or three days to notice it, but the people of Paris had become polite over the last twenty years. They didn't exactly rush up and embrace you and thank you for winning the war for them, but they had certainly become more patient and accommodating. The cab drivers were still complete jerks, but everyone else—shopkeepers, waiters, the police—seemed almost friendly. I even saw a waiter smile once.

So things are changing for the better, and indeed, one can wonder if they were ever really all that bad.

Susan A. D. Hunter, writing in *The House on Via Gombita*, confesses that she was intimidated by the idea of eating out alone in the tiny tourist town of Aigues-Mortes but that her fears were allayed by the friendly reception she received. "One of the waiters," she writes, "a tall willowy fellow in voguish baggy pants, walked me well out into the street when I left and stood watching as I turned up the Rue St.-Louis. He waved a final good-bye and went back inside."

In *Two Towns in Provence*, M. F. K. Fisher writes of the halcyon days at the Café des Deux Garcons in Aix-en-Provence: "Often my girls went there for hot chocolate or a cool silver cup of lemon ice when they must wait for me and could not find me, and the waiters welcomed them gently."

And in the 1800s Mark Twain in *The Innocents Abroad* gives another favorable opinion: "We are getting foreignised rapidly, and with facility. We are getting reconciled to halls and bed-chambers with unhomelike stone floors, and no carpet-floors that ring to the tread of one's heels with a sharpness that is death to sentimental musing. We are getting used to tidy, noiseless waiters, who glide hither and thither, and hover about your back and your elbows like butterflies, quick to comprehend orders, quick to fill them; thankful for a gratuity without regard to the amount; and always polite—never otherwise than polite."

More recently, a friend who is married to a Frenchman and lives in California, mused as we sat on the terrace of the Café Marly admiring the Pei Pyramid: "The French have become so incredibly friendly—what happened?" And this, in spite of the fact that our young waiter was alone serving the entire terrace and couldn't seem to get back to our table to give us more water and sugar for her son's *citron pressé*. (A *citron pressé* is fresh lemon juice served with water and sugar—you need a *lot* of sugar.) But his smile was so sincere and winning and he was such a genuinely pleasant fellow that it was hard to get upset. He reminded me how important it is for serving people to be amiable and how important a smile is. The day I met my friend and her son, a student at Berkeley, for a drink, the sky was blue, the sun was shining, and it was indeed a privileged moment to be in this beautiful capital on a gorgeous autumn day sipping coffee in front of one of the most beautiful museums in the world. Wasn't it a gift not to have this moment marred by a snotty waiter? For a waiter's attitude *can* make or break a dining or drinking experience.

. . . and some not so good

In spite of flattering testimonies such as the above, somewhere along the way the image of the Parisian waiter (or was the waiter the embodiment of all haughty Parisian cabdrivers, storekeepers, and service people?) as the ultimate snotty, intimidating fellow became imprinted on the American mind. Over lunch one cold winter day with my friend Dorie at Le Verre Bouteille, a neighborhood bistro in the seventeenth arrondissement where she tucked into a homey *endive au noix d'agneau*, an endive stuffed with minced lamb and I into a steak tartare (I have decided to order a steak tartare in every reputable restaurant I go to in Paris hoping that someday I'll find the perfect one) we talked about how times have changed. She still remembers a humiliating experience she had with a waiter at Le Pied de Cochon when she was seventeen years old and with hardly a cent to her name. "I'd been to the Pied de Cochon in Washington, D.C., many times where I would order onion soup—only. So when I came to Paris, even though I hardly spoke any French I went to Le Pied de Cochon to get onion soup. I got this really loud waiter who handed me the menu with great bravado."

"What will it be?" he asked her.

"*Soupe á l'oignon*," she replied, without much confidence.

"And to drink?"

"*De l'eau*." she replied, meekly.

"*Une soupe à l'oignon et de l'eau*," he repeated in a booming voice. And then, even louder, intimating that she really was a cheapskate to come to a restaurant and order only soup and water: "*C'est tout?*"

"*C'est tout*," she confirmed, almost whispering. "I was so humiliated I practically burned my tongue on the soup. I couldn't wait to get out of there." This kind of browbeating from the high-handed waiter was unfortunately too frequent in the past. A brief note in the waiter's defense: Dorie couldn't have known that she was in a restaurant and in restaurants you are expected to eat a real meal. Had she gone to a brasserie, she wouldn't have had this problem. Still, the waiter had no reason to embarrass his client, a client who's never been back since!

That was some twenty years ago but recent experiences show that unfortunately the Disdainful Waiter still lurks. (I must note here that on a recent visit to Le Pied de Cochon the service was professional and discreet. My main criticism of the place would be that it is a factory for tourists and not a place where you can expect a warm personal welcome. If you want a warm personal welcome, you go to a small neighborhood bistro where you know the owner.) Food critic and journalist Alexander Lobrano told me of an evening in which he and a friend from New York went to the bar of the Hotel Costes for an after-dinner drink. After they had already sat down, they were told by the waiter that they would have to get up, return to the front door, check their coats themselves, and wait to be seated—and wouldn't be served if they refused!

Lobrano, who is the European correspondent for *Gourmet* and writes a weekly food column for *Time Out Paris*, gets around town so he sees a bit of everything. Another horror story happened to him at the two-star Violon d'Ingres restaurant where he had to send back three bottles of wine all of which were "patently and blatantly" *bouchonnées* (tasting of the cork) and, he says, "the waiter never once apologized." French reviewers have their gripes as well. Wrote one restaurant reviewer in a scalding critique of the service at a restaurant he visited, ". . . is it imaginable that a supposed maître d'hôtel grossly refuses a client who asks him to serve his *côte de bœuf* (rib of beef) in two parts instead of cut in round pieces?"

All of us, tourists and natives alike, are looking for that perfect specimen, the waiter who will serve us promptly with professionalism, courtesy, cordiality. If a restaurant employs only hoity-toity waiters it will end up losing unhappy French customers who will go elsewhere—unless they're masochists. Tourists, though, don't have that kind of time. They will go away with a bad image not only of the restaurant but unfortunately of the French. What a responsibility one lone waiter holds in his hands!

A cultural misunderstanding

While it is true that there are arrogant waiters, it is also true that many Americans don't understand that waiting tables in France is not a stopgap but a profession and that the waiter would find it demeaning to be overfriendly in the "Hi, I'm Ned. Here's your menu. Enjoy" style we are so used to in the States. This is not to say that there are no restaurants and cafés where the waiters are on a first-name basis with their regulars—but that is because the clients *are* regulars and they have established a relationship over a period of time. As a tourist, you won't have time to develop that kind of relationship.

As Frances Gendlin writes in *Culture Shock, Paris at Your Door*: "Being a waiter is a respected profession in France." This professionalism extends to their uniforms; if you look at how waiters and waitresses are dressed, you'll see that it isn't in the T-shirt *du jour*, but easily identified sober black pants or a skirt and a white shirt or blouse.

For me, a restaurant meal represents a relief, one of the only times in the week when no one bothers you—and that includes the waiter. This is because, as one astute observer commented: "Eating out in France is an event and the waiter's part in it is as a professional. He's not going to explain that he's somebody else and is waiting tables because he has nothing better to do. And he's not going to invade your evening with his life story which you don't want to hear anyway." Whew!

One longtime American resident in France contrasted service in France with service at a French restaurant she went to in the States. She was shocked to find that the young waiter, while perfectly pleasant, "had no idea of what he was serving!" This is inconceivable in France, at least in any establishment worth its reputation.

So what should Americans expect when in a French restaurant? "Americans," said one Francophile American who knows both cultures well, "shouldn't be put off by a bit of distance or reserve. However, they should expect good service and when they ask the waiter about what certain dishes are, he or she should be able to tell them."

My days as a waitress

My interest in waiters and waitresses comes from my college experience as a waitress (or do we now say wait person?) at the Martha Cook building, the beautiful Tudor dormitory next to the Law Quad at the University of Michigan where I lived for two years. At that time, we had elegant sit-down meals complete with silver and linen and a wait staff composed of students. When I donned my butter-colored uniform, I realized that although I was the same person to myself, for some of my classmates, very few, I admit, I became invisible as my status dropped from "fellow student" to "server." It didn't matter. I loved the experience. I loved eating down in the basement before the meal with the staff, serving in the dining room and then going back to the kitchen and bantering with the cook and the other waitresses. I loved the bus boys too but that's another story. And I probably loved it because I knew I wouldn't be spending my life waiting tables. Perversely, I loved the fact that people showed their real colors. If I suddenly became invisible to certain people when I became a waitress, they plummeted in my opinion as well.

But the phenomenon of invisibility continues to interest me. Thumbing through the *Everyman Guides, Restaurants of Paris*, I came upon an excerpt from an autobiography by French caricaturist Jacques Faizant in which he describes his experiences as a waiter when a young man. In a humorous scene he tells about the day a customer admired the way he was holding his plates. Gratified by this praise, he decided to show off a bit, and returned to his client's table, laden down with seven plates of jam on each arm, fourteen plates in all, which he proudly displayed to the client and his guests. "But," he wrote, "crowds are fickle. They had resumed their conversation about contemporary art and were no longer interested in my professional acrobatics."

I noticed a similar phenomenon during my brief but extremely educational stint as a cloakroom attendant at the Fleur de Lys restaurant in San Francisco. This is the place where I went with the curtains, remember? Every once in a while I was called up from my downstairs coat-and-hat lair to go into the dining room to sell cigarettes (remember the days of smoking in restaurants?). If I'd been a cigarette machine, it would have been the same. I didn't exist other than as an extension of my wares. *Quelle découverte* for the college graduate that I was! As the evening went on and the finely dressed customers from the higher echelons of San Francisco society laughed and joked and smoked and drank and lingered at the table, I placed private bets with myself on how long it would take the last table to leave. I wondered if they knew how tired we were and how much we all wanted to get out of there (perhaps I'm only speaking for myself here . . .) and then realized they didn't care! And why should they? It was our job.

That experience however gave me more sympathy for the server; even today when sitting at the last table in the restaurant, I can't help but glance at the waiter or waitress to scrutinize his or her thoughts. Does he or she want to leave?

That's how you spy a real professional. A professional waiter will never let you know that he has anything else to do in his life except be there to serve you.

I obviously had not reread my George Orwell *Down and Out in Paris and London*. Orwell, who worked as a dishwasher in Paris restaurants for a time, observed the staff with a cold eye, and wrote: ". . . never be sorry for a waiter. Sometimes when you sit in a restaurant, still stuffing yourself half an hour after closing time, you feel that the tired waiter at your side must surely be despising you. But he is not. He is not thinking as he looks at you, 'What an overfed lout'; he is thinking, 'One day, when I have saved enough money, I shall be able to imitate that man.' "

Many waiters, in fact, are plain tired! "When I started out, I worked fifteen hours a day," Jean-Pierre Athanase, the floor director of Chez Lipp, told me. "I didn't have my first vacation until ten years after I started working and I didn't spend any time with my children until they were almost adolescents." Athanase concedes that he may be part of a dying breed. "Young people now work as waiters four or five years and then they go into something else." Many longtime French waiters, proud of their work, proud of the establishments they work for, and proud of the high standards they hold, have told me the same tale of woe. Waiting tables now is becoming a job whereas it used to be a profession.

A ballet

You may be more immersed in your conversation and food than anything else, which is as it should be when you're in a restaurant, but if you get a chance to look at what's going on behind the scenes, you'll see that in the best of cases the actions of the *serveurs* resemble a ballet where all the movements are perfectly coordinated. In the worst of cases, says journalist Judy Fayard, an inveterate Paris restaurant-goer, "they wander around the room like little lost penguins. They don't know what they're doing. The whole problem is that restaurants can't afford good help so they get inexperienced young kids they don't even bother to train." Remi Picaud at the Union Syndicale de Chambre de Paris confirms that the average age of the waiter now is under thirty and that there are hardly any waiters over the age of fifty left.

Fortunately there are exceptions. Christian David, maître d' of Le Grand Vêfour, one of the finest and most beautiful restaurants in Paris, heads a staff of twenty and has his own firm ideas about what conditions are indispensable for good service in a restaurant. And it's a good thing he does, for Le Grand Véfour is not just any restaurant but a part of French history and classified as an historical monument. When you go to Le Grand Véfour, which began as the Café de Chartres in 1784, you join a long line of illustrious visitors, among them Lamartine, Colette, Cocteau, and Simone de Beauvoir.

A restaurant needs to live up to its history. For David, an indefatigable forty-six-year-old who has been in the restaurant business almost all his life, the fact that he and chef Guy Martin, whose creative cooking recently won a third star for Le Grand Véfour, saw eye to eye on this point was fundamental. "Both of us were very receptive to the history and the charm of this place. He brought the force of his cooking creativity to the kitchen and it was clear to me that the dining room had to be in sync with the rigor of the cuisine. Since I am a perfectionist, my goal is to see that this is done."

He ticked off a list of what to him are the four cardinal points for the success of a restaurant and for good service. First of all, he said, you need "a good correlation" between the kitchen and the dining room. "You have to be able to ask the kitchen for whatever it is you want. You need solidarity between the chef and the staff." Secondly, it's important to have pleasant phone manners as this is the first contact you have with the client. (I can verify the phone manners at Le Grand Véfour because in spite of my rather unclear initial request to speak to Christian David, the person who answered was courteous and professional.) In the third place, the welcome is a crucial moment. "When the guests arrive, the chef, the hostess and I are there to greet them," says David. Finally, he says, "an excellent atmosphere in the dining room with extremely motivated waiters who have a natural *gentillesse*" is a must.

David told me that the wait staff is proud to be able to tell clients about the food Chef Guy Martin has made on any given day and that all of them have tasted the food and can talk about any dish because there is a tasting almost every single day. I appreciate this latter point because I absolutely hate it when I ask, for example, a *commerçant* about his or her wares and the person is unable to tell me where the item in question came from or how to prepare it or anything about it. If you're in the food business and don't know what you're selling, why sell it?

Coke in a carafe

I couldn't wait to ask Christian David my "Coke question." "When you have exquisite cuisine like that concocted by Chef Guy Martin and a customer orders Coke to go with it, what do you, the maître d'hôtel, do?" He seemed surprised by my inquiry. "Everything's a question of mentality," he said. "We have to respect the client's taste. Since people like Coke and clients ask for it, we must give it to them. The client didn't come to get a lecture from us about the marriage of food and drink. Some people, including French people, don't drink wine but like Coke." The only difference is that at Le Grand Véfour, Mr. David will have your Coke put in a carafe as opposed to serving it in a bottle or a can. *Tout de même!* "It's almost the same color as wine and by serving it in a carafe, you avoid calling attention to it." Okay, maybe I'm a snob, but I have to admit that I am shocked that anyone would drink Coke with the refined food Guy Martin or any other top French chef is serving, but of course, in terms of not being a lesson giver, Christian David and his staff are on the right track. Each to his own!

The policy has worked. Le Grand Véfour, which for years had coasted along on its reputation, is now a place where customers feel welcome and not one where they're going to cower because they are being pushed around. "The client is paying," says Christian David. "And the client is right. We don't have the right to be snobbish."

In fact, the emphasis placed on making the client feel welcome is no accident. "It's a long-term policy for the image of our restaurant both in France and abroad. What we have done is reverse the order of things. Some clients are intimidated when they come to Le Grand Véfour. Our pleasure is to welcome them and to make them feel at home. If they want to talk and if they want to know about certain dishes, we're able to tell them what they want to know. If they ask me about the truffle, I can tell them almost everything. But there's not one day that we aren't opening a culinary dictionary or trying to find out more. Respecting people is an *état d'esprit.*"

By the same token, David, like any good maître d'hôtel, is a master at placing people at tables. There may be two or more tables of bankers, journalists, or Japanese on any one day but they won't find themselves seated near each other. Such is the art of discretion.

The morning Christian David is talking to me is a beautiful sunlit one. As we converse on the upper floor of Le Grand Véfour where there are only three tables, I peek through the curtains of the low eighteenth-century room out onto the Palais Royal where the sun is shining on the almost deserted garden. It is truly a magical place to work and it works its magic daily. David tells me he is tired and hasn't been sleeping well and indeed he does look a bit worn out. "But when I start the service, I don't feel the fatigue anymore. It's like acting. Once you're on stage, you are performing and forget everything else."

What waiters find funny or strange or frustrating

Clients may think waiters are everything from "nice," "helpful," "friendly," to "rude," "brusque," and "arrogant," but waiters have their opinions of clients as well. When they've been around as long as fifty-two-year-old Jean Demol, a waiter at the Brasserie Balzar for the last twenty years, they've seen just about everything. As Brasserie Balzar is in the Latin Quarter, Demol has seen plenty of American tourists drinking Coke with French food. Demol is no longer shocked. He calls Coke "the American Beaujolais." Still, he does find it, *"trés bizarre"* that the dinners in question will down three or four Cokes and then ask for artificial sugar with their coffee! These things he finds strange but he doesn't say a thing. However there are certain limits at which he draws the line—and then he has to speak up.

"One night an American came in and ordered a Chateaubriand with a *sauce béarnaise*. When I handed him the plate, he then asked me for ketchup, which he started pouring on the *béarnaise!*" Did Demol let him go ahead and desecrate this most French of sauces? *Bien sûr que non!* "I playfully grabbed the ketchup and explained that the *béarnaise* is a very special sauce and it is eaten as is. I said it in a humorous way and he laughed." The American clearly didn't appreciate that the *béarnaise* is a hot sauce made with white wine, vinegar, shallots, tarragon, and spices to which egg yolks and butter are added and that it is a treat to have one that is made well. It needs no ketchup or mustard or anything else!

The French also make mistakes. "One night a fellow came in with his family whom he obviously wanted to impress and ordered a bottle of Munster. I said, "Of course, and with that I'll give you a nice Sylvaner cheese." By saying it this way, the fellow realized his mistake and saved face.

"These things make me laugh," says Demol, who considers himself lucky to work in a veritable Parisian institution frequented by politicians and professors and students and celebrities, many of whom have been coming for years. "People feel at home here. It's a place with a soul."

But who gives a restaurant or café or brasserie its soul? The people who go to it and the people who work in it. If the waiters don't have it, the place won't either. There aren't a lot of spots like that left. If you find one, give your waiter a *big* tip (see my tip on tipping below). He deserves it.

 INTERVIEW WITH PHILIPPE

HWR: Do you notice much difference in the service in the U.S. and the service in France?

PhR: There's one thing that fascinates me in the U.S. Why do the waiters keep filling up your water glass? I don't want it. I don't brush my teeth when I'm in a restaurant.

A TIP ON TIPPING

The question most tourists ask is: to tip the waiter or not to tip? The answer to this is that unlike in the U.S. where the service is not included in the bill, in France a 15 percent service charge is almost always included in the bill you pay. This 15 percent is then distributed among the various personnel. The tip, however, is not included and is entirely up to the client. If the service is good but nothing special, you don't leave anything. If you are very especially pleased with the service and wish to leave a tip, you can. Regarding how much: in a restaurant where your bill is two hundred French francs, you might leave between ten or twenty francs. If your bill is two thousand francs, you'd be more likely to leave fifty or a hundred francs. No matter what you leave, remember that it's worse to leave a measly tip (one franc or a few centimes) than no tip at all.

The minimum wage for a wait person is a little above forty francs an hour; the tendency these days is for employers to give a flat salary instead of the included 15 percent service charge. Most waiters say this is an unfortunate trend for it hardly incites initiative.

12

Restaurants and Restaurant Manners

Bistros, brasseries, and restaurants · Be your own restaurant critic · The serendipity factor · Memorable meals, both good and bad · Cafés · Screw-you smoking · Splitting the bill and other nit-picking matters · Dogs and children in restaurants · Some other cultural differences · How to eat eyes, slice cheese, and send back wine

Since I make and eat French food every day of my life, and Philippe, for business, often eats out in fine French restaurants for lunch, when we go out to dinner in Paris we very often head to a Chinese, a Japanese, or an Indian restaurant. If we do go to French restaurants, I always order things I don't make at home—*ris de veau*, or *tête de veau*, for example.

Unlike friends of mine who are completely on top of the French restaurant scene, going to them several times a week, tracking the progress of familiar ones and checking out the new ones within a week of their opening, when I do go to a French restaurant I tend to stay with the tried and true. Of course I have my definite idea of what I like in a restaurant and gravitate toward restaurants of a certain type.

The type? An unpretentious place that serves good rustic French food and respectable wine in a setting that hasn't been too tarted up and isn't cold. Or to put it another way, a warm and friendly place! The waiters have been with *la maison* a long time and know what they're doing. They're professional but not obsequious, friendly but not overfamiliar. They don't, for example, congregate in little groups wondering what to do while ignoring your requests nor do they reach in front of you to get your plate. Fellow diners are friendly but not inquisitive, considerate when it comes to things such as not blowing smoke in your face (if they didn't smoke at all it would be even better but let's not dream) or letting their dogs (yes, many French restaurants allow dogs!) climb all over your feet. Does this exist? Of course!

Take the Balzar on the rue des Ecoles in the Latin Quarter, for example. There was a great flap about the Balzar, Lipp's less snobbish sister restaurant, when the Brasserie Flo chain took it over in 1998 but so far it seems to have retained its authenticity and personality. It's got good food and wine, and capable waiters who serve the white-linen-covered tables efficiently and with good humor. When you sit there, you feel that you are briefly "home." For me this is the criterion of a good place to eat.

Bistros, brasseries, and restaurants

A few definitions here. A bistro, from the Russian word for "quick," is a place you can get good homey food. A brasserie originally was a place to drink beer and has become a place where you can get anything from a sandwich to a *choucroute* at any time of day or night. A restaurant is a place where you have a more formal meal (not a salad and a glass of water!) at defined hours. In France, that means you don't drop into a restaurant at four in the afternoon and expect to be served. On the other hand, you can certainly order a salad or a *choucroute* in a brasserie at that time of day. Even in a brasserie, you'll see that some tables have white linen cloths on them and other tables have nothing. If you only want a sandwich or a very light meal, stay away from the white linen. That's for a real meal. And as I explained, for the French, a real meal is not a sandwich or even a quiche.

Be your own restaurant critic

There are many welcoming bistros and restaurants in Paris, each with its own history, its own feeling. Paris has its world-famous restaurants run by great chefs, it also has restaurant chains where the food ranges from so-so to horrible. It has its share of ordinary restaurants, some of which are good and even undiscovered by food writers, although that generally doesn't last very long.

There are a multitude of guidebooks to help you wade your way through all this choice but still in the end you have to decide for yourself. You may be attracted to what is trendy or "in," you may be more interested in the decoration than the food, you may not go to a restaurant unless you've read about it in a newspaper or magazine, you may be obsessed with getting value for money, or you may only be interested in three-star restaurants. (By the way, in case you think that all Frenchmen frequent three-star restaurants [three stars is the respected Michelin guide's top rating], you're wrong. I read somewhere that 93 percent hope that someday they will dine in one of these establishments. Dining in a three-star restaurant is beyond the reach of most people. Three-star restaurants thrive on the clientele of business men and women and tourists. I myself haven't been to that many.)

It's true that guidebooks and restaurant reviews are helpful. Keep in mind, though, that restaurant critics are people like you and me with their own tastes and their likes and dislikes. Make sure that your taste matches theirs! I agree with the advice of Peter Megargee Brown, a lawyer who published his own guide to 143 restaurants in ten countries. In his book, *One World at a Time*, he advises: "Be your own fearless restaurant critic and say to so-called experts, 'I know what I like. I'm over 21 and I say to hell with it.'" My advice would be: Try to enjoy the dining experience even if everything isn't perfect. Don't be so picky that you can't go anywhere. I have dined at restaurants with people who will never be happy no matter what you give them. They *start* the meal knowing they won't like anything. The Unhappy Diner is a sad case indeed. Isn't the whole point of eating out to have fun? Especially in France!

The serendipity factor

My good memorable restaurant experiences are tied to a kind of *je ne sais quoi* factor of serendipity. On a trip to Brittany I stopped in a crêperie in the town of Paimpol, famed because the French writer Pierre Loti wrote a book about the fishermen of the town called *Fishermen of Iceland*. It was a bustling port in his day but when I arrived at around noon, the place looked like an atomic bomb had hit it and everyone had run to the shelter. Not a soul in sight. I walked down one cobbled street and entered a pleasant-looking restaurant. Two smiling women served me and I ate a delicious crêpe all by myself, not minding being alone, watching a table of women friends laughing and enjoying themselves. That night, I ate, alone again, in the restaurant of a lovely hotel by the sea. The food was light and tasty and delicious but for some reason—the serendipity factor?—I didn't enjoy the experience as much. Sometimes simple things are the best, I find.

Other memorable meals at which the serendipity factor came into play include Philippe's and my wedding lunch at the centuries-old Coupe-Chou in the fifth arrondissement in Paris near where we lived at the time on the rue de l'Ecole Polytechnique. Although the food was fine, what stands out in my memory is the beautiful centuries-old decor and the warmth of our two families being together for the occasion. Another memorable meal: to celebrate my French citizenship, which I received in January 1995, Philippe invited me to the Pré-Catalan in the Bois de Boulogne. The food at the Pré-Catalan is delicious, the service professional, friendly, and discreet. The night we went it was snowing, something exceptional in Paris. Seeing the white flakes drift down was perfectly magical, especially in the Bois de Boulogne.

Those were special occasions, in the city. In the country, we have a favorite restaurant we like to go to on Friday nights when we're both tired after the week and I don't want to cook—and Philippe *certainly* doesn't. It's a simple nineteenth-century place with low beamed ceilings and a big fireplace. A perfect fire is always going, poked into life by the *patronne*, who also tends the bar and waits on all the tables. It's impossible to eat *à la carte*. There are three set menus with a *plat du jour* and of course it is expected that you will eat a starter and a dessert. This isn't the kind of place you go to eat a salad. A typical meal there might consist of a homemade terrine of whatever game there is, a fricassee of rabbit, and a selection of cheese or wonderful homemade desserts. All of this for 109 francs, which in Paris would buy you a crummy salad straight from the fridge. There's nothing I like to do better than go to this place when it's cold or rainy outside, take a table facing the fireplace, and sit back and relax. It's in no one's guidebook, it isn't chic, and I guess that's why I like it. It's comfortable and relaxing, and the food is fresh and good and prepared by the chef, who I can see working alone in his kitchen. His desserts are delicious. Philippe and I order a bottle of wine and feel the cares of the week dissolve with the first sip.

Serendipity is stumbling on funny experiences and taking advantage of them. I've always felt sorry for people who don't stray from their guidebooks for fear they might end up in some pit of a hotel or restaurant. The summer our sons were eight and twelve, a perfect age for children to travel, I find, we crossed France from west to east. We started from our vacation spot on the Île d'Oléron and crossed the flat region of the Creuse to get to Auvergne, that mountainous central part of France, which is where three of Philippe's grandparents came from. In the town of Pontgibaud we stayed at a hotel near one of Layfayette's castles. The hotel's most noticeable feature was a parrot that made "boing-boing" noises like a spring every time we crossed its path, which was often, since our feathered friend's cage was located at the head of the stairs to our rooms. When we sat down to the table of the hotel restaurant for our evening meal, Benjamin scanned the menu and solemnly ordered *foie gras* for his first course. We were astonished and surprised, not just because he was only twelve and *foie gras* is a sophisticated choice for a twelve-year-old, but because he was such a picky eater that it never would have entered our minds that he might actually like this delicacy. That experience was proof of his very French genes! Afterwards, on our way to bed, we passed by the parrot, who said "boing-boing, good night" (that's not true, its vocabulary was, sadly, limited to "boing-boing"), and retired to our cavernous rooms, which would never make it into *Architectural Digest*. It's interesting to reflect, all these years later, how those unplanned and unguidebooked experiences are the ones we all remember and enjoyed the most.

Memorable meals, both good and bad

Most of my memorable meals have been in simple unknown restaurants, "normal people's" restaurants with honest food and an ambiance I liked. I probably wouldn't make a special return trip to any of them for the food although it was good. What I liked about them was the particular moment I spent there, the people I was with, and the situation. A village restaurant in Auvergne, a country restaurant in the Eure-et-Loir, even the *routier*, truck stop (not a regular experience), are all places I like to go to eat and prefer to most Parisian restaurants because they feel "real" to me.

The late Ann Barry in her charming book *At Home in France* describes this feeling of the "right fit." Her rental car had broken down on the way to Paris and after finally getting rid of it, exhausted and famished, she looked for a place to eat. She recounted that she had never been in such a "nitty-gritty place" before. It was filled mostly with men who ignored her presence, and she ordered an omelette. "I wanted whatever was filling: an omelette, a *cheese* omelette, french fries. . . . The omelette—a huge, plump mound—was cooked perfectly, the cheese mellow. The fries were crisp and greaseless."

Unfortunately meals can go very wrong as well. One of the worst meals I ever had was right off the Champs-Elysées in a restaurant where a friend of mine and I ordered the ubiquitous *salade de Chèvre chaud*, goat cheese salad. I swear it was on the French equivalent of Wonder Bread, untoasted, and the *Chèvre* was not *chaud* but *froid*. We asked the waiter how he could serve such under-par fare, and he replied, That's what the tourists want. Please! I've also eaten in places where the food was fine but the atmosphere was so chilly that I would rather have been anyplace else in the world. Who needs it? And I've been in tony *à la mode* places where the decor was *très soigné* and all the "in" people were there—but the food ranged from blah to bad. Of course food in those places isn't what it's all about, thank God. But between you and me, I'd rather eat good food with nobodies than horrid food with somebodies.

Cafés

When I first arrived in Paris, I didn't frequent many bistros, brasseries, or restaurants. In those days, cafés were my favorite haunts, as they corresponded to my budget. I wasn't exactly George Orwell but like most young people, neither I nor my friends had money to go to restaurants. We either ate in really cheap student dives that would never get in anyone's guidebook but which were fine for us, or we went to cafés.

What a pity that the number of cafés in Paris has dwindled from 200,000 in 1960 to fewer than 50,000 now. They are an ideal place to gather anytime—in the morning for a croissant, at lunch for a quick sandwich, or in the afternoon or early evening for any kind of drink. At a café you can sit for hours on end watching the world go by. In my first days in Paris I would stand up at the counter in a café eating a Camembert sandwich and drinking a glass of red wine and thinking of how incredibly Parisian it all was. (I don't think that many Frenchwomen actually do that—they are more probably eating a salad and drinking a glass of mineral water to *garder la ligne*, keep slim. *Ligne*, by the way, is the French word for "figure." I love the idea of a line and of "watching one's line" or keeping one's figure, *garder la ligne*.) The café has always been the quintessential Parisian institution. Writing in the mid-1800s, Donald Grant Mitchell in his book *Fresh Gleanings, or A New Sheaf from the Old Fields of Continental Europe* concluded that "to go to Paris without seeing a café would be like going to Egypt without seeing the Pyramids or going to Jerusalem without seeing the Holy Sepulchre."

Most of us associate the Parisian café with the famous artists and writers who frequented them. Personally, when I think of the Parisian café, I think *Philippe*, for that is where I met him, at Le Select, on the boulevard Montparnasse right across from La Coupole. How romantic to meet my future husband at a place where Picasso, Cocteau, Derain, Matisse, Henry Miller, Ernest Hemingway and Scott Fitzgerald gathered to drink, laugh, philosophize, and philander. Of course I didn't know at the time that this person would be anything more to me than a new acquaintance.

Here's how it went: On a balmy summer night, a "kind of" a boyfriend who was, I think, only too happy to get rid of me, led me to a small table on the terrace where this handsome fellow dressed in a white turtleneck and blue blazer was sitting. After introducing us, our mutual friend then discreetly disappeared. Thus it was that I found myself seated on one of those wicker chairs on the terrace of Le Select, not really all that enchanted to find myself alone with my friend's friend. He was good-looking, that's for sure, but he had a sinister expression on his face, with the corners of his lips turned down. I now know that that is his basic expression. I call it his Paris face. It is a face designed to discourage panhandlers, beggars, con men, people asking directions, gypsies in the Metro, and kids washing wind-shields. In fact, the same kids who practically lie on my hood as they wash my windshield, unbidden, don't even *propose* their services to him. Sometimes I even envy that expression. Maybe in another ten years or so I can work up something like that. But back to our meeting: how appropriate, how romantic, how Parisian, to meet in a café. By the time we finished our drinks, he'd asked me to dinner. By the end of dinner, at which we discovered a mutual passion for chocolate cake, we decided we really must see each other again . . . and here I am in Paris twenty-eight years later telling the tale! Still, beyond the nostalgia of having met Philippe in a café, I'm a firm advocate of them and fervently hope that Paris café owners will find a way not only to survive but to restore their cafés to their former glory and place in Parisian life. They're trying: you now find cybercafés, philosophy cafés, even cafés in which you can get a massage! I went to the No Stress Café one day with a friend of mine. It reminded me of New York with its modern, high-tech atmosphere. The food was okay but what interested me most was the massage chair, which I eyed with envy. Had someone else had a massage that day, I would have as well. But no one did. This is a far cry from Picasso and Hemingway but why not? *On n'arrête pas le progrès!* You can't stop progress!

Screw-you smoking

The restaurant, café, brasserie, bistro experience in France would by and large be pretty wonderful were it not for the smoke. From the minute you hit Roissy Airport, where the French can be distinguished from the Americans by their haste to light up as they wait for their suitcases (cough, cough) to the time you get on board to fly back to America, you are assailed by smoke absolutely everywhere you go.

A case in point: We have a bakery down the street from us, which has a few tables and a counter where people can order a pastry or coffee. Nice, *n'est-ce pas?* But 98 percent of the people who sit there sipping coffee smoke like fiends and their smoke wafts right over to . . . *the bread I buy every day*!!! My family will probably be the first in France to drop dead from secondary smoke caused by a *baguette.*

As far as restaurants and cafés go, I figure that when I go to a French restaurant, unless it is a top one and has excellent ventilation and /or enough space to have a truly separate and distinct space for nonsmokers, I will be smoked upon whether I'm in a nonsmoking section or not. I generally return from an evening at a bistro or a brasserie with clothes and hands and hair that reek of smoke even though I wasn't smoking! By the way, the nonsmoking sections of most French restaurants are generally located next to the toilets, far from the front of the restaurant. I have a suggestion for French restaurateurs: put the nonsmokers up front and the smokers in back, which is the way it should logically be. *Non?*

The smoking is bad enough in a restaurant; unfortunately it extends to dinner invitations in private homes as well. I can count on the fingers of one hand and even give you the names of the people who actually ask me if I would mind their smoking *chez moi.* (Sorry, all my French and American and other friends out there— now you know what I think!) I raise this point because in the States not only would you not consider lighting up, you probably wouldn't even dare to ask permission! No such problem in France!

As an American in France, you have to be careful about what you say about cigarettes or you will get the following argument: Oh, you Americans have become so rabid on the subject that people can't even smoke outdoors in your country. My pharmacist told me that while standing on a beach (therefore in the open air) in Los Angeles, he lit up a cigarillo and took a puff while enjoying the view. A jogger ran past him a good ways down the shore and then turned around and returned to harangue him about the smoke. "All I could understand was 'health, health,'" remarked the pharmacist, for whom this zealousness was proof that some Americans have gone off their heads. (Of course you will say that as a member of the health profession he should know better than to smoke but that's being a bit too logical. Incidentally, some of the worst French smokers I know are doctors!)

An American nonsmoker in France really only has two choices: shut up and leave, or be tolerant. The latter entails huge cleaning bills after every visit to a restaurant and regular trips to Lourdes to pray not to get lung cancer from all the secondary smoke.

So now you've been warned. There's nothing to do about it, so just sit back, relax, and enjoy your tobacco-tinged food. And for God's sake, don't complain. You are in the land of *screw-you smoking*!

But this may change. It's been said that everything that happens in the States comes to France ten years later, so there's hope that the antismokers in France, and there are many, believe it or not, may get some clout and some respect. But, for the moment, don't hold your breath—if you have any left.

Splitting the bill and other nit-picking matters

Splitting the bill when you're with a group of Frenchmen is no problem: you divide by the number of people at the table. Splitting the bill with a group of Americans can be an exercise in higher mathematics. I have been at occasions where one person said "I didn't have any wine" and another said "I didn't have dessert." The calculation is then done based on exactly what each person had. Not only is this boring, it is time-consuming. I prefer the French method. Obviously this means that you don't go out to dinner with people who are going to order caviar when you order *pâté* or the most expensive Bordeaux when your budget is more along the lines of the house wine. It assumes that you are all on approximately the same wave length or you wouldn't be together. Cheapskates and bean counters abstain! Of course, I've spoken to several French women who told me that splitting the bill with other French women can also involve higher mathematics and I've heard stories of bean counters among French men as well, which goes to prove one can't generalize—let's say though that *in general* you won't see as much methodical calculation with a group of French people as you will with a group of Americans.

As far as splitting desserts and, oh horrors, main courses, goes, this isn't done in France. This is different from the States where we have such huge portions that people sometimes share a dessert and no one thinks anything about. In France, it's seen as odd to ask for two spoons for one dessert although there are places that will do this without any (visible) fuss. Ordering a main course for two however is definitely on the no-no list.

Last but not least, there's the issue of coffee after the meal. This may sound like a detail but in France coffee is a separate course served after the dessert. Georges Lepré, former chief wine steward at the Ritz, told me a story about how coffee as a separate course was viewed by Americans in the States.

"I ran a restaurant in Pasadena for a short time between my

career at the Grand Véfour and the Ritz and I was very serious about wanting this to be a typical French restaurant with things done the French way. I gathered my young American staff and told them that we would serve coffee as a separate course after dessert. They kindly tried to tell me that they didn't think it would work, but I persisted. After only one evening, there were so many complaints that I had to give up the idea."

Coffee as a separate course is typically French. The coffee is very strong and served in very small cups. People who think French coffee is too bitter or too strong will disagree with me but I think that most American coffee isn't worth a separate course! Frenchmen associate *café au lait*, which many foreigners ask for at the end of their meal, with their morning croissant. It's a free world so you can do what you want. But if you look around you and want to identify who is French, look for the small expresso cups at the end of the meal.

Dogs and children in restaurants

In my experience dogs in French restaurants are treated with much more consideration and affection than children are. (A French friend of mine, upon hearing this observation of mine, opined that it might be "because French dogs are sometimes raised better than American kids!" We then changed the subject so that we would remain friends.)

I got onto this when our children were young and Philippe, who was heavily into his Rudy Giuliani phase, practiced zero tolerance. We would drive up to a restaurant and I would be happy not to be cooking, and contemplating a nice, relaxed meal with the family, when all of a sudden he would give everyone the evil eye and admonish the children to be *sage*. In fear and trembling (I exaggerate slightly), we would sit down at the table and I would spend the entire meal hoping that my offspring wouldn't have the childish idea of running around the restaurant or talking loudly. Are we having fun yet? Hey! However, I do recall seeing many dogs whose masters didn't seem to be upset that they were walking all over the restaurant.

Once, in one of those French fast-food places off the tollway, we ordered *frites*, French fries, for five-year-old David, who promptly doused them with sugar, having taken it for salt. Philippe said: "Now that you've done it, you're going to eat them." (Do I make him sound like a monster or what?) You don't know David, though. Instead of seeing this as a punishment, he thought it was great fun and finished every single one of those *frites sucrées*. To this day Philippe tells the story with admiration.

A girlfriend told me another children and *frites* story. When her kids were young, she liked to take them to restaurants to get away from the kitchen and have a kind of special occasion. But, she told me, the reaction was always either one of open hostility or coldness. One time she and her children were seated, in the back of the restaurant as usual, and had waited a full hour for their order to come. Finally her three-year-old, who had been patiently waiting, stood up on his chair and bellowed: *Ou sont mes frites?!* (*Where are my french fries?!*) Her take on the kid and restaurant situation in France? "In the U.S. they come to the door and ask the kids how they are, and when they get to the table, they pay special attention to them even if they are holy terrors. Here, if looks could freeze, the kids would turn into icebergs."

Generalizations, of course. Well, take it with a grain of salt or not, but in my personal experience I have very few fond memories of eating out in restaurants with my children in France unless it was at an Italian pizzeria. The Italians love children!

The French on the other hand love dogs, so much so that there is no problem taking one to a restaurant (well, most restaurants). You may want to find a baby-sitter for your kid but if you've got a dog, not to worry. "It's lastingly disgusting. It's as disgusting as it was twenty years ago when I first encountered it," says Janet Lizop, an American who has lived in France for twenty years and who has three children and no dog. As for me, I like most dogs unless they're vicious pit bulls, but I don't like dogs in restaurants. I have become resigned to the dog-in-restaurant situation and try to ignore it unless, of course, the dog is slobbering on me. But I, too, am shocked by the cohabitation of animals and food and wonder why the French are so tolerant when it comes to dogs and so uptight when it comes to children in restaurants.

Jean-Pierre Athanase at Lipp (not exactly a place one would expect to find children) agreed that the welcome to children isn't always what it should be. But he also wondered why anyone would want to take a child to a restaurant where there is smoke and noise. As far as dogs are concerned, he told me that at Lipp they have had to tell people not to let their dogs get right up on the bench and lick the restaurant's plates. If they see someone letting his or her dog do this, they offer the dog's owner and the dog a plastic bowl in which the pooch can continue its meal—on the floor. I forgot to ask him about cats.

Some other cultural differences

Even though the restaurant experience in this age of globalization is becoming uniform, there are still some notable differences between France and the States. In France, there's still a proper way to eat food. In the States, anything goes as long as you pay for it. In an article he contributed to the *Washington Post*, Martin Kettle, the Washington correspondent to *The Guardian* in London, observed: "To those who doubt that we are what we eat, compare the experience of restaurant dining on either side of the Atlantic." In an American restaurant, he observes, there is a "remorseless insistence on choice, more choice and still more choice" whereas in Europe it is the opposite. "You get what you are given and don't ask for more." How true. I have to say that I find the portions in the States too gigantic to be true and am convinced this may have some relationship to the fact that such a large proportion of my compatriots are overweight.

Even sicknesses related to digestion vary depending on the nationality: Americans suffer from acid reflux while the French feel the pain in their livers, *mal au foie*! I didn't even know I *had* a liver until I got to France!

How to eat eyes and slice cheese and send back wine

On a trip to the Belle Epoque spa town of Aix-les-Bains on the Lac Bourget, I lunched on the flowered terrace of a restaurant on the edge of a pleasant park. On the menu that day was fried fish from the lake, which I proceeded to order. When the dish was set before me, I looked down at the tiny *eperlans*, smelt, and saw that of course their heads were on them and the eyes as well. How else could you cook such a small fish?

In spite of this logical deduction (am I becoming so French?), I was a bit troubled. Does one eat the whole fish, eyes and all? At that point I'd already downed a couple of fish *avec les yeux* and the thought of eating another twenty-five pairs of eyes was a bit much.

I beckoned for the waitress to come.

"What's the custom here, *s'il vous plaît?*" I asked. "Does one eat the eyes or not?"

And, like my mother-in-law with the rabbit head, she replied, "Some do, some don't."

When my mother-in-law told me the same thing about the rabbit head, I instantly made the decision to throw it away. When the waitress told me that some people eat the fish heads and some don't, I decided to be in the group that doesn't and set about cutting the miniscule heads off of each fish one by one. It takes a long time to eat *la petite friture*, little fried fish, this way. I think that next time I'll consume the eyes.

The point is, though, if you don't know how to tackle things you aren't used to eating, don't be embarrassed to ask. You might find out that there is only one way to eat something. For example, it is bad form to cut off the nose of a triangular cheese and a crime to slice the Roquefort in such a way that the unlucky guy at the end of the table gets only the white.

As far as sending wine or food back to the kitchen is concerned, it's not a problem as long as you haven't imbibed half of your bottle of Bordeaux or eaten three-fourths of your *entrecôte* before making up your mind. Jean-Pierre Athanase at Lipp commented: "Sometimes people expect one thing and get another. For example, our *pied de porc* is reconstituted and so people expecting to lick the bones are disappointed. In that case, we take it back, give the customer something else, and chalk it up as a loss." He also said that it's very easy to spot professional complainers. Very exceptionally, he told me, Lipp will get a diner who is satisfied with absolutely nothing. In that case, after all efforts at diplomacy have failed, says Athanase, "I tell the person that we will pay for his meal but he must leave the premises. Enough is enough!"

By the way, if you go to Lipp you won't get Coke—because there isn't any! Lipp's late owner Roger Cazes decreed he would never serve this beverage with French food and even after his death, the restaurant continues to respect this wish. I'd wager that this is probably one of the last, if not *the* last, restaurant in Paris to hold out on this point.

It's fine by me. I like Coke once in a while but I personally don't think it goes with French cooking because it is too sweet, has too many bubbles and fills you up so you can't enjoy what you're eating. Just one person's humble opinion. Also, while I'm giving out opinions, as an American in gastronomic exile, I really don't like to see iceberg lettuce in French restaurants. When I was young, this was the only head of lettuce you could get. I was amazed when I came to France and discovered all the various kinds of salad greens (lamb's lettuce, dandelion, lolla rossa, frisée Batavian lettuce, chicory lettuce, mesclun, to name but a few). Even with a good vinaigrette, iceberg lettuce will never compare to a tasty *salade de roquette* or a tender *laitue*. I don't know about you but when in France I want *French* food. I can, and do, get my iceberg lettuce (with *gobs* of blue cheese dressing on it) and Coke back in the U.S.A. I like both cuisines—in their respective homes.

 INTERVIEW WITH PHILIPPE

HWR: I've noticed that over the past few years the restaurants you go to for business lunches get better and better. Can you really enjoy good food while talking about banking?

PhR: It doesn't bother me: I am not listening.

HWR: Can you explain why the French love food but kill the taste of it by smoking? And why restaurants relegate nonsmokers to crummy tables right next to the john?

PhR: Because it's depressing. They want you to be depressed that you don't smoke.

HWR: Ah . . . now I understand. In France I have noticed that people don't share food like we tend to in the States. What do you think about people who share food in restaurants, i.e., who order one dish for two?

PhR: If they can't afford a bill for two, only one should go.

HWR: What about doggy bags?

PhR: By Latin standards, it's very vulgar and the contrary of being *grand seigneur*. It means "I want what I paid for." It's the same thing as calculating exactly what you ate when you split the bill with someone.

HWR: You mean you don't like the idea of "Dutch treat"?

PhR: When you see the cuisine the Dutch have given the world, you understand. It's no wonder that the Dutch, who drink café au lait throughout the meal, even if the meal is a delicious confit du canard, gave the world the Dutch treat.

SOME TIPS:

....

On ordering: I used to dawdle about ordering in Paris restaurants but my husband put a quick stop to that. The reason: if you don't order when the waiter comes, you might not see him for another half an hour. That depends on the restaurant, of course, but I've noticed that if you can be ready to order when the waiter comes, it's a big advantage.

On sharing dishes: Unheard of. Viewed as cheap.

On taking kids to a restaurant: Why not, if they're well behaved? You should know, though, that the French definition of "well-behaved children" is not quite the same definition we Americans give (although I can tell you I've seen some pretty rambunctious French children in restaurants . . .). Unless they are French kids and used to long sit-down meals, it is best to take your kid to a café or a brasserie at first.

On taking dogs to a restaurant: Ask first, especially if it's a high-class restaurant. Otherwise, there's generally no problem.

On taking your cigarettes and cigars to a restaurant: No problem in most places.

On the non-smoking, *nonfumeur*, section: Yes, it exists. Just don't be surprised to find it in the back of the restaurant near the toilet. If you want to get up front with the good view and all the fun, you'd better start smoking.

On where to put the bread: The French put it right on the tablecloth.

On the answer to "Where's the butter?": Butter does not come with the bread because butter is seen in relationship to what you eat with the bread, i.e., bread and butter with radishes, bread and butter with oysters. There's a definite advantage to this: if you sit there filling up on bread and butter before a French meal, you'll never make it through!

On drinking coffee: Coffee is a separate course served after the dessert.

On drinking coffee with milk: Coffee with milk, or *café au lait*, is what the French drink for breakfast. It's often served with a croissant or a buttered baguette, which some people dip into their coffee. After meals, though, they drink a small cup of espresso with or without sugar—but without milk.

On ordering decaffeinated coffee: One American told me it doesn't exist in French restaurants. It does and many people order it. It is called *café décaféiné*. Order "oon daykafeenay" or "oon dayka" for short.

On how to deal with a snotty waiter: Call the manager.

On how to reward a wonderful waiter: Give him or her a big smile and a big tip.

On how to negotiate a Turkish toilet should you be unlucky enough to be in a restaurant that still has one: Men don't need any advice on this. The only thing I can tell women is: don't even attempt it if you're wearing a long coat or a long skirt. It's *very* difficult.

13

Big Mac

Le Big Mac · French fast food and street food · Incorporating food from elsewhere · The end of taste buds? · The low-fat trend · The French paradox · Antiglobalization

Le Big Mac—a symbol of globalization and the end of French food

No three words could embody such a symbol of globalization and banality as does le Big Mac, the French name for a McDonald's hamburger. For the French, a Big Mac isn't a harmless hamburger. It is the end of French food—which equals the end of French culture and the French way of life. How telling that when French farmers, led by militant José Bové, got mad about American reprisals against the French for their refusal to accept beef with hormones, they chose to sack a McDonald's under construction as a potent symbol of *la mal bouffe*, bad eating.

In fact, the Big Mac represents many things to many people in France. To many, mainly older, French people it represents the antithesis of French cooking. How strange, they think, this object you can hold in your hands, squirt catsup on, and consume in two minutes. One French sociologist told *Le Monde*, the

French daily newspaper, that in surveys taken of people going into or coming out of McDonald's, he was struck by the justifications the adults launched into for being there, saying it was their first and last time. "You would think they had been to a porno film," he observed. Kids on the other hand love McDonald's and the freedom of not having to sit down to the family table and not having to eat with a knife and a fork.

The older generation is not by any means positively and unilaterally against McDonald's. Jean-Pierre Athanase told me that he takes his grandchildren to McDonald's from time to time "but I also give them *foie gras* and believe me, they can tell the difference!" French chef Bernard Loiseau explained on French TV that he didn't think that McDonald's was the absolute evil and he had even taken a leaf from their book and made his own restaurant more welcoming to children. This being said, you can bet your bottom Euro that neither one of these men would consider eating a McDonald's on a daily basis!

French fast food

If the entire French nation isn't horrified by fast food, it's because the French have always had their own in various versions and in the various regions. What could be more Parisian than the *sandwich jambon beurre* which at its best has a slice of fresh, tasty ham inside a crunchy baguette on which delicious farm butter has been spread. At its worst, the bread is stale, the ham has gristle and the butter is rancid. Many people say that if McDonald's has made such inroads in France, it is because the *sandwich jambon* served in cafés was often substandard and expensive; both young people and people on the run were glad to find an alternative.

In Brittany the quintessential fast food is the crêpe, a thin flat pancake. People eat them all over France. You can eat your crêpe in a crêperie and make a meal out of it with a bowl of cider, or you can buy it from a stand in the street and eat it as a snack.

In Alsace, I love the *flammenküche*, a flavorful tart covered with cream, onions, and bacon. A friend and I discovered this one evening when we weren't hungry enough for a hearty *choucroute*: sauerkraut with sausage and bacon and pork and potatoes; or a *baekenofe*, an Alsatian meat stew that literally means "baked in the oven." So we settled down in our Hansel and Gretel surroundings— Alsace is so picturesque you constantly think you're in a story-book—and were delighted by our find. We drank Alsatian white wine with it. If you don't know Alsatian wines, try them. Reisling, the unpronounceable Gewürtztraminer, Sylvaner. I love them and if I had learned a tad bit more about the vocabulary of wine during my all-too-brief experience with oenologists, I would have the words to tell precisely why. But as you see, I'm not there yet!

. . . and street food

You don't see it so much in the provinces but street food is readily available in Paris and other major French cities, from the sandwich counter at the Prisunic to the Turkish doner kabab, which you see all over the city.

While there's plenty of street food available in Paris, when you get to the country, things become quite traditional and you may find yourself in for the two-hour lunch. Still, even if you find street food galore in big towns, there's a difference between France and the U.S. The difference is that in France people continue to make a distinction between food you eat in the street and a meal, whereas in the States the food you eat in the street *is* your meal—all day long. Snacking full-time the way we do in the States with our cars with their cup holders so we can nosh while on the road is not a feature of French life—yet. French movie theaters didn't used to have popcorn but now do and you see many more candy and soft-drink distributors in public places from schools and gas stations to the Metro.

Be this as it may, snacking is not yet a way of life both in the street and at home as it is in the States. One Frenchman told me he was amazed to see people eating all day long out of refrigerators the size of a truck. By the same token, some Americans who have lived in France for many years find themselves totally left behind when they go to the States. One of my single American friends who has lived in France for almost thirty years told me about a recent stay with her family in the States. "There were no sit-down meals. When any of the family members got hungry, they'd open the fridge to see what was there and take it back to eat in front of the TV." Finally, she told me, "one day I told my family I was hungry." My brother said: "That's terrible, we'll get you some food." And she replied: "No, I'm *long-term* hungry." She continued: "What I was trying to tell my American family, whom I love dearly, was that I wasn't just hungry for food. I was hungry to sit down for a meal. I *enjoy* sitting down to a meal. I look forward to it. I want to be at the table!"

My worst fears about Americans and snacking were confirmed in an article called "Snacking Today: Anytime and Anyplace," by Dirk Johnson in *The New York Times*. One woman told the reporter that she actually saw a person drinking a can of Coke at Mass! The same article said that according to one study only 24 percent of Americans eat breakfast, lunch, and dinner. Compare that to 80 percent of the French, who eat lunch at home and 90 percent who eat dinner at home! And although young people like McDonald's and fast food because they're happy to get away from the family table, as they get older, many of them begin to re-appreciate French food. I saw this in my own home with my two sons who were delighted to go to McDonald's when they were in their teens and now favor a *bonne bouffe*, a good meal, with friends in restaurants serving really good French food. A young press attaché at the French Health Ministry told me that when he was at university in Lyons, he and his friends imbibed more Côtes du Rhône than Coke and they loved to get together to eat the hearty traditional food of Lyons.

French people are always astounded when they go to the States and see the vast number of obese people. It's an unscientific point of view but marathon snacking surely must contribute to the U.S. problem. If the French get into snacking in a big way, *bonjour* the fat French.

Incorporating food from elsewhere

I would be more worried about the French adopting our snacking habits than I am about their penchant for some American foods that can now be seen everywhere in France. The French are geniuses at incorporating food from other countries and putting the French touch to it. Some obvious dishes are couscous from North Africa and chili from Mexico (I never thought I'd see the day) but how about brownies, which you now see in many French pastry shops right along with the *mille-feuille*? By the way, if you want one, call it a *brow nee*.

And, ready for this? Pumpkin pie . . .

The pumpkin pie goes hand in hand with globalization. We're all taking each other's holidays and food and adapting them. When I first came to France in the 1970s, I had a hard time explaining Halloween, which for the French was the night before All Saint's Day, a very solemn occasion on which you visit the graves of loved ones. How could I begin to explain the costumes and the carved-out pumpkins, not to mention things no self-respecting Frenchman would touch such as pumpkin pie and candy corn?

Things started changing a few years ago when I saw my first pumpkin decorating a store window. A year or two later I was astonished to see a huge carved-out pumpkin on a barrel of wine as I walked past the local wine store. Then it suddenly seemed that pumpkins and witches on brooms and scary goblins and ghosts stared out at me from every shop. And the French being French, the displays of everything from witches' pointy hats to specially made Halloween cakes and cookies were *trés artistique*.

But the clincher was the day I bought some of that ready-made pie dough (no comparison to the real thing, but I was in a hurry). On the left end of the package was a bat and a skeleton and a witch on a broom, in the middle the words *pur beurre* (meaning that the ready-made dough was at least made with real butter and not some kind of unidentified oil). On the right—and this is what astounded me—was a recipe for a *tarte Halloween à la citrouille*, a Halloween pumpkin pie. I thought the French *hated* pumpkin pie. Intrigued, I took a closer look at the ingredients which included *crème fraîche* and parmesan cheese and bacon among other things. I yelled at Philippe, who was in the front of the apartment:

"There's a recipe on the box for a *salty* pumpkin pie."

"Thank God for that," he roared back. "*Ce n'est déjà pas bon*," it's already not good. The least thing they can do to improve it is to have it be salty."

The point being, though, that pumpkin has now been associated with Halloween, and mark my words, it won't be long before the French will be eating *sweet* pumpkin pie. We'll probably even be seeing it in pastry shops right alongside the *tartes aux pommes* . . . and the brownie. Anyway, I'd give you the recipe but I don't really think any of my American readers would want to make or eat a *salty* pumpkin pie.

French favorites and the *plat unique*

What is the favorite food of the French? Snails? Frogs legs? Wrong. According to one poll, the first favorite is quiche lorraine (81%) followed by *steak frites* (79%). Next in line is the *pot-au-feu* (79%), *blanquette de veau* (78%), couscous (77%), paëlla (73%), pizza (73%), *gigot*, leg of lamb (72%), *saumon en papillote*, salmon in foil (69%), and *hachis parmentier* or shepherd's pie (69%). Other top favorites are *confit de canard, choucroute*, terrines, and curry.

If the French are worried about globalization, this poll proves they don't need to be. As my son David said when I showed him this list in a special issue of *Cuisine et Vins de France*: "It's normal. The French take things from everywhere and *ils les arrangent à leur sauce*, they make them theirs." Considering that couscous is a North African dish, paëlla is Spanish, and pizza is Italian, one can say that the French have always been global in their tastes. So should they worry about McDonald's?

Many of these favorites are *plats uniques*, one-dish meals. A couscous has semolina or crushed wheat grain, vegetables, and either lamb, beef, or sausage; *choucroute* has sauerkraut, potatoes, ham, and sausage; a *pot-au-feu* has vegetables and meat. In his book *La cuisine du bien maigrir*, French nutritionist Dr. Jacques Fricker sings the praises of the *plat unique*. For him, eating these dishes is an ideal way to lose extra pounds within a weight loss plan. "You take a big plate, put on it a copious helping of one starchy food, a good portion of a green vegetable, a bit of meat (or fish or an egg); finally, you embellish it with a bit of butter or oil. There you are with the ideal 'pyramid' united in one dish," he writes. The *plat unique* has all kinds of health benefits. Not only that, but it's good!

The end of taste buds?

As I mentioned in Chapter 4, "Foraging for Food," right under my very eyes certain products in France are changing . . . and growing. Yogurt is a good example. More and more often I see yogurts that are bigger than they used to be and filled with sugar and artificial flavors. You also see all kinds of ready-made foods such as salads in plastic bags, very convenient when you don't have time to buy or wash a real salad, but without much taste. Frozen food: all you want. You could literally never cook in France if that was your desire. In fact, in France, there is a panoply of food to choose from: frozen, vacuum packed, canned, and fresh. The person who likes to cook and has plenty of time can shop at the market and make traditional dishes such as *pot-au-feu* which require several hours to cook. Working women can stock up on frozen food as can bachelors like my son who have no time or inclination to shop. This is all fine and as long as all the frozen, vacuum-packed stuff doesn't shove out the real thing, why not?

There is one problem, though, and a charming ninety-year-old Frenchwoman I met one day while shopping at Picard, a chain of frozen food stores, expressed it perfectly. We started discussing the

merits of the various frozen food products in the store and her con-
clusion was: "Yes, there's an infinite variety of things to choose from
now. Fortunately I'll soon no longer be here because nothing has any
taste anymore." Isn't that sad?

Which brings me to the tomato, the best example I can find of a
vegetable (or fruit, if you prefer) with no taste. I remember reading
once that a famous French food critic made the rounds of top French
restaurants and judged them on only one criterion: their tomato
salad. That was a few years ago. I wonder what he would find now.
Food and travel writer David Downie comments that French tomatoes "taste exquisitely of nothing. They're just lifeless red blobs on
your plate." The tomatoes I buy at the market are, to be sure, pretty
enough and you can now get them all year round instead of only in
season—but who needs this glowing red object that has about as
much taste as my morning newspaper? If this is what is meant by
globalization, then I'm definitely against it!

I think back often to the elderly woman I met in the Picard store.
I bet that in her day she ate tomatoes that had taste. Taste is indeed
a problem, not only because many products no longer have any but
because many young people don't have taste buds! The younger generation of French kids, brought up by women who work outside the
home and who don't have time to stand around cooking up *bœuf
bourguignon*, is growing up without knowing the savor of classical
French dishes. They don't even have memories of food their mothers and grandmothers made. Philippe Escoffier, the head chef at the
residence of the American embassy in France, says his earliest memories are of the smell of the apple beignets emanating from the
kitchen of his home in the mountainous Savory region. "Children
now," he says, "are too used to fast food and school lunches to know
or appreciate the taste of really good food. Their taste buds haven't

been developed early on and they don't have the basis even to know what simple good food is." The world has changed, he says, and adds: "I'd rather eat a marshmallow than some of the imported mushrooms I find at markets."

The low-fat trend—no go

I have to give credit to the French, though. They didn't succumb in any big way to their momentary flirtation with "light" food. I'll never forget French actress Stephane Audran saying on French TV that she couldn't abide low-fat food. *Quelle horreur!* She said she'd rather have a little pat of real butter than a truckload of low-fat butter, and a little piece of good normal cheese than loads of low-fat cheese. Low-fat products exist and there is indeed a market for them. But, thank heavens, there is still the choice.

The French paradox

The highly touted French paradox, which refers to the fact that the French eat all kinds of foods high in fat and don't drop dead from heart attacks, isn't really a paradox. Think about it: a nation of people who sit down to the table to eat, who eat a bit of everything in moderation, and who drink red wine, which has been proved—in moderation—to be good for cholesterol. Add to that their intake of fruit and vegetables, which the British Heart Association found to be the highest in Europe, and the fact that until recently, they have not been as car dependent as we Americans are. All in all, the French have a healthy diet and healthy lifestyle. When I think of the French paradox, I remember a lunch with an eighty-five-year-old French woman who was as trim and slim and agile as a twenty-year-old. Her secret? "My doctor told me to drink a glass of red wine—Bordeaux—at lunch and at dinner." She does, and is going strong!

Antiglobalization

My personal antiglobalization effort includes going out of Paris on a Friday morning and stopping on the way at the farmer's house to buy eggs and discuss not just food but the weather and the crops and the farmer lady's grandchildren and general chitchat.

On a typical antiglobalization Friday morning, I get in the car and drive to the country, where I start to unwind around Gambais, the town made famous by the serial killer Landru who bought one-way tickets for his mistresses, then killed them and burned their bodies. There was even a film, M. *Verdoux*, starring Charlie Chaplin, based on it. I cannot drive through that town without thinking about the story!

Near Gambais is a pretty farmhouse on the left side of the road where the farmer's wife sells eggs, honey, and *confiture, foie gras*, and chickens and ducks when she has them, to lucky people like me who pass by. You drive off the road slightly and up her driveway. Her house is simple but impeccably clean. Swings outside show that she's been looking after her grandchildren. By now I have stopped often enough that we know each other and shake hands. She tells me she's worried that her granddaughter will fall in the pond so she has to look after her constantly. She leads me down to her cool, impeccably clean basement where her chickens and other fowl are refrigerated, and her jams, gooseberry and strawberry today, are lined up on shelves with a white paper-lace doily on top. She's out of honey and honey bonbons. I'm disappointed for my sweet tooth and for my husband's but console myself at the thought of our preserved waistlines. I tell her I'll get honey the next time around because I want to make *pain d'épices* and we have a serious discussion about what kind of honey I will need for it. Liquid? A strong or mild taste? Not too strong, probably. She then helps me choose a chicken: they're all about the same, she tells me, but the male chicken is more filled out. I don't know why but I choose the female. We emerge from the cool cellar into the daylight and shake hands. I drive off, happy to have my chicken but even happier to have had this exchange. What a difference between this excursion and going to the supermarket and buying some chicken under plastic.

And this is why I agree with journalist Martin Kettle, who writes that "food remains to this day not merely the staff of life but the very stuff of cultural identity and difference."

As long as the farmer's wife is there to tell me how long and even how to cook my chicken and is interested in how I'm going to make my *pain d'épices*, as long as there are markets with *fromagers* proud of their cheeses and who can tell you the best way to eat them, as long as there are people who view food not merely as something to put in your body as fuel but as something interesting and vital and precious, things will be all right. The day food becomes something you can't *talk* about with the people who make it or sell it will be a sad day indeed. I'm counting on the French to see that day doesn't come.

INTERVIEW WITH PHILIPPE

Already somewhat of a chauvinistic Frenchman (although he denies it), Philippe has become (God help us) a chauvinistic European!

HWR: My, you're looking in the pink of health!

PhR: Now that we have the Euro, I am global and you guys will be global too.

HWR: What does the Euro mean for Americans? How about our McDonald's?

PhR: The Euro will *kill* the dollar. [*He angrily swings his head from left to right, his pink face turning to a bright car-nelian.*] Regarding your precious McDonald's, now there will be a tripe restaurant (like Chez Paul) in every small town in America.

HWR: And baseball fields?

PhR: Will become arenas for bullfights.

HWR: And U.S. companies?

PhR: Managed by Italians.

HWR: And barbecues?

PhR: Replaced by boiling meat in water [*he chokes*], but only if the U.K. joins Euroland.

HWR: I can never tell when you are being serious or funny.

PhR: Globalization is not funny. You wanted it, you got it, but it will be *ours*.

Blanquette de veau Rochefort

The anti–Big Mac par excellence: This is a recipe for a family dinner on a cold winter day.

2 pounds veal rib roast with
   a bone or two
1 carrot
1 big onion
2 cloves
Bouquet garni (thyme, bay
   leaf, and parsley)
20 small spring onions
2 tablespoons butter

3 tablespoons flour
2 cups of dry white wine
Small mushrooms
   (champignons de Paris)
Nutmeg
Chopped parsley
2 egg yolks
Crème fraîche
Salt, pepper

(Cont.)

Boil the meat in one quart of water.
(Use best-quality meat and don't forget to add one
or two bones.)
Remove the white foam that forms at the surface.
Add 1 big carrot, 1 big onion spiked with 2 cloves,
and a bouquet garni (thyme, bay leaf, parsley) and
salt and pepper.
Cook for 1 hour or until tender.
(Very important—nothing worse than tough
meat—Ugh!!)
In another pot, plunge the spring onions into boiling
water (3 minutes).
In another pot, melt and slowly mix butter
(2 tablespoons) and flour (3 tablespoons) (this is called
a *roux blanc*) and slowly add 3 or 4 glasses of the
(strained) water in which you have boiled the meat.
Add dry white wine.
Add small mushrooms (champignons de Paris), spring
onions, the meat, pepper, nutmeg, chopped parsley.
Cook 15 minutes.
To make additional sauce, strain a few more cups of
the cooking water mixed with two egg yolks and
crème fraîche.

Place everything on a big plate: the meat in the center, the vegetables around it, the sauce on top. Serve with rice and plenty of white wine (the same you used for the cooking—use a good wine!). This is a really traditional French dish and one I adore when it is well done. It can also be horrible and many French people associate it with the grayish-looking blanquettes they had to eat at the *cantine* (school lunch). Serves 6.

Just in case I've convinced anyone that the world is already global, here's an "I love" list of things that prove the contrary:

What I love in the U.S.
- All breakfasts, whether pancakes with syrup, eggs and bacon and potatoes, or a tasty muffin
- The cocktail hour and all those goodies that fill you up and make you fat
- Wine by the glass
- No smoking in dining rooms

What I love in France
- French cheese
- French coffee

French Fried

- French chocolate
- The French dining experience in a restaurant (*sans* the smoke, of course) because you don't get rushed out for the second service. Once you're there, you're there!

Typically French—
Slow Food in the Provinces

*Kings and presidents · Slow food in the provinces · French
favorites and the plat unique · A little tour of eating in France ·
The pleasure of food*

Living in France has reinforced my conviction that food, the producing of it, shopping for it, thinking about it, and eating of it, remains paramount. After all, isn't this the country where in 1671 François Vatel, the Prince de Condé's chef, took his life when he feared that he wouldn't be able to serve the prince's guests on time? Upon hearing of his suicide, the guests merely murmured that he'd ruined their party. Although more and more open to new tastes from different countries, the French have a long tradition they are rightly proud of and are struggling to maintain in spite of globalization and industrialization.

Nowhere is this tradition of fine food more evident than in the provinces where the food you eat reflects the geography of the region you're in. The Beauce, with its flat rich grain-producing agricultural fields near Chartres, is France's breadbasket. Auvergne, which is poor and mountainous, offers a plethora of hearty food made from potatoes and onions and heartbreakingly tasty sausages. The *carbonnade*, a beef stew made with beer, is bracing on those cold damp winter days in the north of France, while the *bouillabaisse* with its combination of local fish embodies the essence of the Mediterranean. The cuisine of the Touraine and western France is as light as the skies French Impressionists liked to paint there: *tarte tatin*, pike fillet with white butter, a *plateau de fruits de mer*, or a *mouclade charentaise*, mussels in a cream and wine sauce, from the not-well-enough-known region of Poitou. Even evoking the names of these dishes makes me want to get out of Paris and hit the road.

Years ago I bought a book called *La Cuisine des Provinces de France*. On the cover is a luscious-looking stew in a warmly shining copper pot. Inside are recipes from each region, of course, but there are also pictures that evoke the scenery or the most famous monuments of each region. As I gazed at them, I would voyage in my mind to the north of France for onion soup, to the southwest for *foie gras* and *cassoulet*, and to the southeast for ratatouille, *tomates à la provençale*, and *soupe au pistou*. Why would anyone eat at a McDonald's when he or she could feast on a *spécialité du pays*?

Even Paris and the Ile-de-France have their regional specialties. The pot-au-feu is one of them. So before a little "tour de France," here's the recipe:

Pot-au-feu

This is a recipe for a cold winter evening with family and friends. The trick of it is to get the meat tender and not let the vegetables get soggy! This takes plenty of practice so if you fail the first time around, try again. And this is the place to say that *of course* the recipes we give are highly "adjustable."

1 onion spiked with 4 cloves
3 pounds of beef (top rib,
   silverside, shoulder: at
   least 2 of them)
1 pound carrots
A half pound of turnips
4 leeks

A branch of celery
Parsley
Bay leaf
2 pounds potatoes
2 or 3 marrow bones
Salt and pepper

Boil 3 pints of water with salt, pepper, a big onion spiked with 4 cloves.
Add meat, cover and cook gently for 3 hours or until tender (yes!).

(Cont.)

Skim foam every half hour.
An hour before the end of the cooking, add the
unchopped carrots and turnips with a branch of
celery, parsley, and a bay leaf.
A half hour later add 2 pounds of potatoes and the
leeks, thyme, and big bones with marrow (yum).

Serve on a large plate, with the meat in the center and
the vegetables placed around it. Save the cooking
water and use it (strained) with fine vermicelli pasta
for the next day's dinner. Eat the *pot-au-feu* with
French mustard (strong, the kind that makes your eyes
water), pickles (once again, dill, not sweet, and preferably cornichons if you can find them), coarse-grain
salt, and a lot of red wine. Serves 6.

Kings and presidents—from a *tête de veau* to ortolans

We know that Ronald Reagan had a predilection for jelly beans, and
Clinton prefers greasy foods. The taste of French presidents is, to say
the least, a tad bit more adventurous. President Jacques Chirac is
known for his gargantuan appetite and his preference for regional

dishes such as *tête de veau*, veal head. When asked what his favorite dish was, former French president Giscard d'Estaing replied, "Scrambled eggs," which had everyone a trifle mystified. *Scrambled eggs?* Surely this patrician president meant with caviar?

Of course the tastes of these presidents are plebian and their appetites pitiful compared to their illustrious predecessor, Louis XIV, an "illuminated glutton" according to Jean-Robert Pitte in his book, *Gastronomie Française*. Louis XIV's sister-in-law, Madame Palatine, describes one of his meals: "I saw the King eat, and this very often, four plates of different soups, an entire pheasant, a partridge, a huge plate filled with salad, a lamb cut up with its juice with garlic, two good pieces of ham, a plate full of pastries, fruit and jam."

The late president Mitterrand wasn't a king, though he acted like one, but when it came to being right up there with the best of them in terms of appetite, he was—until the very end. Journalist Georges-Marc Benamou in his book *The Last Days of Mitterrand* recounts an eerie scene at which the president, in his final agony from cancer, was partaking of his last Christmas dinner with family and friends. A gendarme presents a plate of a dozen ortolans, tiny birds that are illegal to hunt in France. There aren't enough for everyone and some of the guests decline not at all unwillingly "for," writes Benamou, "they know that eating them is an ordeal." Eating them consists of covering the head with a white towel in order to get the full benefit of the odor and then consuming the entire bird, guts, head and bones. Since the participants must make the bones crack audibly to prove they're not cheating and swallowing the little creatures whole, it is indeed distressing for those at neighboring tables who have to listen. Not for the squeamish. Mitterrand ate them all.

Slow food in the provinces

In my travels from north to south and east to west, I always try to eat as many regional specialties as I can (but rest assured, even if I had the opportunity to eat an ortolan, I wouldn't. I've always said that I eat absolutely everything I come across in France but this is beyond even my limits—not to mention that it's illegal.) The minute I leave Paris, I get into my "I'm no longer in the big city" mode. I feel relaxed as I head off into virtually any other area of France, not because I don't like the capital, far from that, but because living in Paris tends to be wearing. It's good to get out!

Eating regional specialties is also a way to celebrate and appreciate the diversity of all of France's various provinces. As for the food I find on these excursions, you can get bad regional specialties just as you can get bad food in Paris. A badly prepared regional specialty is more disappointing than eating a McDonald's hamburger, in my book, because you are expecting something delicious and nonstandard. One of the reasons standardized fast food like McDonald's has made such inroads is because you always know what you are getting. How sad, for the regional cuisine of France, which is basically a cuisine of necessity made from the ingredients that were at hand, is so flavorful when well prepared.

A little tour of eating in France: Lyons

Although I like almost every region of France I have visited, for some reason I fell in love with Lyons, which has often been called the other French culinary capital.

There's a "Lyons connection" in our family: Philippe got two degrees in Lyons, one in engineering and one in economy, and has always been greatly fond of the city. So it was that I had to hide my disappointment when he first took me there to visit in the early '70s. It was a dismal day and to me all the buildings looked gray and sad. The Saône was small potatoes compared to the Seine. Seeing this city he had raved about so, I really started having serious doubts about his taste.

Then we entered a *bouchon* with friends of his and I began to understand. . . . We ordered not a bottle but a *pot*, as they do in Lyons, of good Beaujolais (the old saw is that Lyons has three rivers, the Rhône, the Saône, and the Beaujolais, and it's true that its proximity to the gently rolling Beaujolais vineyards is part and parcel of its charm.) We then proceeded to eat our *andouillettes* and drink our Beaujolais and I quickly figured out why Philippe was enamored of the place.

Somehow the eating experience was different than in Paris. In Paris the experience of dining can sometimes be sophisticated or worldly or rushed; in Lyons it simply felt authentic. I liked the way that people obviously enjoyed their food and the seriousness with which they got down to the business of eating it. As Balzac observed: "One eats in the provinces without being ashamed of having a good appetite."

I even started feeling guilty about my initial disappointment. I've since been reassured to learn that I was in good company. Charles Dickens on one of his many trips to France in the middle of the nineteenth century, observed, "What a city Lyons is! Talk about people feeling, at certain unlucky times, as if they had tumbled from the clouds! Here is a whole town that is tumbled, anyway, out of the sky; having been first caught up, like other stones that tumbled down from that region, out of fens and barren places, dismal to behold! The two great streets through which the two great rivers dash, and all the little streets whose name is Legion, were scorching, blistering, and sweltering. The houses, high and vast, dirty to excess, rotten as old cheeses, and as thickly peopled." Dickens would have had to live another one hundred years to be able to revise his opinion for there's more, fortunately, than meets the eye in this secret city.

Charles Juliet, a contemporary French writer who moved to Lyons when he was twenty-two, writes that in the beginning years he would walk for hours in the dreary streets where, "veiled with gray, the houses, the sky, the forbidding faces sent me back to my solitude." But, as the years passed, his eyes opened and he found himself going from discovery to discovery, from old houses to monuments to museums to cathedrals. "When a trench for the metro was dug in my street, a sizable mosaic in perfect condition was revealed and I remember the emotion I felt at seeing this trace of a long-buried Roman presence buried five or six meters underground."

I soon became intrigued by this city I had so quickly rejected, and began exploring its various neighborhoods on my own. On one broiling hot August day, I boarded the cable car in the St. Jean district and rode up the steep hill to the Gallo-Roman archaeological museum. It was cool inside and dark after the blinding light of the afternoon so it took my eyes a while to get accustomed. It was there, in that museum, that I took the full measure of the history of this Gallo-Roman city. Right before me was the famous bronze Claudian Table. On it is the Emperor Claudius's plea for the Lyonnais's right to be represented in the Roman Senate in the first century. As I strolled through the museum, I had a view of the Roman theater on one side and underfoot, huge magnificent mosaics discovered in various Lyons houses and underground.

It was on this visit that I really *felt* the city. No one was more pleased than I on subsequent visits to see how much its urban landscape was changing, growing, improving. Now, only two hours on the TGV from Paris, you can literally hop on a train and be there for a hearty lunch and get back to the capital in time for dinner.

The most "typically Lyonnais" thing the city has to offer are its *bouchons*, small restaurants serving the traditional hearty fare of the region. *Mais attention!* As the owner of La Mère Jean pointed out to me, many of the city's restaurants call themselves *bouchons*, but there are only twenty left in the whole city. In 1997 the owners of the real bouchons formed an association called Authentiques Bouchons Lyonnais. If you see that sign on a door, go for it! And if you make the rounds of all twenty, which some people actually do, it's said that you'll never meet up with the same dish, or if you do, it won't be prepared the same way. Here's part of the association's charter, which promises among other things to serve such "popular" and "militant" Lyonnais specialties as:

Salad bowls of tripe, a salad bowl of *clapotons* otherwise known as 'sheep's foot in a remoulade sauce,' pig's snout, lentil salad otherwise known as the 'caviar du Puy,' various sausages provided they are from here, cracklings, warm sausage, cervelat . . .

In addition to that, heavier fare such as tripe gratin, "fireman's apron," quenelle, spinal marrow or "frivolites," hot pork products, "sabodet," poultry poached with vegetables, *pot-au-feu* . . .

Without forgetting the essential: *Cervelle de Canut* (a white cheese with herbs, cream, and white wine), Saint-Marcellin and Picodon . . . For the wine: Beaujolais and Côtes du Rhône in pots please, even if the pots are filled with liters."

Good-bye globalization! And don't eat for days before you dip into a meal of such Lyonnais specialties.

A not-so-solitary meal in Lyons

One night I made my way to a restaurant in Lyons where I sat down to eat *œufs en meurette*, poached eggs cooked in a brown wine sauce, an *andouillette gastronomique avec sauce moutarde*, chitterling in a mustard sauce, and *crème caramel*.

I had underestimated the sheer size of the *andouillette*. It was delicious but too copious for me. As I fiddled with it (the clean-plate lessons of my youth remain), I turned to the couple at the next table and asked them conversationally if they ate *andouillette* where they came from. I could do this since 1) I was alone, 2) they were speaking English, 3) they were on their dessert course and I hadn't seen what had come before and 4) a woman alone can make conversation more easily than when in a couple. Especially my couple as Philippe is not particularly drawn to speaking to strangers . . .

"No," replied the cheerful woman, who turned out to be Welsh. "We eat bangers but not that size," she said, indicating the *andouillette*, three-fourths of which was still on my plate. "And the insides aren't the same. We call that offal and after the mad-cow scare people aren't even eating liver!"

"The closest thing to *andouillette*," she said, "would be faggot with reconstituted dried beans."

Now *that*, I thought, sounds really disgusting and explains why I eat so many things in France that I probably wouldn't touch in any English-speaking country. *Faggot?* Indeed! I told them it sounded pretty offal compared to my delicious gastronomic *andouillette*. Excuse the very bad pun but by this time I'd had much more than I should have of my *pot* of Côtes du Rhône.

As I continued drinking and poking at my *andouillette*, the Welsh couple and I discussed the French educational system (the woman was a professor), which we agreed was rigid. The students she got from France, she told me, were the only ones who had a hard time working as a part of a team. Then we veered off to another topic: how the English would be amazed to see people eating or just starting to think about eating at 9:30 P.M.

Before leaving, the Welsh couple told me that they had dined at a vegetarian restaurant a few blocks away and it wasn't bad at all. Vegetarian, because, it turned out, the man was of that persuasion. I asked him how he fared in a city like Lyons where being a vegetarian is like being a teetotaler in a vineyard. Not too badly, he replied, but of course it's easier in places that are strictly for vegetarians. I bet!

The Welsh couple was followed by a French man and woman. The man ordered the same thing I did, and the woman, a *salade de roquette* and water. I couldn't believe it! First, a vegetarian and then a woman who's ordered only a salad in a restaurant.

What was going on here?

I couldn't bear it any longer and asked the woman, a dainty blond, why she was only eating a salad. She explained that that is what she does to *garder la ligne*. So while her husband wolfed down his heavy three-course meal, she sat there, slowly savoring her greens and sipping her water. By this time, I was about three-quarters of the way through my *andouillette* and had polished off more wine than was good for me and was thinking I should take a page from her book. . . .

Meanwhile, I asked the restaurant's patronne, a slim attractive blond, if it was rare for a woman to like *andouillette*, considering that it has a strong flavor and is rather heavy.

"I eat them all the time," she told me, "but that's because my great-grandmother made them." And, she added, "My two-and-a-half-year-old son *loves* them."

Ah! My investigation into what is typically French and hasn't been killed yet by globalization was progressing. A two-and-a-half-year-old who downs *andouillette?* Of course this shouldn't really have surprised me all that much. Two-year-olds in France also taste Camembert and all kinds of savory things. Maybe that's why their taste buds are well developed and why later on in life they are more gastronomically experimental than Americans are. But I hasten to say that the French do not drink wine instead of milk from their baby bottles! My son told me that when in the States, he was asked if his baby bottle had been filled with wine and if he drank wine. He was eleven at the time and totally flabbergasted to think that anyone could believe that French children drink wine other than the occasional taste offered by their parents on special occasions.

Contemplating these thoughts, I busied myself with finishing my *andouillette.* After all, if a French two-year-old could . . .

Nantes and a lesson in *beurre blanc*

For three years we lived in a suburb of the beautiful town of Nantes during which time I appreciated the lightness of the cuisine, the oysters, the *plateau de fruits de mer,* the fish served with a *sauce au beurre blanc.* The Loire-Atlantique, of which Nantes is the capital, is not really a gastronomic region but the food is good and simple, authentic and light. Nantes has a Breton influence too for it was formerly the capital of Brittany, which explains why you find those typically Breton specialties of crêpes and cider.

We lived in a big house in the suburb of Orvault. It was, unfortunately, the only time I have managed to live in a house in France. I did most of my everyday shopping in the village of Orvault but I made special trips to the Talensac market in Nantes to feast my eyes on the multifarious assortment of fresh fish.

One day, a member of the Orvault Welcome Club knocked on my door to ask if I would like to join them for some of their activities. Gym? A cooking class? When I found out that the cooking class would be on the famous *beurre blanc*, that mysteriously easy-looking but difficult sauce that elevates a fish from mere fish to an art form, I immediately accepted the offer. "*Beurre blanc*," wrote Sanche de Gramont in *The French, Portrait of a People*, "is one of the summits of French subtlety." The class was entirely in French and I was the only foreigner. For the *beurre blanc*, our instructor took out half a pound of salted butter, a mustard glass of vinegar (many French measurements are given in terms of a mustard glass and one never knows which mustard glass!), and a shallot. All I can remember about what she did was that it looked like magic and the class was, on the whole, stunned.

"A real *tour de main*," my neighbor murmured. I nodded my head, wondering if I would ever be able to reproduce the demonstration I had just seen. We took out our paper plates and tasted the *beurre blanc* with bread and drank tea because the person who was supposed to have brought a bottle of Gros Plant, the light white wine of the region, had forgotten it. In less than five minutes, we consumed the work of two hours (for she had also shown us how to make a *poulet provençal*), and was it good!

It's funny because I remember griping a lot when we lived in Nantes about how provincial it was and how there was nothing to do, and strangely enough, now only the good memories remain. In fact, looking back on it I can hardly believe the good fortune we had in terms of both the house we lived in and the baby-sitting situation. I only learned how difficult it is to live with a young child in France once I was in Paris. An incredible, incredible hassle. In Orvault our son Benjamin, a baby then, spent the days I was working with a wonderful neighbor who, in addition to her own brood of five, kept him and two other toddlers. Since she lived right around the corner, I could walk him there and back. Her place was immaculate and her life extremely organized. She sewed and cooked and shopped and gardened—and you'd better believe that at noon the whole family, including my Benjamin in his high chair, were around the table. (At night too, but without my Benjamin, of course.) One day, early on, as I was leaving, Benjamin started making a huge fuss for food. I was panicked but my baby-sitter's experience as a mother and especially as a French mother gave her a perspective I didn't have. "He can wait," she said calmly, grabbing a toy to distract him. No instant eating in that household! *On n'était pas en Amérique!*

Normandy and the *trou normand*

In summer the wedding season is on. Invited to several, we only made it to one, the wedding of my brother-in-law's niece. We were excited to attend because we had been hearing about the plans for almost a year. Held in the small Norman village of the groom's family, this wedding was going to be worth everyone's time. It was a three-day affair; the wedding ceremony and reception were followed by two more days of partying.

The Norman town we stayed in looked like it was straight out of *Madame Bovary*, complete with a mill, stone bridge and rushing stream, half-timbered houses, neat gardens, and a manor house.

· The wedding ceremony took place in a small seventeenth-century church in a nearby village. The bride was ravishing, the groom handsome, the respective parents puffed with pride, the priest young and *sympathique.* The ambiance, even inside the church, was joyful and noisy as people turned to greet each other and then settled down for the ceremony. At one point the young priest took a few oratory precautions, warning the congregation that a certain biblical passage that the bride had chosen to be read "should be viewed in the context of the times in which it was written." My attention, as usual when in church or any other institutional gathering, had been wandering but this got my curiosity up. What on earth could he be referring to? I soon found out when the reader got to a part in his passage that said essentially that the happiest husband is the one who has a woman who keeps quiet. A collective gasp of astonishment and a few chuckles could be heard especially since the bride is a successful lawyer and probably one of the last persons I can think of who would "keep quiet."

But on to more important things: food. The reception was held in a beautiful château and the dinner, which began at ten in the evening and went on well into the night and early morning, consisted of:

Fête de Salades Composées et Crudités Joliment Dressées

Savoureuse Charcutailles de Pays

Assiettée de Saumon Tranché et de Poissons en Terrine

Trou Normand

Canard en Magrets Sauce Vinaigrée de Framboises Fraîchese et sa
Garniture de Petites Pommes Duchesse sur lit de
Champignons en Fricassée et Tomate Provençale

Salade Verdoyante

French Fried

Fromages de nos Terroirs Assortis

Ronde Variée de Saveurs Sucrées en Bouche

Café et son Pousse-café

Soupe Tardive à l'Oignon

This menu is almost impossible to translate because the descriptions of the different dishes are purposely poetic and evocative. Suffice it to say that there were salads and cold cuts and salmon and fish terrines and duck with potatoes and mushrooms and baked tomato halves cooked with garlic and parsley followed by a green salad and cheese and various desserts, coffee and, much later on, onion soup. We missed the onion soup, which was served to those who were still there at six in the morning. As for the *trou normand*, it is a miraculous trick the Normans have invented so that you can go all the way through a meal of several courses without suffering indigestion. The *trou normand* is either a glass of calvados or a calvados sherbet which is served not at the end of the meal but in the middle of it, to enable you to get through the repast without major indigestion. I have a very sensitive stomach and can guarantee you that the *trou normand* WORKS. *Fantastique!*

Incidentally, the above menu looks like a ten-course meal but in fact was "only" seven, as the first three items on the menu were served as a cold buffet and the *trou normand* doesn't count as food.

By the time we were dipping our spoons into the *trou normand*, which in this case was cold calvados sherbet, the *fête* was starting to heat up. A waiter had broken a few sherbet dishes, my tablemates had moved on from a discussion of Americans and religion to the sublime art of the late untranslatable French singer Georges

Brassens. "His songs reflect a simple humanity," commented one guest (and I swear we weren't drunk). The music got louder with each course and guests who felt they'd been seated too long headed to the dance floor to let off some steam.

At eleven we were moving on to the *canard*. Meanwhile, the conversation at our table became more animated. We were now discussing the French writer George Sand, bullfights in Dax and in Spain, Americans and guns, the death penalty in the U.S. (the French have abolished it) . . . and for some reason, religion again.

All of this wining and dining and dancing of course was going on amid a cloud of smoke that anywhere else in the world would have brought out a fire brigade. Not only were there cigarettes but at one point my tablemate pulled out a long lethal-looking cigar at which point I thought I might do something dramatic. Instead, since I have lived in France long enough, I figured that's the price you pay when everyone is having fun. Besides, in practical terms, there were so many people smoking I couldn't stop them all even if I wanted to! So my eyes smarted and my lungs blackened and I thought: It's only one evening. I'll survive. And yes, in spite of the smoke, it was a lovely evening indeed.

And a ratatouille in Provence . . .

Nothing makes me think of the south of France more than a good ratatouille. First of all, if you can pronounce it, you get an award: *rat ta too ee*. Second, if you can make it right, you're doing pretty well, for although it looks simple, there are a few traps. The first one is that if your vegetables taste like cardboard, and unfortunately these days more and more vegetables do because the French are becoming like Americans in that they want aesthetically pleasing vegetables, your *rat ta too ee* will have absolutely no taste in spite of all the trouble you've gone to. The second trap is that some vegetables take longer to cook than others and if you aren't attentive you can end up with one big mess of mush. M. F. K. Fisher in *Long Ago in France* recounts how she learned to make a ratatouille:

> I learned to make ratatouille from a large strong woman, a refugee, not political but economic, from an island off Spain. . . . She cooked on a gas ring behind a curtain at the back of the store, and that is how I first came to ask her questions, because her stew had such a fine smell. She looked at me as if I were almost as ignorant as I was, and after my first lesson from her I bought a big earthenware pot, which I still use.
>
> The ingredients were and still are eggplant unpeeled, and onions, garlic, green peppers, red peppers (if they are procurable), plenty of ripe peeled tomatoes, and some good olive oil. Proportions are impossible to fix firmly, since everything changes in size and flavor, but perhaps there should be three parts of eggplant (and/or squash) to two of tomatoes and one each of the peppers and the onions and garlic. I really cannot say.

She then goes on to give a recipe in which she cooks the vegetables in the oven for five or six hours. This is different from the way I do it, but why not? (Her recipe also omits zucchini for some reason—another mystery.) The thing with ratatouille seems to be: whatever works. If you did it right, it comes out tasting delicious. Some people peel all the vegetables, some peel some but not others, and others peel them all! Some cook all the vegetables together, others cook them separately. This is the way I make it:

Ratatouille

2 onions
1 green pepper
2 garlic cloves
2 eggplants
4 zucchini

Several tomatoes
Thyme, parsley, bay leaf
Olive oil
Salt, pepper

**In a large pot with a few tablespoons of (good)
olive oil sauté chopped onions and chopped green
pepper with a couple of finely cut garlic cloves,
eggplants peeled and chopped, zucchini unpeeled
and chopped, and a few tomatoes,
cut in quarters.
Add thyme, parsley, a bay leaf, salt and pepper.
Cook gently 30 to 40 minutes.**

Goes well with rice or an omelette. Rosé wine goes
nicely with it. Cold ratatouille is also very good.
Serves 4.

Food note: this is a very simplified version; many people cook the vegetables separately.

One can, however, go overboard in one's love for this dish and one's tendency to throw in huge quantities of vegetables, for it expands. What happens is that you end up with ratatouille for days—or weeks. My brother-in-law once got an overdose of rata-touille. I think we must have served it to him for three days in a row on one of his visits. He was practically pleading with us not to do it again! No! No! Please—no more rat ta too ee!! I have since discovered that you can freeze it so that when you make a whole batch, you don't have to torture your family members and guests for days on end but can put it away for later (for other guests??!).

The Pleasure of Food

The French excel in a combination of many things: admirable chefs who create inventive, artfully presented savory dishes with the exceptional produce found in every part of this land, and a nation of guilt-free Frenchmen for whom food is associated with pleasure and taste and conviviality. Compare this to the American concept of food as evil calories that will enter your body and make you fat and unhappy.

"Think of the solemn silence with which a table of Frenchmen greet the arrival of a dish in a restaurant," wrote Sanche de Gramont in *The French, Portrait of a People*. "They might as well be in church." On her trips to France, my late mother always noticed the special air the French had right before sitting down to the table. "They look so happy and expectant, as if something very special is going to happen," she observed.

In the charming book, *L'Ami Fritz*, the Alsatian protagonist, Fritz Kobus, excitedly prepares a feast for his friends. He asks himself: "Is there anything as agreeable in the here below as sitting down to a well-served table in the antique dining room of one's ancestors with three or four old friends; and then, to solemnly tie a napkin under your chin, plunge your spoon into a good soup of crayfish tails, which perfumes the air, and to pass the plates while saying: "Taste this, my friends, you'll tell me what you think. . . . And when you take the big horn-handled knife to cut the slices of melting leg of lamb, or the silver fish slicer to delicately divide a magnificent pike in aspic jelly lengthwise, its mouth filled with parsley, what a contemplative look the others give you!"

The French love food but they especially treasure the conviviality of the table—at any age. Each year in Bréchamps there is a *repas de l'amitié*, a special meal for *les anciens*, the village's senior citizens. On November 20, 1999, forty-eight of *les anciens* (not really all that ancient, as I believe one qualifies for this status from age fifty-five) gathered at the town hall for their annual festive lunch. My mother-in-law, at age eighty-five, was the oldest person there that day. She left the house at noon to walk to the *mairie* and returned at 7:00 P.M. And in between that time here is what she and the others ate and drank:

Apéritif

Petits Fours Chauds

Coquille St. Jacques

Pintade rôtie à l'estragon et à la crème de morilles,
Roast guinea fowl with tarragon and cream of morel mushrooms

French Fried

Accompagnement de pâtes fraiches, *fresh pasta*

Salade

Plateau de fromages

Patisserie

Café–Liqueurs

Vins: Sauvignon, Bordeaux, Champagne

Seven hours and a seven-course meal. Now, that's called taking one's time. Is it possible, even thinkable, that the French, who routinely throw feasts like this, will someday go so global that they lose their taste buds and treat meals like pit stops? Will they stop the *repas de l'amitié* like the one in Bréchamps because the French suddenly fear getting fat or drinking too much or indigestion?

If that happens, and I certainly pray it won't, at least I can say that I was around when it was different, when the French honored the produce of their land, when families and friends still gathered around the table for meals that lasted hours and the company and the food were in harmony.

It is my fervent hope the French won't lose either their taste buds or their incomparable *joie de vivre* when it comes to eating and drinking. If they do, I hope they won't blame the Americans or globalization. Remember that expression from your childhood "the goblins will get you if you don't watch out"? Those would be my final words of warning to the French in this age when the goblins are globalization, standardization, banalization. *Défendez-vous!* Believe it or not, there was a time not all that long ago when we had regular family meals, mom-and-pop diners, and succulent regional food in the United States. It's hard to find originality now, hard to pin down taste in the monotony, predictability, and tedium of all those Howard Johnsons, McDonalds, Kentucky Fried Chickens, and Pizza Huts, food courts and shopping malls. Everything looks the same and tastes the same.

Traveling across the old highways of America in the 1980s, William Least Heat Moon laments the passing of authenticity. He writes, in his book *Blue Highways*:

Old Frankfort did nothing to prepare me for the new Frankfort that spread over the eastern bluffs, where the highway ran the length of one of those carnival midway strips of plastic-roof franchises. It was past noon, and I could have had lunch from any of two dozen frylines without knowing I was seven hundred miles from home. Maybe America should make the national bird a Kentucky Fried Leghorn and put Ronald McDonald on the dollar bill. . . . The franchise system has almost obliterated the local cafés and grills and catfish parlors serving distinctly regional food, much of it made from truly secret recipes. In another time, to eat in Frankfort was to know you were eating in Kentucky. . . . A professor at the University of Kentucky, Thomas D. Clark, tells of an old geologist who could distinguish local cooking by the area it came from and whether it was cooked on the east or west side of the Kentucky River.

That was America "way back when." If I wrote about Simpsons Café and the Normandy Inn in Shenandoah, it is because they are now but a wonderful memory of the days when Main Street in the small town where I grew up was still alive. Too many restaurants like this, which you could once find all over America, have been replaced by fast-food joints and the cafeteria at Wal-Mart.

So a friendly word of advice from a dyed-in-the-wool Francophile. *Attention, les français!* Don't let it happen to you. And don't blame someone else if it does!

 INTERVIEW WITH PHILIPPE

HWR: Do your roots vibrate when you hear the word "*truffade*"*?

PhR: Yes, it reminds me of the good old days when we were defeating the Romans.

HWR: No seriously, what does it do to you?

PhR: Seriously, it makes me want to eat this dish that evokes volcanoes, mountains, the black granite of the churches and even the black tombstones in the cemeteries of Auvergne, land of my roots. It reminds me of St. Pourçain wine and Auvergnat cheese, the best in the world. Will you make it for me again?

HWR: Don't you think it's really fattening? I mean, think about all that cream and all those potatoes.

PhR: Basically that is a very dumb question.

HWR: Watch out, Philippe, some people have no sense of humor when it comes to food or caloric intake.

PhR: So tell them to come to France. They can eat to their heart's desire and never gain a pound.

HWR: What?

PhR: Yes, but they have to walk a lot and they have to sit down to two meals a day and they have to eat them slowly and *enjoy* them.

HWR: Do they have to smoke as well? You know, when in Rome . . .

PhR: It would help.

*A *truffade* is a mouthwatering Auvergnat dish of fried sliced potatoes, with Tomme cheese, cream, bacon, and garlic.

Bibliography

Literature and Essays

Barry, Ann. *At Home in France—Tales of an American and Her House Abroad.* Ballantine Books, New York, 1996.

Bensoussan, Maurice. *Le ketchup et le gratin—Histoire(s) parallèle(s) des habitudes alimentaires françaises et américaines.* Assouline, Paris, 1999.

Bertier de Sauvigny, Guillaume de. *La France et les Français vus par les voyageurs américains 1814–1848.* Flammarion, Paris, 1982.

Brillat-Savarin. *Physiologie du goût (avec introduction par R. Barthes).* Hermann, Paris, 1981.

Bryson, Bill. *Neither Here Nor There.* William Morrow, 1991.

Coffe, Jean Pierre. *Le bon-vivre.* Le Pré aux Clercs, Paris, 1989.

————. *Au secours le goût.* Le Pré aux Clercs, Paris, 1992.

Daninos, Pierre. *Les carnets du Major W. Marmaduke Thompson—Découverte de la France et des français.* Hachette, Paris, 1954.

Dickens, Charles. *Dickens in France—Selected Pieces by Charles Dickens on France and the French.* In Print Publishing Ltd., 1996.

Dournon. *Le dictionnaire des proverbs et dictons de France.* Hachette, Paris, 1986.

Dumas, Alexandre. *Petit dictionnaire de cuisine.* Payot, Paris, 1994.

Erkmann-Chatrian. *L'Ami Fritz.* Hachette, Paris, 1950.

erniot, Jean. *Carnet de route.* Robert Laffont, Paris, 1980.

Fisher, M. F. K. *Two Towns in Provence.* Vintage Books, New York, 1983.

————. *Long Ago in France.* Touchstone Books, New York, 1991.

Gramont, Sanche de. *The French.* Putnam, 1969.

ames, Henry. *A Little Tour in France.* Penguin Travel Library, 1983.

Kerdellant, Christine. *Les chroniques de l'ingénieur Norton—Confidences d'un Américain à Paris.* Belfond, Paris, 1997.

Lazareff, Alexandre. *L'exception culinaire française—Un patrimoine gastronomique en péril?* Albin Michel, Paris, 1998.

Mennell, Stephen. *Français et Anglais à table du Moyen-Age à nos jours* (*All Manners of Food—Eating and Taste in England and France*). Flammarion, Paris, 1987 (Basil Blackwell Ltd., Oxford, 1985).

Nanteau, Olivier. *Portraits toqués*. Archipel, Paris, 1999.

Twain, Mark. *The Innocents Abroad*. Collins, London, 1920.

Wharton, Edith. *French Ways and Their Meanings*. Berkshire House, 1997.

Cookbooks and Guidebooks

Amor, Safia. *A chacun son café—Les cafés thématiques de Paris*. Parigramme, Paris, 1998.

Assire, Jérôme. *Le livre du pain*, Flammarion, Paris, 1996.

Barbier, Nina, and Emmanuel Perret. *Petit traité d'ethno-pâtisserie*. J. C. Lattès, Paris, 1997.

Bertinier, Jacques et al. *Les recettes des authentiques bouchons lyonnais*. Rhone Imp., Lyon, 1998.

Bocuse, Paul. *À la carte—Menus pour la table familiale*. Flammarion, Paris, 1986.

Colinet, Christine, and Helène Mathey. *Cuisine des provinces de France*. Gründ, Paris, 1981.

Constant, Christian. *Le Chocolat*. Nathan, Paris, 1988.

———. *Du Chocolat—Discours curieux*. Ramsay, Paris, 1999.

Courtine. *Le cahier des recettes de Madame Maigret*. Robert Laffont, Paris, 1974.

Eteneveaux, Jean. *Lyonnaise gastronomy*. La Taillanderie, Bourg-en-Bresse, 1996.

Freson, Robert. *The Taste of France*. Stewart, Tabori & Chang, New York, 1983.

Fricker, Jacques. *La cuisine du bien-maigrir, de la forme et de la santé*. Odile Jacob, Paris, 1994.

Gendlin, Frances. *Paris at Your Door*. Graphic Art Center Pub., Portland, OR, 1998.

Guillemard, Colette. *Les mots d'origine gourmande*. Belin, Paris, 1986.

Joseph, Robert. *French Wines—The Essential Guide to the Wines and Wine-growing Regions of France*. Dorling Kindersley, London, 1999.

Lepre, Georges. *Le Ritz—Magie d'un Palace et de ses Vins*. Olivier Orban, Paris, 1991.

Linxe, Robert. *La Maison du Chocolat*. Robert Laffont, Paris, 1992.

Malnic, Evelyne. *Les meilleurs accord gourmands avec le vin rouge*. Marabout, Paris, 1999.

Meneau, Marc, and Annie Caen. *La cuisine des monastères*. La Martinière, Paris, 1999.

Nolot, Pierre. *A la recherche des cuisines oubliées*. Berger-Levrault, Paris, 1977.

Pitte, Jean-Robert. *Gastronomie française—Histoire et géographie d'une passion*. Fayard, Paris, 1991.

Robuchon, Joël. *Le meilleur et le plus simple de la France*. Robert Laffont, Paris, 1996.

Rowley, Anthony. *À table!—La fête gastronomique*. Gallimard, Paris, 1994.

Temmermann, Geneviève de et al. *The A-Z of French Food*. Scribo, Paris, 1988.

Vence, Céline, and Jean-Claude Frentz. *Tout est bon dans le cochon*. Robert Laffont, Paris, 1988.

Viron, Philippe. *Vive la baguette*. L'Epi Gourmand, Le Chesnay, 1995.

Wells, Patricia. *The Food Lover's Guide to Paris*. Workman Publishing, New York, 1999.

ABC des vins. ed. Larousse, 1995.

Restaurants of Paris. ed. Everyman Guides, London, 1994.

French Cheeses—The Visual Guide to More than 350 Cheeses from Every Region of France—Foreword by Joël Robuchon. ed. Dorling Kindersley, London, 1996.